Rivers of Blood

Rivers of Blood

A Comparative Study of Government Massacres

Brenda K. Uekert

Westport, Connecticut
London

Library of Congress Cataloging-in-Publication Data

Uekert, Brenda K.
    Rivers of blood : a comparative study of government massacres /
    Brenda K. Uekert.
       p. cm.
    Includes bibliographical references (p.) and index.
    ISBN 0–275–95165–0
    1. Massacres—History—20th century—Case studies. I. Title.
    D842.U35 1995
    909.82—dc20   95–6946

British Library Cataloguing in Publication Data is available.

Library of Congress Catalog Card Number: 95–6946
ISBN: 0–275–95165–0

First published in 1995

Praeger Publishers, 88 Post Road West, Westport, CT 06881
An imprint of Greenwood Publishing Group, Inc.

Printed in the United States of America

The paper used in this book complies with the
Permanent Paper Standard issued by the National
Information Standards Organization (Z39.48–1984).

10 9 8 7 6 5 4 3 2 1

For those who lost their lives in the skies over Lockerbie, Scotland,

and

for my parents, Eugene and Shirley Uekert, who have supported and encouraged me every step of the way.

Contents

III. COMPARISONS AND CONCLUSIONS

Illustrations

Preface

The title of this book derives from my readings of massacres and the imagery of bodies being swept down the river. In many ways, it is disappointing to know that so few social scientists study issues of government violence and terrorism. Yet, after spending several years studying torture, "disappearances," and massacres, I can certainly understand why so few people undertake the endeavor to study this troubling phenomenon. It is my intent that this project is sufficiently "objective," although I admit maintaining distance and dispassion was indeed a difficult task. I can only hope that this study will make a contribution to the broad field of state terrorism and inspire a person or two.

There are many people who made a valuable contribution to this book. My interests in sociology are a direct outcome of the outstanding sociology program at the University of Wisconsin at Eau Claire. In particular, those who inspired me while I was there include Terence Miethe, Margaret Cassidy, and Jim Williams. I hope the tradition continues. Also, I would like to recognize the university's openness to a diverse range of subjects and, in particular, its support of a course on the Holocaust. UWEC opened many doors for me.

As a graduate student at Syracuse University, I was fortunate enough to study with wonderful people from around the globe, enriching me with a diverse set of views. The dark skies were made a lot brighter by special friends–Cheryl, Holly, Hassan, Nawal, Carla, Maggie, Qian. Thanks for sharing the struggle.

Since 1989, I've had the good fortune of residing in northern California. Over the past few years, I have been privileged to know some exceptional people. In particular, I'd like to acknowledge my comrades at the university–Annette Bethea, Mary Taylor, and Maryan Tooker. We've shared some incredible times and I'm glad to call you my friends.

This book benefited from the resources of the Data Center in downtown Oakland. The center's human rights files made the collection of data a lot less tedious. Also, Julianne Traylor sifted through UN documents for me, saving me hours of time and frustration. My colleague in Sacramento, Don Hills, was kind enough to edit an earlier draft for me.

This project would have been impossible to complete without the support of the Sociology Department at Syracuse University, especially Richard Ratcliff. Others who provided invaluable advice and critiques include Marjorie DeVault, Donna Arzt, Neil Katz, and Gary Spencer. Finally, this work is dedicated to those who were killed in the bombing of Pan Am Flight 103 in December 1988. This book is also dedicated to my parents, who encouraged me to chase dreams.

Part I

The Conceptual Framework

1

Introduction

On December 10, 1948, the nations of the world, horrified by the Nazis' systematic extermination of the Jews and "racially unfit," established the Universal Declaration of Human Rights and proclaimed that "everyone has the right to life, liberty and security of person" (Article 3). The declaration specifically aimed to protect individuals from torture (Article 5) and arbitrary arrest, detention, or exile (Article 9). The authors hoped the world would never witness another Holocaust.

Yet, in the early 1990s, dozens of states continue to practice torture on a systematic basis, arrest and exile citizens for nonviolent activities, build concentration camps for the civilian population, and annihilate entire villages. People are arbitrarily gunned down, stabbed, strangled, poisoned, or hacked to death by the state's security agents. Others are raped, burned, slashed, and electrocuted before being left for dead. Torture, "disappearances," and political killings seem to flourish in today's world.

Based on the Nuremberg Charter,[1] crimes against humanity can be grouped into six categories (Glaser and Possony, 1979). The first of these categories, "crimes against the right to life," includes such things as deliberate and unnecessary killings, crippling, torture, deprivation of food, denial of medical help, massacres, deportations, and forced labor. This study explores one of the most heinous crimes against the right to life, that of government massacres. Massacres may have dual purposes. They may be genocidal in nature, in that the intent of the state is to destroy a particular population. Massacres also may be implemented under the rubric of state terrorism, in which the state's intent is to instill fear in the population. Of course, intent is often difficult to document, as the true motives of the perpetrator are seldom made public.

HUMAN RIGHTS AND THE STATE

The study of human rights and state terrorism invites fundamental questions of good and evil. How is it that people can so readily engage in the torture and murder of their fellow human beings? Hobbes believed that the source of a government's legitimacy lies in its ability to protect its citizens from the fear of violent death. Yet, it is the state that is responsible for a significant proportion of violent deaths.

Theories of the state revolve around two main traditions (Samatar, 1991). In the first tradition, following Hobbes, Locke, and Rousseau, the state is considered to be the ultimate arbiter, bringing peace to humankind and instilling order in society. Weber elaborated this tradition with his vision of the state as an impersonal, legally circumscribed structure that monopolizes the legitimate means of violence. The other tradition, the Marxist tradition, conceives of the state as an extension of class rule, in which the state expresses the interests of the dominant classes in the economy. For Marx and Lenin, the state was a vehicle whose goal was to transform society into a collectivist paradise.

These traditions point to the inherent contradictions of the state. On the one hand, the state must have a monopoly of coercive power to provide a secure environment in which people can thrive. On the other hand, the state can easily turn its coercive instruments against its citizens, denying them basic political and social freedoms (Held, 1989). How then are we to interpret the role of the state in the modern world? If the state were simply a legalistic neutral entity, victims of state violence would consist of people from all walks of life. But as this study demonstrates, state terrorism and massacres target specific groups of people– typically, those who do not belong to the ruling class. Thus, the state reflects the social divisions within a society and is an instrument of class or elite rule (Howard, 1986; Donnelly, 1989; Perdue, 1989). Furthermore, the state advances the interests of those social groups that make up and control it, whether those social groups consist of a particular socioeconomic class, or ethnic or religious group. The state dominates society, while the government ("those who control the official means of coercion, whether or not the control is legitimate") is the central actor in this system (McCamant, 1984: 34).

The state is the only legitimate repository of power and the only unit that can legally employ political violence (Stavenhagen, 1992). International order is based on territorial sovereignty, which enables the state to act with impunity within its own borders (Falk, 1979). Under such an arrangement, each state can impose its own standards when it comes to economic policies, civil liberties, and political rights. Therefore, "human rights are the rights of individuals in opposition to the state" (Howard, 1986: 34). To what extent does each state impose its own standards of morality? Are human rights relative to particular cultures, or are there certain rights that can be considered universal?

Certainly, all people do not share a common morality, and human rights must be based on culture to some extent (Renteln, 1990). Howard (1993) offers the following appraisal of cultural relativism, and its most extreme form, cultural universalism. Cultural relativism can be described as a method of analysis, and an ethical stance, that evolved in the twentieth century to counteract Westerners' belief that their own society was morally superior to all others. Cultural relativism assumes that there is no culture whose customs and beliefs dominate all others in a moral sense. Carried to the extreme, any practice of a society can be theoretically defended merely on the grounds that it is a local custom. In other words, cultural universalism prevails, in which all cultures are considered morally or ethically equal, and there can be no judgments of their comparative worth.

Cultural relativists are opposed by those who believe human rights are universal. In the tradition of Kant, there are simply ways of treating people that are inconsistent with recognizing them as full members of the human community. Henkin (1990) claims that human rights are universal and belong to every human being in every society. Howard (1993) notes that in international law, human rights are considered to be held equally by every individual, and are non-derogable claims against society and the state. Those who advocate a universalistic perspective of human rights point to the widespread acceptance of the principles of the Universal Declaration of Human Rights, a document signed by representatives of nearly every state in the world.

The debate between cultural relativism and universalism has become a left-right/North-South debate (Howard, 1993). The complexity of the nature of human rights can be demonstrated by highlighting the rights of women in society. International law is gender-neutral in theory, yet it interacts with domestic laws and social structures that relegate women and men to separate spheres of existence (Thomas and Beasley, 1993). Men exist as public, legal entities in all states, and enjoy the full extent of whatever civil and political rights exist. Women, however, are in every state socially and economically disadvantaged in practice and in fact, in many places by law (Thomas and Beasley, 1993). In this sense, respect for human rights fails to be "universal" (Cook, 1993). If states cannot agree on the universality of basic rights for an entire class of persons, how can universal claims be upheld concerning individual rights?

Linz (1992) asserts that there will be no consensus on the judgment of human rights performance in different political systems, unless we limit ourselves to a very narrow area to which all human beings might agree. Indeed, the dominant recent trend in the United Nations' international human rights mechanisms has been to address the more severe human rights abuses against the physical integrity of an individual, such as arbitrary executions, "disappearances," and torture (Tessitore and Woolfson, 1988). This study follows Donnelly's (1984) assertion that there are certain practices, such as "disappearances," torture, arbitrary arrests, detentions, and extrajudicial killings, that are entirely without cultural basis. In sum, massacres are crimes against humanity, regardless of circumstance and culture.

BASIC DEFINITIONS

The Guatemala Human Rights Commission/Mexico provides an elaborate definition of a massacre. In particular, the commission notes that massacres are intended not only to eliminate supposed or real opponents, but to terrorize the population into refraining from organizing themselves socially or politically. Furthermore, massacres are often characterized by violence and cruel and degrading treatment. Victims are invariably defenseless. Massacres are not random; rather, they are carried out in a systematic fashion. The commission uses the term *massacre* "when the above characteristics accompany an extrajudicial execution of three or more people" (Guatemala Human Rights Commission/USA, 1989b: 1).[2] To be more exact, *extrajudicial executions* are the "unlawful and deliberate killings of persons by reason of their real or imputed political beliefs or activities, religion, other conscientiously held beliefs, ethnic origin, sex, colour or language, carried out by order of a government or with its complicity" (Amnesty International, 1983: 5).

The terms "state terrorism," "political repression," and "human rights abuses" often are used interchangeably. Repression refers to the use or threat of coercion by governing authorities to control or eliminate opposition (Duff and McCamant, 1976; Pion-Berlin and Lopez, 1991). State terrorism is a subset of repression and is designed to instill fear in a target population. State terrorism is present when: "(1) an actor tends to influence the behavior of a target population; (2) the means of influence involve the act or threat of violence on some victims with whom the target will identify; (3) the deliberate effects of such actions are to induce a condition of extreme fear or terror in the target population; and (4) the actor is the state, its agents, or some approved surrogate group" (Mitchell et al., 1986: 14). State terrorism encompasses a wide variety of acts, such as arbitrary arrests, press censorship, and outlawing of demonstrations and strikes. In a refinement of the concept of state terrorism, Sloan (1984) offers the term "enforcement terrorism" to refer to the more severe, life-threatening acts, such as assassinations, "disappearances," torture, and massacres.

In 1948, the United Nations adopted the Genocide Convention, defining genocide as "any of the following acts committed with intent to destroy, in whole or in part, a national, ethnic, racial or religious group, as such: (a) killing members of the group; (b) causing serious bodily or mental harm to members of the group; (c) deliberately inflicting on the group conditions of life calculated to bring about its physical destruction in whole or in part; (d) imposing measures intended to prevent births within the group; and (e) forcibly transferring children of the group to another group" (Chalk and Jonassohn, 1990: 10). Since the convention, a number of definitions of genocide have been put forward. For instance, Horowitz (1989) views genocide as a policy employed by the state to ensure conformity to its ideology and its model of society. Chalk and Jonassohn (1990) define genocide as "a form of one-sided killing in which a state or other authority intends to destroy a group, as that group and membership in it are defined by the perpetrator" (p. 23).

Notably, early definitions of genocide neglected state attempts to destroy political groups. An important analytical distinction can be made between genocides and politicides. According to Harff and Gurr (1988), in genocide, the state defines victims by communal characteristics, whereas in politicide, victims are defined "primarily in terms of their hierarchical position or political opposition to the regime and dominant group" (p. 360). Conceptually, massacres can be appropriately defined as genocidal or politicidal. In this study, genocidal massacres refers to massacres of persons based on their communal characteristics, such as their racial, ethnic, national, or religious status. In politicidal massacres, persons are targeted for murder because of their real or perceived opposition to the regime and dominant group. Both types of massacre are intended to create an atmosphere of terror as the state kills a part of the victim group "in order to terrorize the remainder into giving up their separate identity or their opposition to the perpetrator group or both" (Chalk and Jonassohn, 1990: 26).

THE SCOPE OF THIS BOOK

This book is divided into three parts: The Conceptual Framework, Case Studies, and Comparisons and Conclusions. Part I includes this introductory chapter, and Chapter 2, which discusses the problem of state terrorism in terms of theoretical and methodological issues.

In Part II, ten case studies are presented. Each chapter is organized in a similar fashion. First, the details surrounding the massacre are introduced. This is followed by a discussion of the historical context in which each massacre took place, and a review of the government and the nature of conflict within society. Next, the perpetrators, victims, and motives of the massacre are identified to the extent possible. Finally, the aftermath of the massacre is discussed in terms of investigation and accountability, and government practices and policies.

The case studies are ordered by the type of political structure and by the nature of conflict. Four of the cases are one-party authoritarian states, while the remaining states adhere to some form of democratic rule. The nature of conflict can be grouped into three general categories: (1) popular nonviolent movements; (2) ethnic-based insurgencies; and (3) class-based insurgencies. Authoritarian states are introduced first, by the type of conflict.

China, the Soviet Union, Ethiopia, and Iraq are authoritarian regimes in which power is concentrated in the hands of a single political party or, as in the case of Ethiopia and Iraq, one individual. Chapter 3 focuses on the Communist regime in

China, and reviews the Tiananmen massacre in the context of a popular nonviolent movement. In Chapter 4, the Soviet Union's massacre of Tbilisi demonstrators occurred in the context of a nonviolent movement based on nationality. In Chapter 5, the She'eb massacre in Ethiopia, a Communist regime that was dominated by Chairman Mengistu, is reviewed in the context of ethnic-based insurgencies. Chapter 6 documents the conditions that led to the Iraqi government's massacre of the residents of Halabja, which occurred in the context of an ethnic-based insurgency, although a war with neighboring Iran complicates the picture.

The remaining six massacres occurred in states that had some democratic form of government. Chapter 7 reviews the conditions that led to the Wau massacre in Sudan, where a weak coalition government was opposed by an ethnic-based insurgency. Chapter 8 analyzes the Meerut/Maliana massacre that occurred in India, a secular state where the government has been opposed by ethnic and religious-based insurgencies. The last four case studies highlight massacres in Latin American states. Chapter 9 examines the El Aguacate massacre in Guatemala, where the government has been challenged by an ethnic-based, in specific, an indigenous-based insurgency. In Chapter 10, the massacre of residents of Cayara in Peru is reviewed in the context of an indigenous-based revolutionary insurgency. Chapter 11 focuses on the Segovia massacre in Colombia, where class-based insurgencies challenge the government. In Chapter 12, the El Salvador massacre of Jesuit priests is reviewed in the context of class-based civil war.

Part III is devoted to the comparison of massacres, a discussion of the character of state terror, a review of outcomes of state terrorism, and policy recommendations. In Chapter 13, a typology of massacres is presented, based on the identity of the victims and motives of the state. Chapter 14 reviews the character of state terror and identifies factors that influence the strategies, targets, and motives. Chapter 15 examines the outcomes of state terrorism, with a focus on the effect of the character of state terror on opposition violence. Finally, Chapter 16 addresses government accountability and develops a list of recommendations that could ameliorate the problem of human rights abuses.

NOTES

1. The Nuremberg Charter (1945) was designed to address Nazi crimes against humanity. It became customary law, thereby applying to all mass crimes ordered from the top, regardless of whether they were committed in times of peace or in times of war and regardless of whether they were perpetrated by soldiers or civilians.

2. See Chapter 2 for a restricted definition of government massacres.

2

The Problem of State Terrorism

In 1994, the United States occupied Haiti in an attempt to restore democracy and end human rights violations carried out by the military regime. In Bosnia-Herzegovina, the Serbs continued their campaign of "ethnic-cleansing," despite the presence of United Nations forces. In Rwanda, the countryside was turned into a province of despair and death virtually overnight.

Few can argue that policies of state terrorism and genocide plague many corners of the world today. Increasingly, domestic human rights practices have become the focus of international debates and struggles. Yet, few scholars focus their studies on the problem of state terrorism. A major obstacle that social scientists encounter is the absence of repression and state terrorism in all of the traditional theoretical models. McCamant (1984) notes the irrelevance of political repression in interest-group models and structural functionalism, which stress consensus; Marxism, elite theory, and dependency theory, which at best acknowledge oppression; and geopolitics, which extols the military. The discussion to follow underscores the formative nature of this subject.

THEORETICAL CONSIDERATIONS

Most often, the concept of state terrorism is used generically, as if there are some universal criteria that allow us to claim that state terrorism is present or absent. But in actuality, state terrorism is a multidimensional concept that includes a variety of strategies, targets, and motives. Two primary questions concern us here. First, what factors influence the character of state terror? Second, what are the outcomes of state terrorism?

The Character of State Terror

In a schematic approach to the analysis of government as terrorist, Lopez (1984) identified the character of terror in terms of the types of acts, the target/message complex, and the technologies available to the state terror apparatus. In a slight variation of this scheme, this section focuses on the strategies, targets, and motives of terror.

Strategies

Relatively little scholarly work has been done in the area of terror strategies. In fact, the major shortcoming of the literature lies in the portrayal of state terror as a generic concept. For the most part, scholars have equated state terror with enforcement terror and have been most concerned with the initiation of terror. In consequence, the literature is devoid of any comparative studies that specify and account for the use of various terrorist strategies. Unfortunately, this limitation requires us to discuss the phenomenon of state terror in very ambiguous terms. In general, there are two perspectives that dominate the literature. In the first perspective, state terror is considered to be a reaction to internal threat. This viewpoint can be contrasted with a second perspective, which considers state terror to be an outcome of regime changes. Note that both perspectives view state terror as an outcome of situational factors.

Gurr (1986) claims that "the necessary condition for state terrorism is the existence of a group, class, or party that is regarded by ruling elites as an active threat to their continued rule" (p. 51). The key factor to consider is the nature of challengers. To be more exact, challengers make claims that challenge the prevailing distribution of power and resources (Tilly, 1978). Gurr (1986) notes three characteristics of challengers that increase the likelihood that the government will resort to terrorist strategies. First, the government is more likely to resort to terrorism when there is considerable latent support for revolutionary challengers. Under these circumstances, terrorism is used as a cost-effective strategy of deterring potential supporters from active involvement in the revolutionary movement. Second, the state may resort to terrorist strategies to counter challengers who rely on terrorist and guerrilla tactics. The rationale for this argument is that terrorist and guerrilla challengers are difficult to combat by conventional military means. But governments simply may feel that their use of terror is a justified means to eliminate violent challengers. In other words, governments may develop their strategies based on the "principle of proportionality," which considers state violence to be justified as long as it is in proportion to oppositional violence (Gurr, 1986; Bushnell et al., 1991). Third, governments are more likely to use terror against politically marginal groups. This argument is based on the premise that groups with weak political ties to the regime can be terrorized at less political cost than others. Walter's (1969) "zones of terror" is a phrase that demonstrates the tendency to direct terror against "expendable" populations. In sum, state terrorism is a reaction to challengers who (1) have revolutionary goals and considerable latent support; (2) rely on terrorist and guerrilla tactics; or (3) consist of politically marginal groups.

A second group of studies on state terror focuses on the regime and, in particular, regime changes. Lopez (1984) notes three types of regime changes that are associated with the initiation of state terror. First, state terror may develop following the deposition of a dictatorial ruler. In these cases, the new regime may use terror to eliminate competing groups, and by doing so, consolidate its base of power. A second regime change occurs as a reaction to pressure for internal change. Here the government undergoes increased pressure for reform of policies and/or the social structure, but chooses to respond to the changing environment by curtailing civil liberties and human rights. The third regime change occurs in the aftermath of a major civil war. Under these circumstances, terror may be used to eliminate groups and persons who oppose the new regime, and as a way to enact radical structural changes. Finally, a fourth regime change, noted by Donnelly (1989), is intra-elite struggles. A divided regime may lead to the emergence of state terror as one faction, or group of elites, attempts to eliminate the support of opposing factions and to establish authority over the political structure. To summarize, state terror may occur as a result of (1) the deposition of dictatorial rule; (2) internal pressure for reform; (3) post-civil war; or (4) intra-elite struggles.

Targets and Motives

Every definition of state terrorism recognizes the presence of a victim, and an audience. The victim is secondary, since the real goal of state terrorism is to intimidate and create fear in an audience, and by doing so, to alter the behavior of the audience. The audience is referred to as the target group. The targets and motives of state terror are inseparable, since the motives determine the targets.

What motivates the state to use terror against its citizens? McCamant (1991) notes three types of struggles that result in state terrorism: (1) the attempt of landholding/business elites to maintain established patterns of extreme domination (economic domination); (2) the use of state power by a dominant ethnic group to impose its cultural mores on other ethnic groups (cultural domination); and (3) the use of state power by an ideological true-believing party to impose its vision on the rest of society (ideological domination). The worst forms of state terrorism occur when there is some overlap between these three struggles.

Economic Domination. Extreme domination of the economic system has been noted by several scholars as a condition associated with state terror. In particular, state terror persists in states where there is a high degree of social inequality and sharp social cleavages (Jackson et al., 1978; Gurr, 1986), and where political and economic power is concentrated in the hands of a small ruling class (Howard, 1986). Proponents of this view point to the high levels of state terror in Latin

America, where social inequality is significant and a small class of elites dominates the economic and political structures. Under these conditions, the primary motive for state terror is the desire of economic elites to maintain the current distribution of resources.

Where the government is motivated to use terror to fulfill economic goals, there are certain types of challengers that pose a particular threat. In general, unionization and land reform are volatile issues from the standpoint of elites, since both are attempts to shift the balance of resources (see Chomsky and Herman, 1979; Herman, 1982; Pion-Berlin, 1984; Howard, 1988; Bushnell et al., 1991). Any opposition movement that seeks to redistribute political power and economic resources is a major threat to economic elites (Petras, 1987; Mason and Krane, 1989). Thus, labor activists, peasant organizers, and groups that advocate the redistribution of wealth are likely to be the primary targets of state terror.

Cultural Domination. A second type of struggle that results in state terrorism is the use of state power by a dominant ethnic group to impose its cultural mores on other ethnic groups. Cultural domination has been linked to genocides, which tend to occur in highly polarized, multiethnic states (Fein, 1984), and in the context of struggles by ethnic or racial or religious groups for power or more equality (Kuper, 1985). Ideological and economic motives play a secondary role. The dominant ethnic group promotes racism and/or nationalism to justify its superiority. The dominant group may also use terror against the minority population to enhance its share of resources.

In cases where state terror is culturally motivated, the government's primary target will be members of the minority population.[1] Gurr (1990) notes three types of groups the state is likely to target: (1) indigenous peoples; (2) separatist nationalities; and (3) ethnoclasses. Indigenous peoples may represent a competing nationalism within the boundaries of the state, and as such, the government may use terror against them to conquer their culture and land (Falk, 1988; Gurr, 1990). Separatist nationalities are cohesive, politically organized, regionally concentrated minorities with histories and culture that demarcate them from the groups that dominate the modern state (Gurr, 1990). Here the government may use terrorist strategies to destroy the political institutions, languages, and customs of the nationalist group in the name of assimilation. Finally, ethnoclasses are groups that have distinct economic roles in societies that are dominated by other ethnic groups (Gurr, 1990). The government may use terror against members of an ethnoclass as a means to secure the economic and political status of the dominant group.

Ideological Domination. State terrorism may be used by an ideological true-believing party to impose its vision on the rest of society. Ideologies refer to total systems of thought held by society's ruling group that obscure real conditions and thereby preserve the status quo (Mannheim, 1949). Once ideologies are assimilated, they serve as a "map" of social and political reality for policy makers, who rely on a few guiding principles to make decisions (Knorr, 1976). Thus, ideological regimes may regard acts of state terror as rational behavior in their quest to create a better world (Fein, 1979).

Genocides have occurred under regimes that promoted nationalist and better-world ideologies (Staub, 1989). In fact, a totalitarian state, in which a regime holds all power and dominates society through its ideology, is a necessary precondition of the genocidal process (Horowitz, 1989). But the relationship between ideology and the broader phenomenon of state terrorism is more complex. In modern times, the primary ideological justification for state terror has been Marxism-Leninism, or some derivative of Marxism-Leninism, and the National Security Doctrine. The dominance of these ideologies reflects the Cold War mentality that divided the East and West for decades.

Communist regimes, which advocate authoritarian principles and revolutionary one-party rule, have long been associated with state terrorism (Dallin and Breslauer, 1970; Rummell, 1984; Sloan, 1984; Harff, 1988; Howard, 1988; Mason, 1989). In these states, Marxism-Leninism is used to justify the party's control over the government, economy, and society (Huntington, 1991). The regime resorts to terror to eliminate alternative ideologies and to assert the party's monopolization of power (Harff and Gurr, 1988). Communist and one-party regimes are likely to direct their terror against individuals and organizations who question the supremacy of party rule or who fail to champion Communist principles.

While conservative scholars point to the threat of Communism and the dangerous doctrine of Marxism-Leninism, others note that anti-Communist ideology, especially the National Security Doctrine, or NSD, is directly linked to terrorist governments in the United States' sphere of influence. The NSD, an ideology developed in the late 1950s and early 1960s in response to revolution in Vietnam, Algeria, and Cuba, declared that domestic subversion and international Communism were essentially the same thing. In order to deter Communism, "subversives" had to be eliminated (Faucher and Fitzgibbons, 1989; McCamant, 1991; Pion-Berlin, 1991). The doctrine was based on the concept of "total war," in which the military plays a dominant role in the "self-defense" of the existing social order (Cáceres, 1989; Perdue, 1989; Bushnell et al., 1991). In these states, the political targets of terror are persons and groups who espouse socialist values.

Shortcomings in the Literature

The brevity of this review of the character of state terror points to several shortcomings. The most significant problem with studies of state terrorism is the lack of specification of terror strategies. In particular, scholars have failed to identify any relationship between terror strategies and the conditions they cite as responsible for the initiation of terror. For instance, are politically marginal groups subjected to the same strategies of terror that are used against revolutionary challengers? Or do governments use different strategies of terror depending on the nature of the regime change? This study will highlight the strategies of terror and explore conditions that may account for variations in the character of terror.

A second shortcoming lies in the fact that scholars have treated the strategies of terror apart from the targets and motives. But will governments use similar terror strategies regardless of motive? Or will characteristics of the target group influence the types of strategies used by the government? Furthermore, can the motives of terror be treated independently? In particular, can ideology be dissociated from culture and economics? This study seeks to elaborate our understanding of how strategies, targets, and motives interact.

The Outcomes of State Terrorism

State terrorism involves violence directed at a victim, with the intention of inducing fear in some target group that identifies with that victim. In this way, the state hopes to alter the behavior of the target group (Mitchell et al., 1986). For the most part, the state identifies the target group as those who challenge the status quo. Thus, the primary concern here is how state terrorism affects opposition movements. In particular, how does state terrorism affect opposition violence? Is state terrorism a "successful" strategy? In other words, does state terrorism deter opposition violence? Or does state terrorism actually stimulate opposition violence? Much of the following discussion is taken from Mason's (1989) overview of the literature on the relationship between government repression and opposition violence.

In general, there are three principal arguments: (1) State terrorism acts as a deterrent to opposition violence; (2) state terrorism stimulates opposition violence; and (3) there is a curvilinear relationship between state terrorism and violence. For the most part, these arguments are based on rational choice theories, which focus on the decision-making process by which persons choose to participate in opposition activity. Thus, the costs and benefits of opposition violence are integral to each argument.

Strong arguments have been put forward for the deterrent effect of state terrorism (Snyder and Tilly, 1972; Hibbs, 1973; Tilly, 1978). In brief, state terrorism supposedly disrupts the organizational capacity of the opposition and raises the expected costs of opposition activities. This high cost of opposition activity reduces the willingness of potential supporters to join opposition leaders in their challenge to the regime. The deterrent effect of state terrorism was demonstrated by Tullock (1971), who depicted participation in revolutionary movements as simply a byproduct of the rational individual's pursuit of private benefit. Since state terrorism eliminates the benefits of participating in opposition violence and adds a significant cost to such behavior, it deters the formation of violent opposition movements.

The deterrent argument has been countered with strong claims that state terrorism has a stimulative effect on opposition violence (Eckstein, 1965; Gurr, 1969). Basically, state terrorism is said to stimulate opposition violence by eroding the legitimacy of the regime, eliminating nonviolent options for participation, and thereby compelling the opposition to resort to violence. Mason (1989) argues that the threat of violence, not the promise of rewards, induces persons to participate in revolutionary violence. This view has been supported by Goodwin (1993), who documented the persistence of mass-based insurgencies in highly abusive states.

Finally, a third group of studies proposes a curvilinear relationship between state terrorism and opposition violence. The literature suggests two particular patterns. First, some social scientists have advocated an inverted U-shaped relationship between regime repressiveness and opposition violence (Bwy, 1968; Gurr, 1969, 1970; Feierabend and Feierabend, 1972; Muller, 1985; Mason and Krane, 1989). According to this view, a low level of state terrorism is likely to be associated with a low level of opposition violence, since a variety of nonviolent tactics are available for the expression of dissent. Opposition violence also is likely to be low when state terrorism is at an extreme level, since organizational capabilities are low and costs are high. Rather, opposition violence is most likely under intermediate levels of state terrorism since organization is possible, and costs are not prohibitive (Muller, 1985). A second pattern suggested by the literature is a U-shaped relationship between state terrorism and opposition violence. Proponents of this view claim that increasing levels of state terrorism initially deter opposition violence but, past some threshold, stimulate such violence by leaving the opposition with no alternative to violence as a means of redressing grievances (Lichbach and Gurr, 1981).

In this review of the outcomes of state terrorism, there is no consideration of variances in the strategies, targets, and motives of terror. But will different strategies produce the same response? Is the scope of terrorism, for instance, whether it is indiscriminate or selective, a factor to consider here? Does the identity of the target group influence the effectiveness of state terror? This study seeks to expand the literature by examining the relevance of strategies, targets, and motives to the outcome of terror.

Goals of this Study

The most fundamental contribution this study hopes to make is the development of state terrorism as a multidimensional concept. Within this realm, there are four specific goals.

1. To identify conditions associated with various strategies of terror.
2. To understand how strategies, targets, and motives interact.

3.   To refine the relationship between state terrorism and opposition violence.
4.   To develop guidelines that further the cause of human rights.

METHODS OF STUDYING STATE TERRRORISM

A review of the literature reveals two distinct approaches to the study of state terrorism.   One approach that has gained considerable enthusiasm is the quantification and ranking of human rights violations in order to assess state terrorism on a global scale. A second approach is that of the descriptive case study analysis, which goes beyond numbers to uncover the dynamics of the terrorist state.   While each methodology has unique advantages, both approaches are limited by the quality and quantity of accurate information, and the degree of comparability between states engaged in different forms of terror. A review of the two basic methodologies follows.

Quantitative Approaches

A comprehensive data set on state terrorism should provide "information sufficient to make judgments about the phenomenon itself and its relationship to other aspects of the political process" (Mitchell et al., 1986: 2). Currently, such a data set does not exist.   In fact, numerous social scientists have recognized the limitations of using quantitative data in studying state terrorism (Rubin and Newberg, 1980; Safran, 1981; Scoble and Wiseberg, 1981; Bollen, 1986; Claude and Jabine, 1986; Goldstein, 1986; Gurr and Scarritt, 1989; Barsh, 1993). The development of a comprehensive data set on state terrorism elicits three types of problems. First, many of the most violent states practice severe censorship and are closed to investigation (Goldstein, 1986).   Thus, no data set could ever be exhaustive, since human rights data simply are not available for some states (e.g., North Korea, Iran, Libya). Second, government involvement in terrorist acts may be difficult to identify since the deeds may be carried out in the name of paramilitary groups, death squads, or vigilantes (e.g., in Colombia, Guatemala, or the Philippines). Third, the lack of consistent numerical data across states means that a data set dependent on quantitative variables (such as the number of violations, or number of victims) would be incomplete and unreliable. Quantification is extremely difficult since some of the best sources of data, such as Amnesty International and Americas Watch, intentionally avoid counting human rights violations and adamantly contest the use of comparisons and ratings.

Despite these reservations, the use of ranking scales and composite indexes has gained prominence in the field of human rights. For instance, in its second annual *Human Development Report* in 1991, the United Nations Development Program (UNDP) ranked countries according to a "Human Freedom Index" (HFI) based on the work of Humana (1986). The ranking set off a wave of criticism as numerous member states objected to the universal use of a rather subjective index developed by one Western academic (Barsh, 1993). Another popular ranking of human rights is that of the Freedom House, under the direction of Raymond Gastil (1985), which publishes a yearly survey of political rights and civil liberties around the world. The Gastil index was used in the World Bank's *World Development Report 1991*, which declared that "liberties" resulted in strong economic growth (Barsh, 1993). However, the index, which relies on a rating scale of one to seven, tends to reflect the extent to which a country follows the American political system and the degree to which it adheres to capitalist principles (Scoble and Wiseberg, 1981; Mitchell et al., 1986; Barsh, 1993). As such, the index more accurately measures poverty than repression (Barsh, 1993).

In addition to ranking schemes, a few social scientists have attempted to devise their own measures of state terrorism or government repression. Wolpin (1986) devised a composite index of global state repression and categorized countries according to the level of repression (violent, institutional, or minimal). However, it is not clear how each country was labeled. Yet another attempt to use quantitative data appears in the work of Duff and McCamant (1976). The researchers devised elaborate criteria to measure violence and repression in Latin America. However, two problems arise from the work of Duff and McCamant: The categories they develop are not mutually exclusive and do not translate into interval data; and many of the measures derive from unacknowledged press reports that cannot be duplicated with any degree of reliability.

In sum, current data sets suffer from Western biases, the lack of comparable and accurate data, and the multidimensionality and controversial concept of "state terrorism." The development of a valid and reliable data set must come to terms with several questions. How can "state terrorism" be operationalized in an unbiased manner? How should weighting schemes be developed? For instance, is the massacre of five persons equivalent to ten cases of torture, or to 50 cases of censorship, or to one assassination of a prominent figure? How should variances in government involvement be evaluated? Or should acts committed by private citizens, but with the tacit support of government agents, be treated the same as acts committed by regular forces? How will the data set account for changes in human rights policies and practices over time? Finally, how will the lack of statistics and inconsistencies in current reporting tools affect the reliability of the data?

Case Study Approaches

The majority of studies on state terrorism are case studies that rely on historical data. There are literally hundreds of examples of state terrorism and genocide. Stalin's system of terror, the Nazi Holocaust, mass killings in Indonesia (1965-

1966), the Khmer Rouge's killing fields in Cambodia (1975-1979), massacres in Uganda under Idi Amin (1971-1979), and the killings and "disappearances" of thousands of civilians in Argentina (1978-1979), are only a few examples of some of the more notable cases of state terrorism or genocide.

Walter (1969) was one of the first to study the process of terror, producing an anthropological study of terror within the Zulu kingdom. Arendt (1966) and Fein (1979) have written excellent accounts of totalitarian systems and the Holocaust. Conquest (1968) produced a definitive study on terror in the Soviet Union under Stalin. Political repression in America and nineteenth-century Europe were subjects of books by Goldstein (1978, 1983). Other examples of case studies include Denemark and Lehman's (1984) analysis of state terrorism in South Africa, Zwick's (1984) review of militarism and repression in the Philippines, and Pion-Berlin's (1984) discussion of state repression in Argentina. Certainly, there are many more case studies that have contributed to our understanding of the dynamics of state terrorism.

Just as political and ideological biases have infiltrated indexes and ratings of human rights, many of the case studies take on a political agenda, implying that state terrorism is a phenomenon applicable only to certain types of government. Some researchers suggest that acts of terror are intrinsic characteristics of authoritarian regimes (e.g., Schapiro, 1972; O'Donnell, 1973; Perlmutter, 1981) or totalitarian governments (e.g., Arendt, 1966).[2] Furthermore, some social scientists have attributed worldwide state terror to either the Soviet Union's Communist government (e.g., Dallin and Breslauer, 1970), or the United States intelligence community (e.g., Herman, 1982). Other case studies take a regional approach, such as Howard's (1986) study of Commonwealth Africa and Schoultz' (1982) review of Latin America. In general, the case studies lead readers to believe that state terrorism is confined to certain regions of the globe (Latin America, Africa) or to certain types of government (authoritarian, totalitarian, communist, capitalist).

Research Design

The approach advocated here consists of comparing one particular event across a wide variety of states. State terrorism encompasses everything from arbitrary arrests, threats to one's family, torture, "disappearances," and assassination. Since the goal of state terror is to produce a climate of fear, many of these actions remain hidden and undocumented. For instance, individual cases of torture may go unsubstantiated as the victim fears retaliation from the perpetrator. "Disappearances," as the name implies, are nearly impossible to document since the victims are seldom found.

While individual cases are difficult to document, one particular act of terrorism, that of a massacre, often produces a substantial amount of evidence, especially forensic clues to the crime as well as witnesses who are able to call attention to the act. Furthermore, massacres may be followed by public criticism and international condemnation, thereby encouraging some kind of independent investigation and, possibly, an official government response. Massacres exemplify the character of state terrorism and provide a wealth of information regarding the circumstances under which the state resorts to violence against its unarmed populace. Therefore, massacres are the focal point of this study.

The Massacres

In order to analyze government massacres, some restrictions were necessary to ensure comparability. The study considers the problem of legality and excludes killings carried out under legal means. For instance, thousands of executions for criminal offenses have occurred in Iran since 1979 (Amnesty International, 1987). Since it was not uncommon for several "criminals" to be executed at once, some may consider these executions to be massacres. However, the executions were carried out under legal pretenses, and it is not the intent of this study to examine the issue of capital punishment. Therefore, the massacres considered here are extrajudicial executions in the strictest sense. That is, they are *unlawful* killings.

State terrorism and massacres may take place in an international arena. For instance, the Libyan government's assassinations of exiles on foreign soil inevitably draw another government into the crime. Similarly, massacres committed during war, such as Soviet massacres in Afghanistan, involve complex issues of international conflict. Massacres that directly involve the peoples or government of another state are not addressed here. Rather, the government massacres considered in this study are domestic massacres—they are committed within the perpetrator state's borders and claim victims who are members of that state.

Another element to consider in a government massacre is the role of the government itself. Government involvement can range from the toleration of terror actions of vigilante groups to the use of government decrees that enable the armed forces to legitimately terrorize individuals and groups in an organized manner (Lopez, 1984). In some cases, it is simply impossible to substantiate government involvement. For example, many "vigilante" killings in the Philippines appear to take place with some coordination by the armed forces, yet there is often no direct evidence that definitively implicates the government (Amnesty International, 1988h). In other cases, there is uncertainty as to whether the crime can be attributed to government or guerrilla forces. Therefore, the massacres selected for this study were relatively well documented, and the degree of government involvement was substantiated through credible sources.

A final consideration is time. The world changes considerably from decade to decade. Therefore, the massacres selected here occurred within the same time interval. Specifically, the years 1987, 1988, and 1989 were chosen to hold the time variable relatively constant. This time frame was also chosen to allow for a five-year interval in which any evidence and government action should be definitive.

The Comparative Method

There are two basic methods of comparison, as outlined by John Stuart Mill (1950). In the "method of agreement," several cases that share the phenomenon to be explained also have in common the hypothesized causal factors, even though they vary in other ways. By comparison, the "method of difference" contrasts cases in which there are a number of overall similarities but the phenomenon to be explained is present in one case and absent in another (Skocpol, 1984). Each approach has its share of limitations.

The method of agreement is less powerful for establishing valid causal associations than is the method of difference (Skocpol, 1984). But the method of difference requires the designation of a control case, in which the independent variables in the negative case are identical to the independent variables in the positive case. This is an especially difficult task, since history does not always oblige in providing identical circumstances. In reality, social scientists tend to incorporate both methods into their analysis.

Although the method of difference has greater explanatory power, it requires a deductive approach utilizing well-established theoretical models to designate the control variables. As stated above, sociological theories have tended to ignore the problem of government repression and state terrorism, and therefore, a deductive approach is inappropriate. In the absence of comprehensive models, an inductive approach, which identifies various conditions and explores patterns, is particularly useful. The method used here is a variation of the method of agreement, where y is the government massacre (or in general, state terrorism) and x is the social structure. This method, demonstrated in Figure 2.1, allows several comparisons to be made. First, massacres within the same social structure can be compared (Case 1A can be compared with Case 1B). Second, massacres can be compared across social structures (Case 1A can be compared with Case 2A).

The Selection of Cases

The method of agreement guided the selection of cases. Although the designation of particular social structures will be an inductive product of the comparative analysis, certain assumptions were made to ensure the presence of analogous social structures. First, states with similar government types were expected to have comparable political and economic structures. For example, one-party regimes should have similar social structures that allow them to be contrasted with democratic governments. A second assumption is that states with similar

Figure 2.1.
Variation of the Method of Agreement used to Compare Massacres

Case 1A	Case 1B	Case 2A	Case 2B	Case 3A	Case 3B
a	d	g	j	m	p
b	e	h	k	n	q
c	f	i	l	o	r
x1	x1	x2	x2	x3	x3
y	y	y	y	y	y

histories are likely to share certain features, such as a high degree of inequality, or the presence of marginal populations. History and geography tend to be intertwined, so we would expect the social structures of South American states to be comparable, and quite different from the social structures of African states. Therefore, government type and geographic region became the primary elements that were used to produce a purposive stratified sample.

The first task in drawing a sample of massacres was identifying the population. For this purpose, the *Amnesty International Report* for 1987, 1988, and 1989, were used to create a master list of government massacres (see Appendix). Unfortunately, this list is by no means exhaustive. For instance, a further analysis of the human rights situation in Colombia revealed 82 government massacres in 1988 alone (Washington Office on Latin America, 1989; Wirpsa, 1989), while only three massacres were specifically mentioned in the Amnesty reports for the same year. Certainly, a more inclusive list is desirable; however, the Amnesty reports are the best source of human rights violations on a global scale and provide substantial information on 92 massacres occurring in 34 states over a three-year period. Furthermore, the Amnesty reports, though limited, tend to review massacres that are relatively well documented and where government involvement is substantiated, two criteria of the cases studies here.

Once the master list was compiled, the next phase of the sample selection process was the development of a stratification scheme that would result in a heterogenous sample. In order to do so, the states in which at least one government massacre occurred were grouped by region and type of government. The type of government derives from Kidron and Segal's *The New State of the World Atlas* (1987), which identifies each state by six major types of government: multiparty parliamentary, restricted parliamentary, one-party, despotic, military rule, and praetorian. This classification is only a rough guide to various broad categories of distinction, and its usefulness is limited to the sample selection process.[3] For example, the term "multiparty parliamentary" refers to nearly all varieties of democracies and includes a diverse group of states, such as the United States, Italy, Uganda, and Argentina. "Restricted parliamentary" is applied to governments whose parliamentary institutions are qualified by controls or limitations, and includes Bangladesh, Mexico, and South Africa. The term "one-party" government is self-evident and includes Communist governments in China and the Soviet Union, the Ba'th government in Iraq, and the National Liberation Front government in Algeria. The term "despotic" government refers to regimes in which a single personal authority is in control of the institutions of power, and includes Paraguay, ruled by Stroessner for several decades, North Korea, formerly under the authority of President Kim Il Sung, and Kuwait, a monarchical despotism ruled by the emir. Military governments encompass military regimes such as those of General Pinochet's Chile, and General Babangida's Nigeria. Finally, "praetorian" refers to governments in which military or paramilitary rule is exercised through civilian institutions, and includes such states as Guatemala and Panama. Table 2.1 lists the states with at least one massacre by region and government type.

Without question, more than ten massacres fit the criteria for inclusion in this study. Ideally, the sample would be selected on a random basis and be representative of the greater population. Table 2.2 shows that nearly all of the massacres occurred in states administered under three types of government: one-party, multiparty parliamentary, and praetorian. By descending order, the massacres were prevalent in states in the Americas, Africa, and Asia and the Pacific.[4]

Although a politically and geographically representative sample was desirable, the availability of data dictated the selection of cases. A stratified random sample would have required the identification of a subpopulation of massacres. This subpopulation would include only those massacres that were sufficiently documented and for which background information was available. The identification of such a subpopulation would have demanded a methodical and thorough assessment of all 92 massacres, a task well beyond the means of this study. Therefore, various Amnesty International publications were used as a screening device.

The *Amnesty International Newsletter*, a monthly publication that reports major developments in human rights throughout the world, along with Amnesty country reports, provided extensive documentation on some of the worst violations of human rights. In particular, massacres that claimed dozens of victims, involved the use of poison gases, or became the subject of government investigations received considerable attention. A review of these publications also revealed that the quality and quantity of information was related to geographical region. For example, there was limited information on African states, partly due to the lack of independent presses in many of those states. At the same time, there was an abundance of quality data on the human rights situation in most Latin American states. This disparity influenced the selection of cases by limiting the number of

Table 2.1.
Table of States with at Least One Documented Government Massacre, 1987-1989

Region	State	Government (end-1986)
Africa	Sudan, Uganda	Multiparty parliamentary
	Benin, Burundi, Ethiopia, Madagascar, Somalia	One-party
	Liberia	Praetorian
	Mauritania, Nigeria	Military
Americas	Bolivia, Brazil, Colombia, Peru, Venezuela	Multiparty parliamentary
	El Salvador, Guatemala, Haiti	Praetorian
	Chile, Suriname	Military
	Mexico	Restricted Parliamentary
Asia and the Pacific	India, Philippines, Sri Lanka	Multiparty parliamentary
	Afghanistan, Burma, China,	One-party
	Bangladesh	Praetorian
Europe	United Kingdom	Multiparty parliamentary
	Soviet Union, Yugoslavia,	One-party
	Romania	Despotic
Middle East and North Africa	Algeria, Iraq	One-party

Table 2.2.
Distribution of States with at Least One Massacre,
by Region and Type of Government

Region		Type of Government	
Americas	11	One-party	12
Africa	10	Multiparty parliamentary	11
Asia and the Pacific	7	Praetorian	5
Europe	4	Military	4
Middle East and North Africa	2	Restricted parliamentary	1
	34	Despotic	1
			34

African states and increasing the number of Latin American states to be included in this sample.

As mentioned above, the best documentation exists for the most notorious cases. In general, massacres are extremely controversial, with governments typically denying their involvement, accusing opponents of perpetrating the act, or denying the event altogether. In addition, many massacres remain hidden and are never discovered. Therefore, a truly representative sample would have to include alleged government massacres that have never been proven. But this study absolutely depends on the quality documentation of the massacres. For this reason, the majority of massacres included in this sample are particularly notorious and, as such, particularly well documented. Several of the massacres were selected because they provoked international criticism and became the subject of intense scrutiny. These massacres included the chemical bombing of a Kurdish village by Iraqi forces, the Soviet use of poison gas against Georgian demonstrators, the Tiananmen massacre in China, and the massacre of Jesuit priests in El Salvador. Still other massacres gained notoriety when official government investigations were authorized and the facts surrounding the massacre came to light. Four cases were selected for this reason: the massacre of Segovia residents in Colombia, the massacre of Muslims in India, and massacres of peasants in Guatemala and Peru. These eight cases did produce a politically diverse sample but excluded massacres in Africa. Therefore, two of the better-documented African massacres, the killings of Eritreans in Ethiopia and a massacre of Dinkas in Sudan, were included in the final sample.

Overall, the massacres are fairly representative of the geographical and political distribution of the greater population. The selected massacres occurred in Central America (El Salvador and Guatemala), South America (Colombia and Peru), Asia (China and India), Africa (Ethiopia and Sudan), Europe (Soviet Union) and the Middle East (Iraq). Four of the massacres occurred under one-party governments (China, Ethiopia, Iraq, and the Soviet Union), four under multiparty parliamentary rule (Colombia, India, Peru, and Sudan), and two under praetorian governments (El Salvador and Guatemala).

The massacres vary in both numbers and characteristics of the victims. While eight individuals were the victims of a massacre in El Salvador, more than 5,000 persons were killed in the chemical bombing of a Kurdish village. Each massacre, committed by government security forces or by persons acting on their behalf, had victims and targets that were easily identifiable. Table 2.3 summarizes the final sample of ten government massacres

A Note on Sources

Massacres are controversial events that typically result in contradictory and biased reports. Which sources are most reliable and factual? Claude and Jabine (1986) pointed out that "the chief antidote to unreliable information in the field of

Table 2.3.
Summary of Selected Massacres

LOCATION	DATE(S)	NUMBER OF DEATHS	VICTIMS
Beijing, China	June 3-4, 1989	at least 1,000	pro-democracy demonstrators
Segovia, Antioquia Colombia	Nov. 11, 1988	at least 37	Segovia residents
San Salvador, El Salvador	Nov. 16, 1989	eight	priests and staff
She'eb, Eritrea Ethiopia	May 12, 1988	200 to 400	Eritreans
El Aguacate, Chimaltenango Guatemala	Nov. 24, 1988	19 to 21	peasants
Meerut and Maliana, Uttar Pradesh India	May 22-23, 1987	dozens	Muslims
Halabja, Sulaimaniya Iraq	March 16-17, 1988	at least 5,000	Kurds
Cayara, Ayacucho Peru	May 14, 1988	at least 28	villagers
Wau, Bahr al-Ghazal Sudan	Aug. 11-12, 1987	hundreds	Dinkas
Tbilisi, Georgia Soviet Union	April 9, 1989	19 to 60	Georgian demonstrators

human rights reporting derives from the multiplicity of independently published assessments by nongovernmental organizations" (NGOs) (p. 555). Some of these voluntary groups include Amnesty International, Cultural Survival, the International Commission of Jurists, the Minority Rights Groups, and the Human Rights Watch Groups (e.g., Americas Watch, Asia Watch, Middle East Watch). In general, the NGOs emphasize particular issues, such as the rights of indigenous persons or the use of the death penalty, tend to overlook human rights violations by armed insurgencies, and often report from a liberal perspective. But in their entirety, the reports of such NGOs are considered highly reliable and are used here as the primary source for the documentation of each massacre.

Another source of information is the United Nations (UN). In particular, the Special Rapporteur on Summary or Arbitrary Executions, S. Amos Wako, was particularly active on contacting governments concerning alleged massacres. In

1989 alone, Wako contacted 48 governments about summary or arbitrary executions. In addition, several of the massacres were the focus of discussions at the Sub-Commission on Prevention of Discrimination and Protection of Minorities. Other massacres received UN attention because of the special status of some governments, such as Guatemala, which was under the advisory services item, and El Salvador, which had a Special Representative.

Finally, government sources were used in a critical manner. Goldstein (1986) notes that "obstruction is the normal contemporary governmental response to attempts to gather data on human rights violations" (p. 618). It was not unusual for the government to publish an account of the massacre that contradicted findings from NGO and UN reports. When inconsistent reports did arise, the NGO and UN reports, commonly based on independent investigations and eyewitness accounts, were regarded as more credible than government sources. For the most part, the government's version of events and its response to independent accounts are part of the data to be analyzed and are considered a good indicator of the government's commitment to human rights.

Limitations

On the one hand, quantitative approaches to state terrorism tend to be ahistorical and limited by the availability and reliability of data. On the other hand, case studies, which highlight the unique conditions that give rise to a particular genocidal or repressive state, seldom provide a framework that can be used to compare other states. The approach advocated here, the comparison of a number of government massacres, also has limitations.

A major problem of quantitative approaches, the lack of reliable data, also limited this study. In particular, the availability and quality of data determined the population of massacres from which the cases would be drawn and eventually selected. As such, this study compares some of the most notorious massacres, ignoring massacres that were less well known. Thus, the final sample may not be truly representative of all massacres.

Case studies uncover the dynamics of the terrorist state and provide extensive documentation of significant historical events. The same kind of detailed analysis will not be found in these relatively brief case studies. One of the main objectives of this study was to develop generalities that may account for variances in government massacres, and more generally, the character of state terror. For this purpose, a comparative study of several massacres was more appropriate than the detailed analysis of two or three cases. Yet, the comparative method is limited, in the sense that the results of such analysis often take the form of generalizations, which don't exactly fit all cases, since each case is unique.

This study, like all studies of genocide and state terrorism, is limited by the degree of government secrecy and denial. Some of the more intriguing questions revolve around the issues of motives and goals. Yet, governments seldom acknowledge their gross violations of human rights, or if they do, they legitimize their actions by claiming to act in defense of the nation. Other governments continually deny the events or engage in a conspiracy of silence. Certainly, this study is limited by the lack of government openness.

Finally, the greatest limitation of this study is its lack of explanatory power. The method of agreement is used to identify patterns and conditions that *may* influence the nature of government massacres in particular, and the character of state terror in general. However, these conditions do not determine government massacres and state terror. Thus, the reader should not assert that the conditions identified as significant are causal. Rather, this study is more descriptive and exploratory in nature. The findings from this study may be used in future models that do provide greater explanatory power.

SUMMARY

This study addresses (1) the character of state terror; and (2) the outcomes of state terrorism. The character of terror was reviewed in terms of the strategies, targets, and motives of terror. Two theses were presented in regard to the initiation of terrorist strategies in general. First, state terrorism is a response to internal threat. Second, state terrorism is an outcome of regime change. The motives of terror were discussed in economic, cultural, and ideological terms. Economic motives refer to the attempt of landholding/business elites to maintain established patterns of extreme domination. Cultural motives are equated with the use of state power by a dominant ethnic group to impose its cultural mores on other ethnic groups. Finally, ideological motives refer to the use of state power by an ideological true-believing party to impose its vision on the rest of society. This review of the literature demonstrates the need for an exploratory study that specifies the particular strategies of terror and the interaction among strategies, targets, and motives.

The second focal point, the outcomes of state terrorism, was discussed in terms of opposition violence. Three principal arguments were presented. First, state terrorism deters opposition violence. Second, state terrorism stimulates opposition violence. Third, there is a curvilinear relationship between state terrorism and opposition violence. These arguments are based on rational choice theories, which focus on the costs and benefits of participation in opposition activity. Overall, the literature points to the need to clarify the concept of state terrorism in relation to opposition violence.

In this study, the method of agreement was used to develop a stratification scheme that allows for comparisons between cases within similar social structures, and between cases with different social structures. One particular event, a government massacre, was chosen as the unit of analysis. Massacres tend to be relatively well documented and often elicit a government response, thus enabling the researcher to explore the character, or strategies, targets, and motives of terror. A stratified purposive sample, relying on the availability of quality information, resulted in the selection of ten massacres, occurring under three different government types, throughout various regions of the world. This approach, although limited by the actual selection of cases and extent of documentation, avoids some of the problems involved in using solely quantitative evaluations or a few detailed case studies.

NOTES

1. Note that "minority" refers to distinct racial, ethnic, or nationalist groups that do not have equal political and/or economic status within society; it is not to be confused with numerical minority, since technically, some minority groups form the majority.

2. In authoritarian states, power is held by an individual or small group of leaders with formally ill-defined limits (Linz, 1992), and the state's resources are heavily concentrated in the military and police (Sloan, 1984; Mason, 1989; Mason and Krane, 1989).

3. In general terms, one-party, military, and despotic regimes may be considered authoritarian, while multiparty parliamentary, restricted parliamentary, and praetorian governments adhere to some form of democracy.

4. Actually, more massacres were recorded in Africa (29 massacres in ten states) and Asia and the Pacific (28 massacres in seven states) than in the Americas, which had fewer massacres (25) in more states (11).

Part II
Case Studies

3

China: Tiananmen Massacre

China is an authoritarian state where power rests in the hands of the Communist Party. A popular nonviolent movement emerged in the late 1980s to challenge the party's authority, which was weakened by divisions within the leadership. In this context, the government endorsed the use of force against demonstrators, culminating in the Tiananmen massacre. The ensuing crackdown, combined with strategic political purges, guaranteed the continuation of Communist rule.

THE MASSACRE

The Tiananmen massacre may be the best-documented massacre in recent history. Events preceding the actual killings were broadcast throughout much of the world, as the media focused their attention on the democracy movement and Soviet-Chinese relations. Journalistic accounts document the following scenario. On the evening of June 3, Red Army troops descended on Tiananmen Square in Beijing, where thousands of citizens had been demonstrating for political reform. As troops entered the western part of the city, soldiers allegedly fired indiscriminately at groups of unarmed citizens and armored vehicles plowed through the streets (Wong, 1990; Yim, 1991). Contrary to popular belief, most accounts claim that the majority of those killed lost their lives on the periphery of Tiananmen Square, specifically along western Changan Boulevard, and in the western suburbs (Munro, 1990). The killings ended during the early morning hours of June 4, when armored personnel carriers entered the square and the demonstrators began leaving (Abrams, 1990).

Despite the lapse of time, the actual number of victims of the massacre will never be known. According to some, an exact body count is impossible to obtain since the government prohibited hospitals and mortuaries from disclosing fatality figures, troops airlifted some of the dead to unknown locations, and soldiers reportedly burned some of the bodies in Tiananmen Square

(International League for Human Rights, 1989). However, the government did print an official count of the dead, reporting about 300 deaths (Kristof, 1990). But information accumulated since the massacre indicates that well over 1,000 people may have lost their lives (Abrams, 1990). The majority of dead were workers or Beijing residents who died mainly on the approach roads in western Beijing (Munro, 1990).

HISTORICAL CONTEXT

The People's Republic of China (PRC) was founded on October 1, 1949, marking the date of the revolutionary triumph of Mao Zedong (Tse-tung) and the Communist Party. In 1958, Mao undertook the "Great Leap Forward" campaign, which combined the establishment of rural communes with a crash program of village industrialization. These efforts failed, causing Mao to lose influence. In 1966, Mao and his supporters launched the Great Proletarian Cultural Revolution and for the next decade, intellectuals and students were sent to forced labor programs in the countryside, and the Red Guards ruled the streets. By the mid-1970s, the aging Mao found himself between two factions fighting for succession. Mao chose the reformist Zhou Enlai to succeed him, but Zhou died in January 1976. Deng Xiaoping was expected to replace Zhou, but upon Mao Zedong's death later that year, Mao's widow and three of her colleagues ("the gang of four") temporarily seized control of the government. Just weeks after Mao's death, Deng Xiaoping was "depurged" and by 1982 had established himself as the paramount leader of China. As the decade came to a close, the Deng government was faced with internal political struggles and the largest mass movement in China's history.

Government

China's political system is a closed one that thrives on patriarchalism. As such, the Communist government suffers from several ingrained problems. For one, there is the abuse of authority, including various forms of corruption. The government operates in secrecy and has enormous control over the economy, encouraging officials to manipulate the system for their personal gain. There also is a widespread perception that children of cadres get the better jobs and special benefits (Stavis, 1988). The system is impaired by the phenomenon of "local emperors," or local officials who exercise absolute power over citizens under their jurisdiction. Finally, there are no institutionalized means to select a successor, resulting in factional power struggles within the leadership (Stavis, 1988).

In China, all political authority rests with the Chinese Communist Party (CCP). The ideology of the CCP was outlined in 1979 by Deng Xiaoping: (1) Keep to the socialist road; (2) uphold the dictatorship of the proletariat; (3) uphold the leadership of the Communist Party; and (4) uphold Marxism-Leninism and Mao Zedong thought (Stavis, 1988). The CCP ideology applied to all segments of society, including education, the media, the military, and economic institutions.

Under Deng, Communist ideology was almost totally reinterpreted, and sweeping economic changes were set in motion in the early 1980s. In the latter half of the 1980s, these reforms produced high inflation and social unrest. Meanwhile, the government was increasingly divided, both generationally and ideologically. By 1989, the government experienced a crisis of authority and a major power struggle between the various factions of the leadership.

Reforms

In the early 1980s, political authority was consolidated under Deng Xiaoping. In 1980, four members known to be critical of Deng's policies were removed from the Politburo, while two of his proteges were promoted to the Politburo Standing Committee (Yim, 1991). In 1981, Deng Xiaoping became chairman of the military commission of the central committee, giving him control over the army. By 1982, Deng had successfully consolidated his rule. Hu Yaobang and Zhao Ziyang headed the Communist Party and the state bureaucracy, respectively, thus securing the "second echelon" of the leadership.

The government's economic reforms were intended to increase productivity by decentralizing the economy and creating a "socialist commodity economy" (Dittmer, 1989). In 1978, Deng Xiaoping began a series of reforms, first returning control of the agricultural sector to individual families and, in 1984, modernizing the urban industrial sector. In the 1980s, China had the highest rate of economic growth in the world (Hartford, 1990; Hore, 1991). While economic reforms transformed society, political reforms were virtually nonexistent. In the 1982 constitution, freedom of religion, the inviolability of personal dignity and of the home, freedom of speech, and privacy of communication were guaranteed (Yim, 1991). In reality, popular protests were typically greeted with arrests, violations of civil rights, and purges (Stavis, 1988; Lee and Cooper, 1991). For instance, in 1978 the Democracy Wall movement arose in urban centers. The government reacted by arresting and imprisoning scores of dissidents, writers, and human rights advocates (Jayawickrama, 1990).

After 1984, China's economy was highly unstable. The government frequently changed development strategies and reform policies, inflation remained high, and disparities in income widened (Guocang, 1989). In 1986, several important leaders began to advocate political reform, in particular, the democratization of the political system.   In December, widespread student demonstrations for democracy and human rights shook the country. In January 1987, conservative forces put clear limits on reform. Hu Yaobang, the general secretary of the Communist Party, was forced to resign, and China entered a period of criticism against "bourgeois liberalization" (Stavis, 1988). Hu's ouster was seen by some observers as delivering a major blow to reformists who backed economic changes, and marking a shift toward the view of conservatives who believed Deng's reforms had moved too fast (Yim, 1991).

Divided Leadership

Against the backdrop of deepening domestic crisis, the Chinese Communist Party held its National Congress in fall 1987, the party's first since 1982. The Congress heralded the rise to power of a new generation of Chinese leaders and seemed to reaffirm the course of economic reform that had been adopted by Deng.   Deng, 83, resigned most of his key party posts at the end of the Congress.   On paper, he turned over the reins of leadership to his protege, Premier Zhao Ziyang, who was elected CCP general secretary (Yim, 1991). But a secret agreement had been reached that, despite Deng's retirement from the Politburo, all major decisions must receive his approval, despite his retirement (Dittmer, 1990). Thus, Deng Xiaoping and his peers, who had retired only on the condition that they could name their successor, had ultimate political authority based on patriarchalism and personal influence (Dittmer, 1990).

In effect, the Politburo Standing Committee found its powers usurped by Deng and the senior leaders. Once these party elders forged an alliance with Premier Li Peng and others, many of the personal followers of Zhao Ziyang and Hu Qili, who headed key central institutions, contested the rule of Premier Li Peng and the "shadow cabinet" (Walder, 1989). Finally, Deng's poor health prompted the issue of succession, for which no coherent plans to transfer power to the next generation of leaders existed. The CCP became split generationally between its nominal power, which rested with the Politburo, and its real power, existing in the form of a "shadow cabinet," led by the aging leader Deng Xiaoping (Jencks, 1991).

The CCP leadership was also split ideologically on the issue of economic reform.   In general, some members of the party leadership believed that economic reforms had gone too far in undermining Maoist ideology, the basis of China's socialist system (Dittmer, 1989; Hartford, 1990). The reformers, led by Zhao Ziyang, advanced capitalist, free-market plans while a conservative minority advocated central control. In fall 1987, the reformers emerged in a strong position and retail price reform was initiated. In May 1988, the government removed price controls on basic foodstuffs as part of its effort to wean the nation from an economy dominated by central planning in favor of one governed by free-market forces. Months later, China's inflation rate had reached its highest level in nearly 40 years (Yim, 1991). High inflation was accompanied by an increase in crime and corruption, which undermined the position of the reformers. In February and March 1989, the reformers shifted their attention to human rights as the regime imposed martial law on Tibet for the first time since 1959 (Dittmer, 1989). A power struggle became obvious, with the conservatives able to advance their position of central planning (Lee and Cooper, 1991). The party Politburo convened a meeting of the "central work conference" in Beijing in September 1988. The conference decided to recommend to the central committee of the party that the planned price reform be postponed for at least two years. A week later, this recommendation was approved by the Communist Party Central Committee. The move also reflected the increased influence of Premier Li Peng among the upper echelons of the CCP (Yim, 1991). Thus, by 1989, ultimate power was exercised by a group of about 20 people in their seventies and eighties who obtained their power from their positions in the Communist Party and the People's Liberation Army over the past five decades (Stavis, 1988; Shambaugh, 1992). The CCP was clearly riven by two overlapping cleavages, one ideological and the other generational (Dittmer, 1989). The power struggle between the hard-liners and reformers, the "shadow cabinet" and the Politburo, was compounded by a possible succession crisis and the collapse of Communism in Eastern Europe and the Soviet Union. The increasingly isolated regime soon found itself facing the largest demonstrations in the history of the People's Republic of China.

In the spring of 1989, mass demonstrations rocked Beijing and several major cities. Initially, Zhao Ziyang made conciliatory advances to the movement leaders and put forward two proposals concerning reforms of the political structure. The Politburo rejected Zhao's proposals, which included a call for the retirement of all senior cadres over age 75 (Dittmer, 1989). Zhao's failure within the Politburo and the extreme demands of the democracy movement spelled a downfall for Zhao's conciliatory approach. In response, Deng and the Politburo Standing Committee took action to strip Zhao of all his power and placed him under virtual house arrest (Dittmer, 1989).

The government replaced Zhao's negotiations with silence. In response, protesters escalated their tactics, adopting a hunger strike that increased their credibility and embarrassed the regime in front of an international audience. Li Peng's declaration of martial law was met with widespread resistance. The authority and legitimacy of the CCP leadership were clearly being eroded. The divided leadership proved unable to reach a consensus on a strategy to cope with the situation and eventually relied on the use of force to maintain its legitimacy.

The Democracy Movement

The democracy movement arose in the context of a collapsed Communist ideology, the stagnation of party politics, and the dislocations of economic reform (Guocang, 1989). The mass appeal of the movement was mostly an outcome of the government's economic reforms, which resulted in high inflation, a widening gap between the rich and the poor, and rampant corruption (Gelber, 1990). In particular, the students were able to capture the active participation of the masses by highlighting the regime's failure to deal with political corruption (Guocang, 1989; Sun, 1991). The movement also expanded as a result of government indecisiveness and inaction.

The democracy movement erupted in April 1989, when students at Beijing University used the death of Hu Yaobang to showcase demands for political reform. The CCP responded with a condemning editorial in the *People's Daily* of April 20 in which Deng claimed the demonstrations were led by "people with ulterior motives" engaged in a "premeditated conspiracy" aimed at negating the socialist system (Dittmer, 1989: 7). The editorial sparked the largest demonstration in 40 years of CCP rule.

On April 24, tens of thousands of Beijing University students began an indefinite boycott of classes. Three days later, in the largest rally since the start of the unrest, between 100,000 and 150,000 demonstrators marched through the capital. The demonstrators called for numerous political reforms, including freedom of the press, speech, and assembly. They also sought increased funding for education, the publication of the wealth of top party leaders, and the formal rehabilitation of Hu's reputation (Yim, 1991).

In a conciliatory gesture toward the students, the Politburo member in charge of propaganda and the press, Hu Qili, authorized nine major Chinese newspapers to give increased coverage to the student protests. On April 29, Chinese government officials met with a group of handpicked student leaders to hear their demands, but the meeting was later dismissed by many students as inadequate (Yim, 1991). Meanwhile, the student movement began to address more populist issues, such as relief from inflation and an end to corruption (Yim, 1991).

The movement became extremely visible on May 4, when about 100,000 Beijing students demonstrated to celebrate the seventieth anniversary of the first student movement in China's history. Smaller rallies were staged the same day in a number of other Chinese cities. When the government refused to acknowledge the students' demands, several thousand students began a hunger strike in Tiananmen Square, timed to coincide with the scheduled May 15-18 summit meeting between Mikhail Gorbachev and top Chinese leaders.

In May, the movement spread to more than 20 provincial capitals. By May 17, the Beijing demonstration swelled to over one million people, the largest pro-democracy demonstration since the founding of Communist China

(Goldman, 1989). On May 18, Premier Li Peng and party leader Zhao Ziyang visited Tiananmen Square to speak with the hunger strikers. Despite the visit, the Beijing vigil showed no indication of abating. On May 20, Premier Li Peng responded to the movement by declaring martial law. Large troop contingents began entering the capital, while the military moved to occupy television and radio stations and the premises of the official newspapers. A day later, the hunger strike ended but the movement continued to grow. Meanwhile, an unofficial union, the Beijing Workers' Autonomous Federation (BWAF), appeared on the scene, alarming the Communist leadership, who feared the beginnings of the "Polish disease."[1]

Despite martial law, the demonstrators proved unwilling to leave the square, and the troops lacked the will to crush through the crowds of people. On May 26, Deng called more army units to the outskirts of Beijing, raising the number of troops surrounding the capital to 200,000. The number of protesters encamped in the city's central square dwindled the same day to about 20,000. On May 29-30, a group of Chinese art students erected a statue in the square, based on the Statue of Liberty and nicknamed the "Goddess of Democracy." On June 2, the movement was invigorated when more than 100,000 people turned out in Tiananmen Square for a rally led by a popular singer (Yim, 1991).

In the early morning hours of June 3, several thousand unarmed soldiers began a march through the capital. In the face of civilian resistance, the army troops fell out of rank and retreated. As the day progressed, dozens of tanks and armored personnel carriers and thousands of combat troops armed with automatic rifles and machine guns moved toward the central square from several points around the city (Yim, 1991). As evening approached, the troops descended on the square and the massacre began. The massacre and ensuing nationwide crackdown coincided with the reappearance of Deng, who had not been seen in public since his May 16 meeting in Beijing with Gorbachev (Yim, 1991).

PERPETRATORS, VICTIMS, AND MOTIVES

The Tiananmen massacre was carried out by government troops from around the country, under direct orders from the Communist leadership. The victims of the massacre were students, workers, and other citizens who were in the area of Tiananmen Square. The motives appear to be twofold. First, the massacre reasserted the authority of the Communist Party. Second, the massacre effectively consolidated the power of the conservative leaders in the government.

Perpetrators

The People's Liberation Army (PLA) did not immediately respond to the civilian leadership's orders to carry out the martial law decree. On May 20, the Thirty-eighth Army group was forced to retreat from Beijing, leading Yang Shangkun to deploy group armies from all military regions around the capital (Cox, 1989-90). According to some, the Twenty-seventh Army, considered loyal to Yang and the conservative faction of the leadership, ultimately executed the order to clear Tiananmen Square (Dreyer, 1989). In the end, the campaign involved at least 150,000 soldiers from 18 provinces and two municipalities (Brook, 1992). The soldiers were acting under the direct orders of the hierarchy of the PLA. The hierarchy of the PLA is intertwined with the leadership of the CCP, and Deng Xiaoping had authority over the armed forces.

To what extent was the massacre planned? Given the number of troops, the use of substantial armored support, and the inclusion of marksmen among the troops, it would seem the government was more than willing to shed blood (Brook, 1992). Although the government advocated violence, many of the killings may have been the unintentional result of undisciplined soldiers (Brook, 1992). Despite this fact, the decision to use force was made by Deng Xiaoping and Communist leaders of the government, and therefore, they are ultimately responsible for the killings.

Victims

The victims of the massacre were citizens who were on the streets at the time government troops pushed toward the square. Most of the victims were workers and students who were indiscriminately attacked because of their participation in or presumed support of anti-government demonstrations. The troops did not distinguish between movement participants and bystanders. Everyone who was in the path of the troops was killed, regardless of personal involvement in the movement.

Although the massacre was carried out in an indiscriminate manner, members of the Beijing Workers' Autonomous Federation were particularly targeted. On June 2, authorities declared the BWAF to be a "counterrevolutionary" organization. The federation's tents were the first target of attack by the PLA forces that arrived in the square, and many of its members were arrested in the weeks and months thereafter (Asia Watch, 1990).

The Tiananmen massacre was unique in recent Chinese history because of the amount of bloodshed involved. Yet, previous government responses to protest movements show a pattern in which students and political activists were commonly subjected to arrest and imprisonment. For instance, the Communist leadership launched the Anti-Spiritual Campaign of 1983 and the Anti-

Bourgeois Liberalization Campaign in 1987. Each of the campaigns included an ideological agenda and the arrests of political activists and dissidents. Thus, the use of government repression against political opponents was a constant element in Chinese society.

Motives

The most obvious reason for the massacre was to put an end to the demonstrations and reassert the supreme authority of the Chinese Communist Party. The demonstrators showed no respect for the Communist authorities when they refused to adhere to martial law. Furthermore, it is likely the Communist leadership felt vulnerable and internationally isolated, given recent signs of liberalism in Yugoslavia, Poland, Hungary, and the Soviet Union (Lee and Cooper, 1991). Although the demonstrators' demands were reformist in nature, Deng believed that the movement was revolutionary and that the movement's intent was to "negate the leadership of the party and to negate socialism" (Deng Xiaoping, 1989/90: 138). Thus, following the failure of conciliatory approaches, the Chinese leaders felt force was necessary to reassert their authority over the populace.

An underlying motive of the massacre is related to the crisis of authority within the leadership itself. Tiananmen Square became the battlefield among China's leaders as they struggled for individual power (Gong, 1990). The demonstrations were supported by one faction of the leadership that hoped the movement would enable Zhao Ziyang and his supporters to usurp control over Deng Xiaoping and the "shadow cabinet" (Zuckerman, 1990). The failure of the democracy movement and ensuing massacre and crackdown were used to legitimate the authority of Deng and the conservative members of the CCP. Deng and his supporters were able to purge party members who had supported the movement, and by doing so, consolidate the power of the conservative faction, led by Li Peng and Yang Shangkun. Thus, it would appear that the conservative faction promoted the use of force not only to destroy the movement, but to consolidate its own power within the Communist leadership.

AFTERMATH

The Chinese government moved to criminalize the democracy movement. Thus, any investigations and prosecutions were directed against movement participants. The crackdown on dissidence and the revamping of Communist ideology continued into the early part of the 1990s.

Investigation and Accountability

China does not have an independent judiciary. Judges are answerable to party-dominated committees, and the verdicts themselves are usually decided before the trial even begins (Asia Watch, 1990). The judiciary is used as an instrument of the party to further its policies. The legal system was used to punish movement participants and had absolutely no role in investigating the government's actions in the massacre.

The Chinese government came under tremendous international criticism following the massacre. At this level, the government portrayed the massacre as an unavoidable mishap: "Troops, while marching into the city, had been besieged and attacked by ruffians, and could not but resort to emergency measures to quell the rebellion, and that although the troops had exercised the maximum restraint to avoid injuring the masses nearby, some civilians had been inadvertently wounded as the ruffians were mingled in the crowd, which was an unavoidable mishap" (UN Doc. E/CN.4/1990/22). According to the government, movement participants constituted "a rebellious clique and a large quantity of the dregs of society . . . who wanted to overthrow our state and the party" (Deng Xiaoping, 1989/90: 154-55). Thus, the government justified its actions by labeling the pro-democracy participants as "thugs," "hooligans," "counterrevolutionaries," and "chronic troublemakers" (Weisskopf, 1989; Shi, 1990).

The government also portrayed the movement as part of an international conspiracy against China. In particular, anti-China forces in the West were given the credit for engineering the movement. In fact, Deng claimed that one of the goals of the movement was to "establish a bourgeois republic entirely dependent on the West" (Deng Xiaoping, 1989/90: 155). If one were to believe this claim, then the government's actions could be viewed as defensive, aimed at protecting the state from external enemies. Deng and the Chinese government have continued to justify and legitimize the Tiananmen massacre.

Government Practices and Policies

Following the massacre, the Chinese government outlined its priorities at the Fourth Plenum: (1) completely stopping disturbances and stabilizing the situation everywhere; (2) rectification of the economic environment; (3) strengthening political and ideological work; and (4) strengthening party building (Dittmer, 1990). These priorities were carried out by criminalizing the movement, and in consequence, eliminating the opposition through purges, arrests, and executions. The CCP also strengthened its control over society and government by engaging in a new round of ideological indoctrination, revamping the security forces, and asserting controls over the economy. The criminalization of the democracy movement was carried out on several fronts.

China's criminal justice system contained several elements that aided the government's crackdown on dissidence. First, there was no such thing as the presumption of innocence. Penitence was essential, and any attempt to argue innocence was generally taken as evidence of a "bad attitude" and further proof of guilt. Torture was used to extract confessions. The system of legal defense was inadequate, and criminal detainees were expressly denied access to a lawyer throughout the period of pre-trial custody and interrogation (Asia Watch, 1990). The system also relied on a procedure known as "verdict first, trial second," which allowed for the adjudication of the case and the sentencing of the prisoner prior to the actual trial. Random arrests were made under "shelter and investigation" regulation, which allowed the authorities to detain suspects without charge for renewable periods of three months (Drinan and Kuo, 1992).

Under this legal system, at least 10,000 people were arrested and detained in the crackdown on pro-democracy demonstrators (Southerland, 1989a). The majority of those brought to trial were convicted on charges of "counterrevolution" and generally received prison terms from ten years to life imprisonment. Others were sentenced to three-year terms of "re-education through labor," a form of incarceration that was dispensed solely on the authority of the police and for which no appeal to the courts was possible (Asia Watch, 1990). Although the actual number of arrests has never been made public, the Chinese government eventually released more than 800 prisoners and claimed 334 people were still being held in jail (Kazer, 1990). In addition to arrests and imprisonment, executions were reported. Approximately 50 executions were publicized (Guocang, 1989). Workers and peasants accounted for all officially announced executions through the end of 1990.

Six months after the massacre, the government launched a new wave of investigations designed to capture "anti-government rioters" and Communist Party "scum" who supported the movement (Southerland, 1989b). Martial law was formally lifted in Beijing in January 1990. In the spring, the Chinese government launched a massive nationwide campaign to "crack down on serious crime." As many as 986,000 people were arrested in the "anti-crime" campaign, which included a new wave of charges brought against leading students and intellectuals (Human Rights Watch, 1991). The government reimposed state controls over all aspects of free expression, adopted measures to monitor its citizens overseas, and tightened restrictions on religious and ethnic groups within the country (Human Rights Watch, 1990, 1991). In October 1989, two legal measures were issued by the state council that restricted the right to organize: Regulations on the Registration of Social Organizations and the Law of the PRC on Assemblies, Parades and Demonstrations. Both documents were aimed at preventing the re-emergence of any kind of mass public activities (Asia Watch, 1990).

The criminalization of the movement enabled the leadership to discredit the factional opposition within the Central Committee (Dittmer, 1990). Deng and his supporters purged party members who had supported the movement and made Zhao Ziyang the scapegoat for what had happened (Lee and Cooper, 1991). Hu Qili also was purged.

On the ideological front, students and workers were required to attend routine political meetings to make confessions and support the government's use of force against the demonstrators (Drinan and Kuo, 1992). The government also directed a new wave of censorship. According to the *People's Daily*, 12 percent of the nation's newspapers and 7 percent of the publishing houses were closed following the massacre, with nearly 80,000 individuals convicted for "illegal publishing" (Shambaugh, 1991). Students were singled out for special attention. The entering class at Beijing University was cut by 60 percent, and all incoming students were required to undergo a year of military training (Pomeranz, 1990).

In 1990, the government revamped its security agencies and strengthened their loyalty to the CCP. Within the PLA, personnel changes in the High Command and senior officer corps were accompanied by an intensive political indoctrination campaign among the rank and file (Shambaugh, 1991). The People's Armed Police (PAP), who were so incapable of responding to the demonstrations, underwent reorganization, accelerated training in riot control, added new non-lethal weapons to their arsenal, and increased their public presence (Shambaugh, 1991).

In the economic realm, the government reinforced the economic retrenchment that had been under way since the Third Plenum in 1988. The renewed centralization of the economy and the drive against inflation substantially removed economic decision-making from local governments, rural collectives, and private enterprises while benefiting state-owned enterprises (Dittmer, 1990). In September 1989, wages were cut for workers in the cities and bonuses were cut in many factories (Hore, 1991).

In 1991, thousands of political prisoners remained in prison, including hundreds of prisoners of conscience. At least 26 prominent pro-democracy activists were sentenced to terms of imprisonment after highly publicized trials. Torture of detainees by police and harsh prison conditions were frequently reported. Public meetings and demonstrations remained severely restricted (Amnesty International, 1992a).

In 1992, the power battles within the CCP leadership were once again apparent. In October, three key hard-line ideologues were swept from high party positions. Also stepping down from the Central Committee were eight of 14 current members of the ruling Politburo, including President Yang Shangkun. The changes were endorsed at the closing session of the party's Fourteenth National Congress and were considered part of a gradual transfer of power to a successor generation (Holley, 1992). It was also rumored that Deng turned against the three hard-liners after deciding that they were placing obstacles in the way of economic reforms (Holley, 1992).

Throughout 1992, the Chinese government maintained its hard-line stance toward political dissent. On July 21, in the most important political trial in China since the "Gang of Four" was tried 12 years earlier, the Beijing Intermediate People's Court sentenced Bao Tong, a leading reformer and former aide to deposed Party Secretary Zhao Ziyang, to seven years in prison. In Tibet, suppression of pro-independence activists escalated at the end of February, when groups of policemen conducted surprise raids at the homes of Lhasa residents. A record number of demonstrations were reported, not only in Lhasa but also in rural areas. On August 11, as part of a continuing campaign to improve its human rights image, the Information Office of the State Council issued a *White Paper on Criminal Reform in China*, which claimed that the government had succeeded in transforming criminals into law-abiding citizens by productive labor and "humane handling of prisoners in accordance with the law" (Human Rights Watch, 1992).

In October 1992, the Fourteenth Congress of the CCP convened, the first since the Tiananmen massacre. Most of the leading conservatives who opposed Deng's market-oriented reforms were retired, and the Congress decided to abolish the committee's Central Advisory Commission (CAC), headed by Deng's most powerful rival, Chen Yun. A significant element of the reshuffle was the effective removal of the Yang brothers, the country's military commanders.

DISCUSSION

What accounts for the government's use of force in the context of a popular movement? The movement had considerable urban support, but its reformist goals and nonviolent tactics did not seem to merit the regime's use of terror. Instead, an intra-elite struggle within the party leadership best explains the events that led to the massacre. In particular, the movement posed a threat to one faction of the leadership, while the opposing faction could have benefited from the success of the movement. In response to the challenge, Deng used force against the demonstrators, launched a new wave of terror to eliminate "counterrevolutionaries," and purged movement supporters from the regime. These actions effectively consolidated his power and reasserted the supremacy of the central Communist government.

What factors influence the character of terror in China? Authoritarian rule has led to a comprehensive system of terror that is founded on the dominant ideologies of Marxism-Leninism and Maoism. The authority of the party absolutely rests on its ability to control information and eliminate alternative ideologies. For this reason, speech, movement, and thought are regulated.

When dissent has emerged, the party typically responds by launching a campaign of terror, which includes the arrest and imprisonment of dissidents, ideological indoctrination, and purges.

Is terrorism a successful strategy? The Communist Party continues to monopolize power in China. In this respect, state terrorism has upheld the authority of the regime and thus can be deemed successful. However, the party's authority is tenuous and demands the continuation of ideological controls and occasional enforcement terror. Furthermore, there is a cyclical relationship between state terror and dissent. When the government relaxes its controls, movements emerge to challenge the party's authority. The regime then responds by launching a new wave of terror, which temporarily quiets the masses. This pattern indicates that party authority may not survive without the use of terrorist strategies.

The Communist Party in China has the option of implementing reforms that would open the political system and legitimize its rule. Would such reforms make the use of terrorist strategies unwarranted? The next case study focuses on the character and outcomes of terror in the Soviet Union, an authoritarian state that has moved in the direction of democratic rule.

NOTE

1. The "Polish disease" refers to Poland's Solidarity movement, which toppled the Communist government.

4

Soviet Union: Tbilisi Massacre

The Soviet Union was an authoritarian state, although the government moved in the direction of democratic rule. Political and economic reforms led to a deeply divided party leadership. In this context, nonviolent nationalist movements began to assert their demands for regional autonomy. The Tbilisi massacre was carried out in an effort to re-establish central control over the republics. The massacre was followed by inconsistent government policies, an increase in nationalist sentiment, and eventually, a coup that sealed the demise of the Soviet state.

THE MASSACRE

On April 4, a series of rallies began in the Georgian capital of Tbilisi. At the same time, a hunger strike by 158 militant Georgians advocating secession from the Soviet Union turned into a nationalist outpouring to demand greater autonomy (Keller, 1989a). On the night of April 9, special riot troops (Special Units of Internal Troops of the USSR Ministry of Internal Affairs) entered Tbilisi's Lenin Square, where 8,000 Georgians had gathered to demonstrate. According to press reports, the troops resorted to violence against unarmed civilians in their effort to clear the square. Eyewitnesses and videotape recorded soldiers grabbing women by the hair and releasing canisters of poison gas under their noses, causing the "sudden death" of at least four victims (Remnick, 1989b). Other survivors spoke of soldiers dragging people behind a row of shields and beating them to death with riot clubs and shovels (Remnick, 1989b).

Official sources cite at least 19 deaths as the result of the massacre, although other sources list the number at over 60 (Amnesty International, 1989g). According to health officials, about 4,000 persons sought hospital treatment, most of them complaining of headaches, respiratory problems, and skin irritations they attributed to the poison gas (Ottaway, 1989). None of the soldiers was reported to have been hurt by the gas, and doctors believed they had taken an antidote (*New York Times*, 1989b).　Officials from the Military and Internal Affairs Ministry refused to give medical professionals and the public any information on the components of the poisonous gas.　One month after the massacre, American medical specialists traveled to Tbilisi and identified three gases used in the massacre (Ottaway, 1989).[1]

HISTORICAL CONTEXT

The former Soviet Union, made up of 22 major ethnic groups consisting of more than one million people each, had one of the most diverse and heterogeneous ethnic populations in the world (Lane, 1992).　The Russians formed the largest group and dominated culturally and politically (Lane, 1992). The primary conflict in the Soviet Union revolved around the autonomy and independence of the nationalist republics.　The source of the conflict dates to the founding of the state and the forced incorporation of the nationalities into the new union.

Government

The Soviet Union was founded in 1917, following the revolutionary triumph of Lenin and the Bolshevik wing of the Communist Party.　The Union of Soviet Socialist Republics (USSR) was established as a federation in 1922.　The death of Lenin in 1924, precipitated an intraparty struggle between Joseph Stalin and Leon Trotsky, who was banished from the Soviet Union in 1929.　Stalin further consolidated his power by a series of purges in the late 1930s, liquidating prominent party leaders, military officers, and cultural and political leaders of the nationalities (Gitelman, 1990).　Upon Stalin's death in 1953, Nikita Khrushchev emerged as the new power.　Khrushchev was forced into retirement in 1964 and replaced by Leonid Brezhnev as First Secretary of the Communist Party.

In 1982, Brezhnev's death sparked a series of succession crises.　Yuri Andropov presided over the Soviet empire for just over a year until he died in 1984.　His successor, Konstantin Chernenko, died a year later.　Finally, in 1985, Mikhail Gorbachev became the youngest man, at the age of 54, to take charge of the Soviet Union since Stalin.

Gorbachev inherited a government that did not allow dissent of any kind.　It was a closed system in which all authority rested with the Communist Party in Moscow.　It maintained this system by controling education, the press, the economy, and all social organizations.　Political dissidents were regularly subjected to arrest, imprisonment, and in some cases, psychiatric abuse (Amnesty International, 1989i).　In 1979, Soviet military forces invaded Afghanistan, and did not completely withdraw until 1989.　In this context, Gorbachev embarked on an extraordinary program of reforms. Yet his focus on economic and political reforms ignored the concerns of the nationalist republics. The failure of economic reforms and the erosion of Communist ideology led to power battles between various factions of the Soviet leadership. By the late 1980s, Gorbachev's authority was clearly in doubt.

Reforms

Perestroika, or "restructuring," and *glasnost*, or "openness," became the cornerstones of Gorbachev's reform program. The economic reforms were designed to decentralize the economy and increase productivity by utilizing free-market principles. But the Soviet peoples found few benefits from the new economy. In addition to a falling standard of living, people had great difficulty obtaining basic consumer goods (Lih, 1989). Under *glasnost*, society was opened to diverse ideas and the media became an influential instrument of change. *Glasnost* also expanded the political arena. New and unofficial organizations emerged, public forums aired critical concerns, and all aspects of the Soviet polity were up for debate (Burg, 1989).

Gorbachev's political reform program contained significant inconsistencies. On the one hand, he moved toward the *demokratization* of the country, but on the other hand, he initiated legislation to crack down on dissent. The June 1988 Party Conference led to several electoral changes, including the creation of a new supreme legislature, the Congress of Peoples Deputies. The conference also reiterated the Communist Party's monopoly of political organization, even though the creation of the new legislature caused many to question the dominance of the party (Lane, 1992). Overall, the political changes meant a shift of power from the party to local soviets. Authority was clearly being transferred away from the central party structure to the states, and traditional top party bodies like the Politburo began to meet less and less frequently (Lih, 1990).

While the political system was opened considerably, the Gorbachev government began to crack down on dissent. In July 1988, the Presidium of the Supreme Soviet adopted two decrees intended to curb dissent. Despite espousing a greater openness, the July decrees were drafted and passed in virtual secrecy, being published only in the Supreme Soviet Record and not in the mass media (Fitzpatrick, 1989). Decree No. 504, a "Decree on Demonstrations," gave local government officials the discretion to approve the purpose of a demonstration and the constitutionality of a given group, thereby essentially banning all street rallies and public meetings by undesirable groups (Fitzpatrick, 1989). At the same time, Decree No. 505 was issued "On the Obligations and Rights of the Ministries of Internal Affairs while Preserving Public Order." The decree increased the powers of the special Internal Affairs Ministry (MVD) troops and codified previous police practices. Under the new decree, these forces had the right to search and detain without a warrant, to bear arms and use special crowd-control methods to stop demonstrations and disorders, and to seize control of communications facilities and buildings during emergencies (Amnesty International, 1989i; Fitzpatrick, 1989).

Gorbachev's policies in dealing with the nationalities problem were clearly ambiguous. From all appearances, the Communist leadership was simply unprepared to confront the true dimension of the problem (Burg, 1989). The June 1988 conference followed 18 months of sometimes violent ethnic unrest, yet the conference adopted a vague resolution calling for devolution of greater autonomy to the republics and the creation of an unspecified central government organ to deal with nationality issues (Burg, 1989). Gorbachev had no definite plan in regard to the nationalist movements, and in July, he announced that the nationalities plenum would be delayed until mid-1989.

While the nationalities problem was left unsolved, the decrees inhibiting dissent and the loss of central authority signaled major threats to *glasnost*. In 1989, the official Soviet press began to brand nationalists as "anti-Soviet," "extremist," and "adventurist." Conservatives in the republics as well as in Moscow wanted Gorbachev to crack down harder on nationalists and to slow the reforms (Trimble, 1989). In March 1989, elections to the Congress were held, marking the first competitive elections in the Soviet Union since 1917. During the election campaign, "preventive detention" and "administrative arrest" were widely used against people supporting unofficial candidates or advocating electoral boycotts (Amnesty International, 1990c).[2] Although dissident candidates gained some seats, pro-government deputies maintained a strong hold on the Supreme Soviet. In the elections, Gorbachev was named president. By the end of the 1980s, the government faced widespread dissatisfaction with economic and social conditions, and increased political activity among the masses (Lane, 1992). At this juncture, the most important question facing the Soviet government was whether it could recapture the loyalties of its citizens or whether it would ultimately lose control (Beissinger, 1988).

Divided Leadership

In Gorbachev's first year in power, substantial personnel changes were made. In an attempt to consolidate power, eight of the 11 Central Committee Secretaries were purged, five of the 12 members of the Politburo were replaced with Gorbachev supporters, and nationally, tens of thousands of officials were transferred or dismissed (Crouch, 1989; Smith, 1992). In September 1988, a new round of personnel changes was carried out and in April 1989, over 100 Central Committee members were purged, leaving the coalition of reformers in a relatively more secure position (Willerton, 1990).

Gorbachev's consolidation of power showed a strong bent for centralization. The government's highest leadership position went to Russians who had little knowledge of events outside Russia. The republics had no voice in the new administration and their grievances went unchecked (d'Encausse, 1993). Despite the centralization and consolidation of power, Gorbachev's authority depended on his ability to build a ruling coalition in the Politburo, and it is here that he had the greatest difficulty (Smith, 1992). As the role of the Communist Party deteriorated, the Politburo became a battlefield to determine who would control the future of the Soviet Union.

By the late 1980s, the middle of the political spectrum had evaporated and the government was polarized into liberal and conservative camps (Smith, 1992). The failure of Gorbachev's economic reforms, the loss of legitimacy of Communism, and successful *demokratization* of the political system led to the organization of various factions and groups within the Soviet power elite. In July 1989, a group of liberal deputies to the new Congress of People's Deputies formed the Inter-regional Group. This faction, led by Boris Yeltsin and Andrei Sakharov, among others, pushed for faster political and economic reforms (Smith, 1992). The reformers were opposed by a conservative faction that included Party Secretary Yegor Ligachev and Defense Minister Dmitri Yazov. In 1990, the conservative forces organized around a new faction known as Soyuz (Union), which found support among members of the armed forces, Russian-speaking minorities, and those who opposed the disintegration of the Soviet Union (Roxburgh, 1991).

While various factions fought for political control of the Soviet agenda, Gorbachev moved to increase his personal authority. As the decade drew to a close, central authority appeared to disintegrate. Demands for regional independence became impossible to ignore and ideological splits within the Communist leadership threatened to make the country ungovernable (Lih, 1990).

The Nationalist Movement

The source of conflict between the ethnic nationalist groups and the Soviet government lies in the coerced incorporation of the republics into the Soviet Union. Along with the loss of their nation-state, many of the republics also experienced forced changes in their alphabet, the neglect of indigenous literary works, and the Soviet antireligious campaign (Hunter, 1990). While under the domain of Moscow, formally the republics had their own constitutions, national plan, and budget, and separate Communist parties. In the late 1960s, the nationalist movements arose, largely in response to the perceived threat of "Russification" (Hajda, 1988). In the mid-1980s, Gorbachev's call for openness and changes in the electoral system enabled activists among the nationalities to reassert their demands for greater autonomy from the Moscow government (Burg, 1989).

As the economy deteriorated and dissatisfaction among the public grew, the nationalist movements' demands for independence became potent. The Transcaucasia (Georgia, Azerbaijan, Armenia) soon demanded autonomy from the

Soviet state (Hajda, 1988). The Baltic republics had strong independent national movements, and in November 1988, the Estonian legislature declared Estonia a sovereign state and asserted its right to veto central legislation adopted in Moscow. During the course of 1990, 15 republics declared themselves to be sovereign (Lane, 1992). Many of the republics faced demands for independence and autonomy from internal ethnic groups as well. For instance, Georgia had secessionist movements among its large minorities, including the Abkhaz, Ossetians, and the Azerbaijanis (Hunter, 1990).

In Georgia, the conflicts among the republic, the Soviet government, and internal regions was complex. In 1921, Georgia was incorporated into the Soviet Union. Faced with Georgian nationalist resistance, Stalin created the Abkhazian Autonomous Republic and declared it independent from 1921 to 1931. Abkhazia was later incorporated into the Georgia Republic. In reality, the Abkhazian Republic consisted of less than 20 percent Abkhazians, and nearly 50 percent Georgians (Human Rights Watch, 1992). The remainder consist mostly of Russians and Armenians (Burg, 1989).

In 1978, the Abkhazian Republic sought to secede from Georgia and join the Russian Republic. In the late 1980s, Abkhazia again declared its intention to secede from Georgia, complaining that Georgia had forgotten it (d'Encausse, 1993). Meanwhile, the Georgians accused the Abkhaz of sabotaging interethnic relations by keeping the Georgians out of all leadership positions in Abkhazia. Georgia charged Moscow with exacerbating the conflict and using it as a pretext to intervene in Georgia (d'Encausse, 1993). The conflict between Georgia and its autonomous republic had a direct influence on the level of protests in the Georgian capital (Russell, 1991).

On February 18, 1989, several thousand people marched in Tbilisi to protest the idea of secession by the Abkhazians. Not satisfied with asking to secede from Georgia, the Abkhazians increased the stakes, demanding to be granted the status of a sovereign republic, an independent status giving them equality with the Georgians. However, the main purpose of the demonstrations of February, notably that of February 15, was to recall Georgia's forcible annexation to the Soviet Union in 1921 (Burg, 1989; d'Encausse, 1993).

On April 4, a crowd estimated at 20,000 men and women of all ages overran the square and neighboring streets around the building of the Council of Ministers. At the same time, a group of militants claiming to represent an illegal party, the Georgian National Democratic Party, went on a hunger strike. In a few days, the crowd quickly grew to more than 100,000 and a quasi-general strike paralyzed all public services. As the protests grew, the Georgian demands shifted from autonomy to independence (d'Encausse, 1993). On the night of April 9, government troops entered Tbilisi and announced a curfew. Minutes later, the troops went into action (d'Encausse, 1993).

PERPETRATORS, VICTIMS, AND MOTIVES

The Tbilisi massacre was committed by members of the special Internal Affairs Ministry (MVD) troops. From all accounts, the troops were ordered into Tbilisi by conservative members of the Moscow leadership, upon the request of Georgian authorities. The victims included demonstrators who were in Lenin Square, including Georgia militiamen who were trying to protect the demonstrators. The motives appear to be twofold. First, the massacre was intended to destroy the Georgian nationalist movement and make an example of it for the other republics, and by doing so, to affirm the authority of the Moscow government. Second, the massacre and crackdown on the nationalist movement may have been an attempt to push the balance of power in favor of the conservative faction.

Perpetrators

The deliberate use of poison gas suggests that bloodshed was not merely an accidental outcome of the military effort to clear the square but part of an overall plan that took into account the deaths of civilians. There is no doubt about the perpetrators of the crime—Special Units of Internal Troops of the USSR Ministry of Internal Affairs. These troops acted at the discretion of the Internal Affairs Ministry, which was under the authority of the Moscow government. While the soldiers committed the actual crime, there was a great deal of controversy surrounding the origin of the orders.

All of the evidence documents Gorbachev's absence during the decision to use force in ending the Tbilisi demonstrations. On April 7, Party Secretary Ligachev called a meeting with selected Politburo members, including Viktor Chebrikov, who presided over the Politburo, and the Defense Minister, General Yazov (Roxburgh, 1991). Notably, the conservative group excluded one of Gorbachev's main supporters, Prime Minister Ryzhkov. The group agreed to send the special riot troops to Georgia, and put the hard-liner General Rodinov in charge of operations (Roxburgh, 1991). Meanwhile, the Georgian party leadership called for federal assistance to clear the square.

Gorbachev was informed of the massacre upon his return from London. Reportedly, the president had in principle earlier ruled out the use of force (d'Encausse, 1993). The massacre clearly indicated that Gorbachev lacked authority over his close collaborators (d'Encausse, 1993). Although the decision to intervene may be attributed to local authorities, the intervention was endorsed in Moscow at a very high level by both civilian and military authorities (d'Encausse, 1993).

Victims

The victims of the massacre were Georgian nationalists who were in the area of Lenin Square. At least 11 Georgia militiamen were killed or injured, reportedly trying to protect demonstrators from the riot troops (Amnesty International, 1989g). The government's dissent decrees showed its growing intolerance of political opposition. The Tbilisi victims were killed because of their assumed political beliefs and actions, which promoted Georgian autonomy from the Moscow regime. Although there was an ethnic component in the conflict, it seems clear that troops were sent in to stop the demonstrations, not to attack Georgians per se. The nationalist movements, in the end, were political movements that threatened the legitimacy of the Soviet regime.

Motives

Since the alleged perpetrators of the crime never discussed the reasons for their actions, their motives can only be imputed by examining the context in which the massacre occurred. The most obvious motive would have to be the elimination of the Georgian nationalist movement. Not only would the massacre subvert the Georgian movement, but the Soviet government hoped the attack would also warn nationalists throughout the country that the Communist Party would not tolerate actions that threatened its rule (Olcott, 1991; d'Encausse, 1993).

But another factor, which suggests an ulterior motive, involves the divided nature of the Soviet leadership. The Tbilisi massacre provided a battlefield in which conservatives fought to revamp Communist central control over the republics, while the liberals pushed for faster economic and political reforms. It was clear that Ligachev and Chebrikov intended to put an end to the nationalist extremists, with or without Gorbachev's consent (Roxburgh, 1991). By doing so, the conservative faction exercised its authority and hoped to receive enough support to shift the administration's policies to its advantage. However, this attempt at consolidating the conservatives' power base within the leadership failed.

AFTERMATH

The Tbilisi massacre was the subject of legislative investigations at the regional and federal level. Both investigations assigned blame, but neither was followed by prosecutions. A criminal case was also opened into the matter, although little is known about the actual investigation. Meanwhile, the massacre gave a conclusive impetus to the Georgian nationalist movement, and independence was declared exactly two years after the massacre, which became known as "Bloody Sunday." In the Soviet government, Gorbachev moved toward an increasingly authoritarian style of rule. The nationalist republics continued to assert their demands for independence, and on December 31, 1991, the Soviet Union was officially dissolved.

Investigation and Accountability

The publicity surrounding the Tbilisi massacre caused public outrage and tested the government's political reforms. The government's initial reaction was to legitimate the massacre by claiming that the troops acted in self-defense. At first, officials representing the government of the Soviet Union alleged that demonstrators provoked the troops with bricks, stones, and metal objects and that most of the victims died in the ensuing crush (Keller, 1989a). The official news agency TASS said that the security forces acted "strictly in accordance with instructions on the non-use of weapons, and precautionary measures were taken, especially with regard to women and children" (Amnesty International, 1989g). Government officials also denied that any chemical agents had been used to fight demonstrators in Georgia (Keller, 1989b).

Immediately following the massacre, the Tbilisi area was off-limits to the press and a curfew was put in effect. The curfew was finally lifted one week after the event, at which time tanks and troops were withdrawn from the area. On April 11, several leaders of the Georgian protests were formally sentenced to jail, after "hasty trials without legal representation for the defendants" (Fein, 1989). Four days later, thousands of people, many carrying black flags, joined funeral processions through Tbilisi (*New York Times*, 1989a).

As the facts surrounding the massacre became evident, legislative inquiries were carried out at the national and regional level. While each body presented reports containing accurate descriptions of the massacre, the assignment of blame differed. In addition, the investigation carried out at the national level resulted in a battle between conservative and liberal members.

The regional investigation was carried out by the Georgian Supreme Soviet. The investigation found that Moscow was in constant communication with the regional Communist Party leadership and played a key role in an operation that was "of a punishing nature, having the appearance of a deliberately planned slaughter of innocent people carried out with extraordinary cruelty" (Remnick, 1989a). The committee called the event "one of the saddest in the history of the Soviet state" (Remnick, 1989a). The report went on to say that the principle blame lay with the republic, "but at the same time responsibility lies with officials of the central organs of power" (Remnick, 1989a). The report, a relentless, detailed study of closed-door government decision-making, indicated sympathy for the nationalist cause. The report blamed General Igor Rodinov, the military commander in the Transcaucasus region, for making the decision to use poison gas and clubs and recommended criminal proceedings against the regional military leaders involved (Remnick, 1989a).

The commission appointed by the national legislature, the Congress of People's Deputies, said that two leaders of the republic at the time, Dzhumber Patiashvili and Boris Nikolsky, requested permission to disperse the crowd, while Defense Minister Dimitri Yazov and Viktor Chebrikov, as the leadership's "duty officer," made the final decision to send in troops (Remnick, 1989a). The commission concluded that at least a dozen of the 19 fatalities were due, at least in part, to the use of poison gas (Remnick, 1989a). In addition, members of the investigating commission claimed that attempts to resolve several key questions about the massacre had been hampered by a lack of cooperation from the military and Internal Affairs Ministry (Keller, 1989b). Lead players refused to appear before the investigating committees and preferred to grant interviews in which no one could dispute their version (d'Encausse, 1993). Following the report, supporters of Yazov, Chebrikov, and Ligachev attempted to discredit the report by producing leaflets denouncing the committee's chairman, Anatoli Sobchak, a lawyer from Leningrad and a leading progressive in the Congress (Remnick, 1989a).

The massacre produced no significant change in the balance of political power, although it led to a change of leadership in Tbilisi. President Gorbachev sent Foreign Minister Edvard Shevardnadze, a Georgian and former Communist Party leader in the republic, to Georgia as a troubleshooter. Shevardnadze promptly fired some local leaders, including Patiashvili and Nikolsky, accusing them of losing contact with the people and resorting to force instead of dialogue (*The Washington Post*, 1989). In September, General Rodinov was transferred to the military's academy in Moscow. Also in September, Chebrikov was dismissed from the Politburo, although the action was not related to the massacre. In April 1990, the government passed a law that took away from the minister of the interior the freedom to dispose of the MVD freely as he wished (d'Encausse, 1993).

While these purges and legal reforms seemed to demonstrate the government's willingness to deliver some type of punishment to those responsible for the massacre and to prevent such events in the future, other personnel decisions indicated otherwise. For instance, the Georgia party chief was replaced by the republic's KGB chief, a clear signal that Moscow intended to control events in the republic more closely (Burg, 1989). Furthermore, Dmitri Yazov remained defense minister, and Gorbachev came to his defense when he was attacked during his confirmation hearings in the Supreme Soviet (Remnick, 1989a). Finally, no government or military personnel were ever prosecuted for the Tbilisi killings.

Government Practices and Policies

Government policy immediately after the Tbilisi massacre moved in the direction of authoritarian rule. In May 1989, the Congress of Peoples Deputies convened in Moscow. Gorbachev reiterated his insistence on subordinating regional interests to the national interest and offered no new proposals to meet the growing demands for greater regional autonomy. Instead, he used his control over what one delegate criticized as an "aggressively obedient majority" of the delegates to ensure that the Congress adopted only officially sponsored positions and elected a less independent group of its members to sit in the new national legislature, the Supreme Soviet (Burg, 1989). In September, the Communist party finally convened a long-awaited special meeting on nationality problems, at which time Gorbachev offered the republics only vague promises of an unspecified form of political sovereignty (Olcott, 1991).

In the early 1990s, the Soviet leadership began to move in two apparently contradictory directions. It attempted to transform the Union into a federation of self-governing republics, but at the same time, created an executive presidency that would rule by emergency decree (Hirst, 1991). In the spring of 1990, Article 6 of the Soviet constitution was removed, which had guaranteed the Communist Party's monopoly of power. In October, the Law on Public Associations was approved by the Supreme Soviet of the Soviet Union, giving legal recognition to a multiparty system. The Communist Party became increasingly marginalized from the political process, and central authority appeared to be on the verge of disintegrating. The party was badly splintered ideologically and swiftly losing its stronghold over Soviet society (Lih, 1990). The central government had become so weak that its ability to govern was questionable, with republic leaders becoming the locus of genuine power (Cosman, 1991).

While the party disintegrated and Communist ideology no longer held the nation together, Gorbachev pursued policies aimed to increase his authority. Toward the end of 1990, Gorbachev openly aligned himself with conservative forces calling for "law and order" and for "presidential rule." A dozen areas of the country were placed under states of emergency. In December, Foreign Minister Shevardnadze resigned, warning about the "danger of dictatorship." Gorbachev's declining popularity only encouraged the conservative forces, who began a war against his policies and the liberals in his administration (Roxburgh, 1991).

Meanwhile, the Soviets continued to use lethal force against unarmed civilians. Armed forces killed civilians in Baku, Tadzhikistan, in 1990. In January 1991, Soviet tanks attacked peaceful civilians in Lithuania and Latvia, resulting in 22 deaths and hundreds of wounded. Investigations into these types of events were met with official opposition, and their findings were ignored. (Cosman, 1991). On March 6, 1991, General Prosecutor Nikolai Trubin officially closed the criminal case on the Tbilisi massacre due to lack of evidence.

In August 1991, a coup led by the elite of Gorbachev's administration prevented Gorbachev from signing the Union Treaty, his solution for keeping the country together by allocating more powers to the republics. But generational and ideological divisions in the military resulted in the coup's failure (Hough, 1991). Defense Minister Yazov, implicated in the Tbilisi massacre, was arrested for his role in the coup attempt. On December 8, Russia, Ukraine, and Belarus created the Commonwealth of Slavic States. On December 17, Boris Yeltsin and Gorbachev announced the Soviet Union's official dissolution, and on December 31, the Soviet Union was replaced by the Commonwealth of Independent States (CIS). By the end of 1992, ten of the former Soviet republics were united in the CIS. The three Baltic nations and Georgia and Azerbaijan rejected that option.

Meanwhile, in Georgia the nationalist movement had coalesced, partly as a result of the Tbilisi massacre (Burg, 1989). The Georgian Supreme Soviet legalized the formation of opposition parties and delayed regional and local elections to allow the newly formed parties a reasonable chance to succeed at the polls (Smith, 1992). In May 1990, the National Forum, the umbrella organization for an estimated 150 groups, voted to elect a Congress to negotiate Georgia's independence. Two years after the massacre, on April 9, 1991, Georgia became an independent state.

Georgia was immediately faced with its own secession movements. In the winter of 1990-91, war broke out for control over South Ossetia. In July 1992, an agreement was reached among government officials from Russia, North Ossetia, Georgia, and representatives of the self-styled government of South Ossetia. Meanwhile, in Abkhazia, tensions erupted into ethnic violence in 1990, when the Abkhaz Supreme Soviet declared independence from Georgia. On July 23, the 1978 Abkhaz constitution was suspended and the constitution of 1925, according to which Abkhazia had the status of a union republic, was reinstated. Throughout 1992, Northern Abkhazia was controlled by Abkhaz forces, while the Georgian National Guard controlled the capital (Sukhumi). Hundreds of people lost their lives in the conflict, many of them civilians who were victims of summary executions and sniper fire (Human Rights Watch, 1992). In 1992, Georgian President Zviad Gamsakhurdia, who was responsible for serious human rights violations, was ousted from office, bringing on a new era of political and social chaos.

On March 10, 1992, the Military Council transferred its legislative and executive powers to a newly created State Council, chaired by Edvard Shevardnadze. In November, Shevardnadze was confirmed as head of state and given ultimate executive power. The battle over Abkhazia continued, and the government was threatened with the loss of more territory when the South Ossetian parliament voted to leave Georgia and apply to join Russia. In 1993, Sukhumi fell to Abkhazian separatists, and relations between Russia and Georgia deteriorated.

DISCUSSION

Why did the government use force against Georgian demonstrators? The nationalist movements posed a significant challenge to the central government. But the movements were reformist and nonviolent, which calls the government's use of force into question. The most significant factor to consider in this context is the intra-elite struggle within the leadership of the regime. A hard-line faction pressed for a return to central Communist rule, while a liberal faction pushed for faster political and economic reform. The use of force in Tbilisi was ordered by key conservatives in the party in an attempt to shift the balance of power in their favor and put an end to nationalist demands.

What was the character of terror in the Soviet Union? The strategies of terror changed dramatically in the Gorbachev era. The most noticeable difference was the tolerance of free expression, a byproduct of *glasnost*. At the same time, legal and political reforms greatly diminished the problem of political prisoners and arbitrary police action. However, the government's passage of repressive legislation indicated its willingness to use terror as a means to curb dissent. As dissent increased, the regime attempted to eliminate the threat to its authority by reestablishing controls over political organizing, arresting dissidents, and using force against unarmed civilians in the republics. The use of terrorist strategies served an ideological purpose, as the party attempted to assert supreme authority over the state.

Did state terrorism effectively uphold the power of central authorities? The Soviet government failed to establish a clear and consistent policy regarding the republics. Within the Gorbachev administration, divided elites continued to battle over the direction of policy. The Soviet leadership moved in contradictory directions by attempting to create a federation of self-governing republics, while at the same time establishing an executive presidency that would rule by emergency decree. The government failed to implement any consistent pattern of terror, Gorbachev failed to consolidate his base of power, and a coup led to the collapse of the Soviet state.

The Soviet case demonstrates the dangers of inconsistent policies and divided leadership. If authoritarian regimes have difficulty eliminating popular challengers, how well do they perform in the context of armed insurgencies? The next case study examines the government of Ethiopia, where the Mengistu regime was opposed by regional ethnic-based insurgencies.

NOTES

1. The poison gases included chloropicrin (a chemical agent used during World War I), CN, and CS (two types of potent tear gas) (Keller, 1989b).

2. "Preventive detention" could be imposed by the militia or riot troops, without the sanction of a court or procurator, for up to three hours. In areas where a curfew was in force, it could last up to 30 days. "Administrative arrest" of up to 15 days could be imposed by a single judge without the right of appeal (Amnesty International, 1990c).

5

Ethiopia: She'eb Massacre

Ethiopia was an authoritarian regime dominated by the leadership of Mengistu Haile Mariam. The Communist government was challenged by several regional ethnic-based insurgencies, including an Eritrean nationalist insurgency that sought greater autonomy. The government relied on terrorist strategies to establish control over the minority population. In this context, the She'eb massacre was carried out in retribution for a guerrilla offensive. State terrorism failed to deter the insurgents, who eventually captured the capital and oversaw the transformation of Eritrea to an independent state.

THE MASSACRE

In the spring of 1988, Ethiopian troops engaged in heavy fighting with opposition forces following an intensification of the conflicts in the provinces of Eritrea and Tigray. In Eritrea, the Eritrean People's Liberation Army (EPLA) captured the town of Afabet and threatened to take over still more territory. According to survivors' accounts, on May 12, government troops massacred between 200 and 400 civilians in the Eritrean village of She'eb, located 35 miles northwest of the strategic port city of Massawa (Amnesty International, 1988a). The reports state that about 80 people were crushed to death by tanks, while as many as 320 civilians were killed by gunfire, from both tanks and foot soldiers (de Waal, 1991). In the following days, government troops allegedly killed at least 100 other civilians in 30 other villages in the vicinity (de Waal, 1991).

HISTORICAL CONTEXT

The root of the Eritrea-Ethiopia conflict lies in the unique history of Eritrea, which was an Italian colony from 1889 until 1941. Fascist Italy invaded Ethiopia in 1935, forcing Emperor Haile Selassie into exile in 1936. Ethiopia was annexed to Eritrea, then an Italian colony. In 1941, British troops routed the Italians, and Haile Selassie returned to Addis Ababa. Ethiopia was then under the protection of Britain until 1952. In 1950, the United Nations voted to federate Eritrea with Ethiopia, and in 1962, Eritrea became a mere province in the state of Ethiopia. Ethiopia, which was never colonized, carried out the annexation of Eritrea by destroying its unique political and cultural institutions (Kaplan, 1991). Its elected Parliament, national flag, systems of justice and education, independent press, and free trade unions were dismantled (Amnesty International, 1991a). The government further suppressed Eritrean culture by imposing Amharic, the language of the Ethiopian regime (Tseggai, 1988).

The destruction of Eritrean society was met with the birth of armed opposition forces in what was to become Africa's longest-running civil war. The Eritrean opposition forces sought their own state and objected to the central government in Addis Ababa, which was traditionally dominated by the Amharic-speaking Christians, who constitute most of the upper class (Woldemikael, 1991). The government, for its part, was resistant to a peaceful settlement of the conflict and instead pursued an aggressive and brutal strategy to maintain its supremacy.

Government

For nearly 58 years, Ethiopia was ruled by Regent and then Emperor Haile Selassie. In 1974, charges of mismanagement of drought relief sparked a revolution that ended in the overthrow of Selassie and the installation of a committee of representatives from various branches of the armed forces, the Provisional Military Administrative Council (PMAC), or Dergue. From 1974 to 1978, the Dergue institutionalized its authority throughout the state. From 1979 onward, the Dergue, under the leadership of Lieutenant Colonel Mengistu Haile Mariam, developed civilian political institutions in an effort to enhance the state's legitimacy.

The new revolutionary government embarked on an ambitious program to institutionalize its rule throughout the state. First, all remnants of the former regime were destroyed and replaced with new state organs, using Marxism-Leninism as a blueprint for state power organization (Ottaway, 1987). Second, the government launched a period of "Red Terror," which culminated in the assassination or "disappearance" of all political opponents. By the end of the Red Terror, all state authority rested in the hands of a single undisputed leader, Mengistu Haile Mariam.

Establishing Institutional Control

The Dergue began its domination of Ethiopian government by eliminating all vestiges of the former regime. The first set of proclamations issued by the new government created new offenses, increased the government's powers, and brought the judicial process more closely under its control. Special penal and criminal procedure codes were established, and special courts tried people accused of offenses against the revolution (Clapham, 1988). Parliament was dissolved, the constitution was suspended, and members of the former government and political activists were summarily executed. Civilian organizations, from labor unions to political parties, were abolished and replaced with state organs (Kebbede, 1992).

Central control and socialism were achieved through the nationalization of all banks, insurance companies, and rural land (Henze, 1985). To promote its ideology, the Dergue introduced compulsory Marxist-Leninist instruction throughout the country. In 1974, colleges and schools were closed and students were sent to the countryside to implement land reform and political restructuring. The rural land reform was followed by an urban land reform, in which all urban land was nationalized and all houses except those occupied by the owners were confiscated (Ottaway, 1987).

The move toward socialism and Marxism-Leninism was accompanied by the creation of an extensive system of control. The first institutions to be set up by the Dergue were the peasant associations and urban-dwellers associations (*kebeles*). These organizations were structured in a hierarchical manner. For instance, any town large enough to need two or more *kebeles* had a *keftenya* to supervise them, while the 24 towns large enough to have two or more *keftenyas* were administered by a city council (Clapham, 1988).

The primary purpose of these organizations, in which membership was mandatory, was to monitor the population and provide authorities with intelligence (Dines, 1988). Each association and *kebele* had its own police force, court, and prison. Control of the population was maintained throughout the *kebele's* auxiliary organizations, such as the youth association, which had compulsory membership and required its members to attend all celebrations and demonstrations organized by the authorities. The *kebeles* were also charged with handing over quotas of conscripts for the Ethiopian army (Dines, 1988). Despite the fact that the *kebeles* were the main system of control for the Dergue, these organizations had considerable autonomy and could be manipulated by political opponents. Indeed, the *kebeles* played a major role in the Red Terror, which decimated political opponents of the Dergue.

The Red Terror and Monopolization of Power

In the mid-1970s, the Dergue, primarily a military committee, found its authority questioned by opposition movements. One organization, known as MEISON, cooperated with the Dergue, but its hidden agenda was to build up its own strength as an opposition movement. In mid-1976, MEISON split, with one faction forming the Marxist-oriented Ethiopian People's Revolutionary Party (EPRP), which advocated civilian rule (Ottaway, 1987). The EPRP soon engaged in a campaign of "White Terror" that included the assassination of labor union, *kebele*, and Dergue officials. This period was distinguished by demonstrations, the disruption of facilities, and struggle for control of the *kebeles*.

Following the EPRP's attempt to disrupt the official celebrations marking the third anniversary of the emperor's dethronement, the Dergue declared the EPRP an "enemy of the revolution" (Harbeson, 1988). The government decided to eliminate the threat from the EPRP by launching a Red Terror campaign. The Dergue armed the *kebeles* in 1976 and called for them to administer "revolutionary justice" to counter-revolutionaries (Schwab, 1985). *Kebele* units loyal to the Dergue and neighborhood defense squads served as instruments of terror and intimidation (Keller, 1988; Henze, 1989a). From 1976 to 1978, the Red Terror campaign culminated in the detention, torture, execution, and "disappearance" of tens of thousands of people (Amnesty International, 1991a). A whole generation of young leftist intellectuals, students, and workers opposed to the regime were killed, and by the beginning of 1978, the urban opposition had been decimated.

While the Dergue's authority became firmly established within the state, the Dergue itself was enveloped by power struggles. The head of the new provisional military government, Lieutenant General Aman Andom, was deposed and replaced by Brigadier General Teferi Benti, who was executed in 1977. From 1975 to 1977, a series of assassinations gradually defined the nature of power within the Dergue. Between July 1975 and September 1976, over 100 members of the Dergue and military officials who worked along with it were executed (Schwab, 1985). By 1977, the power struggle reached a climax. In February, seven leading members of the Dergue were shot and killed by Lieutenant Colonel Mengistu Haile Mariam and his supporters (Schwab, 1985). Later that year, the last Dergue member who represented any threat to Mengistu, Vice-Chairman Atnafu Abate, was killed (Clapham, 1988). By liquidating his opponents, Mengistu successfully monopolized all power and would rule Ethiopia with an iron fist for the next 14 years.

Enhancing State Legitimacy

Following the Red Terror campaign, the government turned its attention to increasing central control and enhancing the state's legitimacy (Keller, 1988). The *kebeles*, which had been rather autonomous, were stripped of some of their authority. The Dergue exercised tighter control over the *kebeles'* financial and administrative matters and deprived them of their security functions (Henze, 1989a). Meanwhile, Mengistu began to legitimize his authority by creating a government party and moving toward constitutional rule.

In 1979, Mengistu announced the formation of the Commission for Organizing the Party of the Working People of Ethiopia (COPWE), whose first congress took place a year later. Under the proclamation that established it, the chairman of the PMAC, Mengistu, was appointed as chairman of COPWE, and all of the powers and duties of COPWE were personally vested in him (Clapham, 1988). The Workers Party of Ethiopia (WPE) was formed in 1984. By this time, the government had already established mass organizations. For example, the Revolutionary Ethiopian Women's Association (REWA) claimed a membership of over five million and the Revolutionary Ethiopian Youth Association (REYA) claimed almost four million adherents (Ottaway, 1987). Thus, by 1984 Mengistu had successfully built mass organizations that responded to his absolute authority.

In 1987 a new constitution was adopted. The constitution declared the establishment of the People's Democratic Republic of Ethiopia (PDRE), which operated under a one-party system, and granted the president of Ethiopia enormous powers. For all practical purposes, the founding of the PDRE was a largely symbolic event in which there was no real transfer of power to civilian institutions (Clapham, 1988; Pateman, 1990b). Similarly, the infusion of civilian cadres in the WPE reflected more a ceremonial than a real transfer of power from a military administration to a civilian one (Harbeson, 1988). In the end, the power of Chairman Mengistu remained essentially unchanged.

Civil War

The Ethiopian government faced insurrection movements from three main fronts: the Eritrean People's Liberation Front (EPLF), which had been fighting for independence since the early 1960s; the Ethiopian People's Revolutionary Democratic Front (EPRDF), a rebel coalition whose dominant member was the Tigrayan People's Liberation Front (TPLF); and the Oromo Liberation Front (OLF), which sought greater autonomy for the Oromo, the dominant tribe in southern Ethiopia. Armed opposition in Tigray and in Oromo areas had been maintained since 1975 and 1976, respectively. The guerrilla movements struggled against a government that actively targeted civilians for reprisals and had an overall strategy designed to pacify the population into a state of submission.

Eritrean Insurrection

The federation of Eritrea with Ethiopia was met with armed insurrection. The Eritrean Liberation Front (ELF), an exclusively Muslim movement, was founded in 1960. The ELF soon attracted a substantial number of Christian Eritreans, largely as a result of the proscription of the Tigrinya language in education and the arbitrary rule of Ethiopian officials (Markakis, 1989). But the ELF became splintered by strains between Christians and Muslims and at the end of the decade, lost its support to a far more radical movement, the Eritrean People's Liberation Front (EPLF).

The EPLF was formally proclaimed in February 1972 as a "unified" competitor to the ELF (Henze, 1985). On the night of January 31, 1975, the two Eritrean liberation organizations launched an offensive against the newly arrived Ethiopian troops. A year later, the Eritrean forces controlled more than 90 percent of the Eritrean countryside and conducted military operations with ease inside most of the Ethiopian-controlled towns and cities (Tseggai, 1988). By the end of 1977, the two rebel forces controlled nearly all of Eritrea.

With victory in sight, the two rebel forces could not agree on a plan for consolidating their gains and turned their weapons against each other. The disunity of the rebel forces led to the recapture of Eritrean territory by Ethiopian troops, which greatly benefited from Soviet and Cuban support. By 1978, the Ethiopian government regained control of all major Eritrean cities and communication routes (Henze, 1985).

Two years later, the battle between the rebel forces was resolved, with the EPLF, better organized and less associated with Islam and Arab support than its ELF rival, now the sole nationalist movement in Eritrea (Clapham, 1988; Woldemikael, 1991). At a second National Congress held in 1987, the EPLF defined its political program, called the National Democratic Program (NDP), which declared its intent to create a state based on a multiparty system and with supreme legislative power vested in a democratically elected national assembly (Leonard, 1988). The EPLF built an impressive organization and boasted Africa's best grass-roots famine relief and health care network, an agricultural extension service, an education system, and a well-documented record of protecting human rights (de Waal, 1991; Kaplan, 1991). Its armed forces, the Eritrean People's Liberation Army (EPLA), an entirely voluntary and literate force, rarely engaged in urban guerrilla warfare but instead concentrated its efforts on fighting government troops in the field (Pateman, 1990a; Amnesty International, 1991a).

The EPLA continued to fight the Mengistu regime throughout the 1980s, but it was not until March 1988 that it launched a major offensive, capturing numerous towns and gaining control of much of the area. In response, the government declared a state of emergency and proceeded to bomb the rebel-held towns (Markakis, 1989). More than 18,000 Ethiopian troops were captured or killed in several intense weeks of battle, and the EPLF was able to capture all but a handful of urban centers (Keller, 1990). The government massacre of She'eb civilians occurred as Ethiopian troops found themselves in retreat.

The Government's War

The Ethiopian government fought Eritrean rebel forces by combining developmental and political strategies with brute military force. These developmental and political strategies were intended to pacify the Eritrean civilian population and included an "Ethiopianization" scheme, "villagization" and mass relocation, the use of food as a weapon, and the administrative division of Eritrea. Meanwhile, the military campaigns included indiscriminate attacks on civilians as well as military offensives against the rebel fronts.

Military Campaigns. In 1975, Ethiopian troops were on the defensive in Eritrea. As they continued to lose territory to the ELF and EPLF forces, the troops reverted to reprisals against the civilian population in many towns and villages under their control. The scope and intensity of these reprisals were staggering. More than 100 villages were set on fire and hundreds of thousands of Eritreans were forced to seek shelter in the surrounding mountains and neighboring countries (Tseggai, 1988). The government's early defeat was countered with a massive military offensive.

In August 1977, Mengistu called for a "total people's war" against the "aggressors and the secessionists" (de Waal, 1991). The government, engaged in a border war with Somali forces, obtained substantial Soviet military support and Cuban combat assistance. In 1978, the Ethiopian troops successfully defeated the Somali forces. Armed with sophisticated weaponry, the revamped military forces turned their attention to Eritrea. In mid-1978, the government launched its first major offensive and during the next five months recaptured all of the region (Clapham, 1988; Markakis, 1989).

In January 1982, the government launched its most ambitious offensive, the Red Star Multifaceted Revolutionary Campaign, in an effort to eliminate the "anti-freedom, anti-unity, anti-people and anti-peace bandit gangs" (Clapham, 1988). The Red Star campaign sought to combine the military defeat of the EPLF with economic development programs intended to provide the resources necessary for the economic reconstruction of the region. The government hoped to turn the population against the EPLF by arming workers and peasants, giving them military training, and providing them with political education. At the same time the national army was expected to deal a death blow to the Eritrean rebels (Keller, 1990).

Militarily, the Red Star campaign failed, and in 1986 and 1987, the government adopted a strategy that consisted of constant military patrols, small-scale offenses, and bombing "everything that moves" in the EPLF-controlled areas (de Waal, 1991). Napalm and cluster bombs were used against the civilian population (Dines, 1988). In early 1988, the rebel fronts in Eritrea and Tigray decisively gained the military initiative. The government responded with repeated attacks on civilian targets, culminating in the She'eb massacre (de Waal, 1991).

The occasional military offensive complemented a persistent policy of arbitrary arrest and imprisonment. Those arrested were often picked up in the streets or in the fields and taken straight to prison, where torture was commonly practiced (Dines, 1988). In Eritrea, many of the political prisoners were tried in secret by Special Courts Martial, Special Courts, and emergency military courts. Under these trials, defendants were often denied legal representation, statements made under torture were admitted as evidence, and judges exercised little or no judicial independence. Many of these political prisoners were reportedly summarily sentenced to death and swiftly executed (Amnesty International, 1991a).

Pacification Strategies. Military campaigns, accompanied by the arbitrary rule of Dergue "law," failed to halt the Eritrean liberation movement. In fact, insurrection movements continued to flare not only in Eritrea, but in Tigray and the Ogaden as well. The government attempted to re-establish control over these areas through techniques designed to change the composition of the population itself. A prime example of this strategy was the secret "Ethiopianization" campaign, developed in 1977. Under this scheme, the government simply replaced Eritreans in powerful positions with Ethiopians (Woldemikael, 1991).

In 1984, widespread famine helped secure government legitimacy for its "villagization" and mass relocation plans. Under the "villagization" plan, over twelve million peasant farmers were moved from isolated homesteads or hamlets into larger villages (Amnesty International, 1991a). In the resettled areas, members of the WPE were heavily involved in political indoctrination and *kebeles* maintained repressive control of the population (Keller, 1988). The process included the nationalization of all possessions and the collectivization of production (Kebbede, 1987). Although Eritrea was spared from massive relocations, the government attempted to remove as many Tigrayans as it could (Kebbede, 1992). The massive relocation of Tigrayans from the north to areas in the south also accomplished the breakup of the homogeneous southern population (Dines, 1988). The result of the "villagization" plan was greater control over the population (Keller, 1988).

While the Ethiopian government moved millions of peasants from the north, a different tactic was used in Eritrea. The civil war resulted in the flight of up to a million Eritreans to Sudan and elsewhere from the occupied areas. The government decided to fill the loss of Eritreans by importing people from Ethiopia into the towns and suburbs. New arrivals received public housing and jobs, creating yet more Eritrean refugees (Dines, 1988). This strategy exemplified the Dergue's ambition to destroy Eritrean culture and advance an Ethiopian nation, with a common language and culture (Dines, 1988).

From 1984 to 1988, control of famine relief was a major component of the pacification strategy pursued by the government (de Waal, 1991; Kebbede, 1992). The Dergue and rebels were criticized for holding back or blocking famine relief efforts. The distribution of food was left entirely to the government, which refused to transport relief food to areas it did not adequately control. The famine-struck citizenry was at the mercy of government troops for its survival, enabling the troops to distribute food as a reward or withhold it as punishment.

Still another pacification strategy used in Eritrea was the attempt to solve the conflict by dividing the population administratively. The Dergue's first plan for dividing Eritrea was its nine-point program for Eritrea, announced in 1976. Under this plan, Eritrea was to be divided into seven national districts (Henze, 1985). More than a decade later, Mengistu's constitutional government devised a divide-and-rule proclamation under which Eritrea was to be subdivided into three administrative regions, roughly corresponding to the main ethnic clusters in the area (Markakis, 1989). The administrative division of Eritrea was simply an attempt to eliminate the Eritrean problem by eliminating Eritrea itself.

PERPETRATORS, VICTIMS, AND MOTIVES

The She'eb massacre was carried out by regular government forces. Those who fell victim to the troops were Eritrean civilians. The massacre, carried out in reprisal for EPLA advances against the Ethiopian troops, was part of a broader scheme aimed to pacify the civilian population.

Perpetrators

Who was responsible for the She'eb massacre? Those who carried out the actual killings were conscripts, many of whom were probably obtained by forceful and deceitful means (de Waal, 1991). The troops, based in garrisons, had little contact with and few ties to the Eritrean population. They had been known to loot villages, burn houses and crops, and slaughter animals (Dines, 1988). But the She'eb massacre was not an isolated incident carried out by undisciplined soldiers.

In the mid-1970s, reprisal massacres were common as Ethiopian troops were forced to retreat from Eritrea. Indiscriminate arrests, killings, bombings, massacres, and the persistent violation of human rights were institutionalized in Ethiopia. No government soldiers or officials have ever been reprimanded for the extrajudicial killing of civilians. The police, military, courts, and prisons are integrated into a system that promotes the arbitrary arrest, torture, and killing of civilians. The military hierarchy, headed by Mengistu himself, was ultimately responsible for allowing, condoning, and ordering acts such as the She'eb massacre.

Victims

The victims of the She'eb massacre were Eritrean men, women, and children who were unable to hide from the tanks and bullets. Victims were not "selected" in any manner. Eritreans of all ages and ethnic groups were among the dead and injured. The killings were genocidal in nature, since the victims were attacked only because of their ascribed status as Eritrean.

Massacres typically followed rebel attacks on government troops. In brief, all Eritreans were held responsible for EPLA attacks. Reprisal killings were not unique to Eritrea. In Tigray and Ogaden, unarmed villagers and nomads were extrajudicially executed by Ethiopian army units for acts committed by rebel forces (Amnesty International, 1991a). Under the philosophy of collective responsibility, all Eritreans were "naturally guilty" of supporting the opposition group simply because they were Eritreans. Therefore, age, ethnicity, gender, and "guilt" were not relevant in these arbitrary killings.

Motives

Ethiopian troops and government officials did not offer motives for their behavior; neither did they feel the need to defend their policies. If the She'eb massacre is isolated from its broader context, it appears to be an act of retribution against civilians who were suspected of supporting the rebels. In general, it is not known whether the massacre was a planned act or a spontaneous reaction. The motives behind the She'eb massacre must be inferred from the social conditions that prevailed at the time.

The primary goal of the regime was the maintenance of the current political order, which assured Mengistu's position as the supreme leader of Ethiopia. In order to do so, Mengistu had to establish control over the Eritreans and all other "nationalities" and ethnic groups. Mengistu's mechanisms of control included instilling a climate of terror through massacres, arbitrary arrests, extrajudicial executions, torture, and imprisonment. Overt terror was accompanied by an administrative scheme to redistribute the population in such a manner as to eliminate civilian support for the insurgents. In essence, "villagization" and mass relocations were used to destroy cultures that were not compatible with the Ethiopian (Amharic) culture and language. Thus, the She'eb massacre appears to have been carried out as part of an overall plan to destroy the rebels' base of support, and by doing so, to assert the authority of the Mengistu regime.

AFTERMATH

The government continued to engage in the massive violation of human rights while persistently evading responsibility for its actions. The She'eb massacre was followed by several more massacres and the intensification of war in Eritrea and the rest of Ethiopia. In 1991, as peace talks between the EPLF and government were under way, President Mengistu fled the country, ending 14 years of authoritarian rule. The EPLF was given the responsibility of governing Eritrea while the other rebel organizations struggled to govern the Ethiopian central government.

Investigation and Accountability

The Ethiopian government had no internal mechanism that could investigate and prosecute government officials for any type of criminal behavior. All legislative and judicial powers rested with President Mengistu. The purges and assassinations of Mengistu's opponents highlighted a system of "law" based on the personal whims of the executive. In short, the government and its officers were not held accountable for human rights violations. The She'eb massacre was never acknowledged by the Mengistu government.

In the United Nations, Ethiopian officials were requested to respond to various charges of human rights violations. In a general declaration to the UN concerning alleged killings by government forces in Eritrea, an official government statement conveyed that "it was the dissident groups which were engaged in acts of terrorism, banditry and killing of innocent individuals and that it was those same groups that were the source of allegations brought against the government" (U.N. Doc. E/CN.4/1990/22). In general, the Mengistu government considered any international comment on its human rights record as interference in its internal affairs and national sovereignty. The government typically reacted to any criticism with silence, evasion, misinformation, or false denials (Amnesty International, 1991a).

Government Practices and Polices

The Ethiopian government increasingly found itself in a precarious situation. Just two days after the She'eb massacre, the government declared a state of emergency in Eritrea and Tigray that would remain in effect for the rest of 1988 and all of 1989. Meanwhile, government troops continued to target civilians, and massacres were documented in Hagareselam, where 340 people were killed, and in Maikinetal and Adua, which claimed over 100 deaths (Amnesty International,

1991a). Despite the state of emergency and arbitrary force exercised by government troops, the various rebel forces continued to gain substantial territory.

In May 1989, the Mengistu regime suffered a major political crisis when most of the top leaders of the armed forces attempted a coup. The coup failed after three days of fighting, but Mengistu's authority was clearly eroded. Four months later, peace talks were held between the government and EPLF, accompanied by a ceasefire. However, fighting intensified throughout the rest of Ethiopia. By the end of 1989, the EPRDF, led by the Tigrayan People's Liberation Front, made a remarkable advance southward. The government forces relied on the same tactics that it had used in previous years, including indiscriminate bombing of civilian targets (Human Rights Watch, 1991).

In 1990, fighting resumed between government forces and the EPLF. In February, the government suffered a major defeat with the loss of the port town of Massawa to the EPLF. During the fighting about 200 civilians were killed, many of them while being kept hostage as "human shields" by the retreating government forces (Human Rights Watch, 1991). While the EPLF staged some impressive victories, the EPRDF continued to make important advances and in early 1991, launched a major military offensive against the Mengistu government. On May 21, as rebel troops encroached upon the capital, President Mengistu fled the country. Within a week, Addis Ababa fell to the EPRDF and Asmara, the Eritrean capital, fell to the EPLF, marking the end of 30 years of civil war.

Mengistu's departure left Ethiopia with no government and no independent civilian institutions that could fill the void. The EPRDF held the reins of Ethiopian government while the EPLF formed a new administration in Eritrea, which it governed as a separate area. Both were provisional governments scheduled to hold office for a two-year transitional period, leading up to multiparty elections in Ethiopia and an internationally supervised referendum in Eritrea to decide whether it should be fully independent.

In 1992, the main partners in the Ethiopian coalition government were the EPRDF and the Oromo Liberation Front (OLF). The electoral process took place against a backdrop of nine months of intermittent military clashes between EPRDF and OLF forces and an explosion of rural violence in the southern part of Ethiopia. Shortly before the elections, the OLF withdrew from the government. On June 20, elections were held in 12 of the country's 14 new regions. However, the elections were so flawed that many dismissed them as meaningless (Human Rights Watch, 1992).

Both the Eritrean and Ethiopian governments engaged in human rights violations in their efforts to establish authority. In Eritrea, the EPLF arrested hundreds of former government and ruling party officials and soldiers, and expelled about 120,000 people from its territory. At the end of 1991, several hundred people were still detained without charge or trial (Amnesty International, 1992a). Throughout 1992, the Ethiopian Transitional Government arbitrarily arrested and detained political opponents. Although the level of human rights violations is admirable when compared with the Mengistu reign of terror, the governments still lack an independent judicial and legislative apparatus, which is considered essential for the development of a democratic and humanitarian state.

In April 1993, the people of Eritrea voted overwhelmingly in favor of independence from Ethiopia. The vote marked the end of a 30-year struggle. The formal declaration of independence took place on May 24, the second anniversary of the fall of Mengistu. Issaias Afewerki, leader of the EPLF, was sworn in as president.

DISCUSSION

What motivated government troops to massacre civilians in the town of She'eb? The massacre was carried out as troops retreated and served no purpose other than revenge. In the broader context, retribution massacres were relatively common in Eritrea and other regions where insurgencies battled government forces. The strategies used in Eritrea and elsewhere indicate a cultural motive. In particular, the government forced members of the minority group to relocate to government-controlled villages, transferred populations to create a pro-government populace, and engaged in indiscriminate enforcement terror against the target population. In Eritrea, the overall intent of the government's strategies was to destroy Eritrean culture and advance an Ethiopian nation with a common language and culture.

What factors influence the character of terror in Ethiopia? Certainly, the Dergue and Mengistu dictated the strategies of terror. The Mengistu regime attempted to eliminate all alternative ideologies and opposition parties by controlling all institutions and executing political opponents. The primary purpose of terror was ideological, and an extensive system of control was set up to monitor the population. In addition, the government, dominated by one particular ethnic group, attempted to impose its culture on other ethnic groups, and thus, nationalist and minority groups were subjected to an added dimension of state terror.

Did state terror succeed in eliminating the challenge to the Mengistu government? The regional insurgencies continued their battle against the regime, while the government's credibility fell as a result of its inability to deal with famine. Mengistu lost the support of military leaders and was forced to flee the country when rebels overran the capital. By all accounts, state terrorism did not deter the opposition, and in the long run, the government proved unable to assert its authority through terror.

The Ethiopian experience suggests that authoritarian rule and terrorist strategies are not sufficient to defeat ethnic-based insurgencies. But can a strong leader and extreme levels of terror produce a different outcome? The next case study introduces the character of state terror in Iraq, where the authoritarian regime, under the dictatorship of Saddam Hussein, is opposed by a nationalist insurgency.

6

Iraq: Halabja Massacre

Iraq is an authoritarian regime where power is in the hands of a single leader, Saddam Hussein. The authority of the Ba`th regime is challenged by a nationalist-based insurgency that struggles to gain autonomy for the Kurdish population. The Halabja massacre occurred as the government's war with neighboring Iran came to a conclusion. The massacre was followed with the intensification of state terrorism, which decimated the guerrilla movement. However, the Kurds, with assistance from the international community, have continued their opposition to the Iraqi regime.

THE MASSACRE

The Halabja massacre occurred in a disputed area of conflict. Due to the Iraqi war with Iran, and the disputed nature of the territory in question, journalists were provided access to the area and documented the following scenario. In mid-March 1988, the Kurdish *peshmergas* ("those who face death"), with support from Iran's Revolutionary Guards, seized the Iraqi town of Halabja, located in the Sulaimaniya province near the Iraq-Iran border. The town had swollen to a population of 70,000 by refugees from a Kurdish village to the west that had been destroyed by the Iraqi army (Middle East Watch, 1990). On March 16 and 17, Iraqi forces dropped cluster bombs, containing a combination of mustard gas and other internationally outlawed chemical substances, on the residential areas of Halabja. Approximately 5,000 people were killed, the vast majority being Kurdish women, children, and elderly who could not escape the gas (Amnesty International, 1989a).

The Halabja massacre was followed by similar assaults on several nearby townships and villages, including Khormal (People for a Just Peace, 1988). Journalists allowed into the area reported seeing "hundreds of unwounded corpses strewn in the streets" (Gowers and Johns, 1988). Halabja was turned into a virtual ghost town when the survivors were relocated to a newly constructed village called "Saddamite Halabja," located 12 miles from the old town and surrounded by military posts (Kelsey, 1989).

HISTORICAL CONTEXT

Iraq consists of three main distinct ethnic and religious groups: the Arab Sunni minority, which controls the government; the Arab Shi`a majority, which has no real power; and the Kurds, whose population is scattered over Iraq, Iran, Turkey, and Syria (Atarodi, 1991).[1] The current conflict between the government and the Kurds dates back to 1922, when Britain incorporated Kurdish provinces into the new state of Iraq. The Kurds, a non-Arab ethnic group with its own language and culture, numbers between three million and four million in Iraq. The Iraqi Kurds have generally promoted the idea of a "Grand Kurdistan" or some kind of autonomous region within Iraq (Farouk-Sluglett and Sluglett, 1991). The Iraqi government has vehemently opposed the secession of Kurdish areas.

Government

In World War I, an Anglo-Indian force occupied most of the country, which was then part of the Ottoman Empire. Britain was given a mandate over the area in 1920, and two years later, recognized Iraq as a kingdom. In 1932, the mandate was terminated and Iraq was admitted to the League of Nations. In 1958, Iraq's monarchy and parliament were overthrown in a military coup that left the king, his family, and former prime minister dead. In March 1963, the Ba`th Socialist Party orchestrated a coup, killing the leader of the military junta, Abdul Karem Kassim. Months later, the Ba`th members of the revolutionary council were driven from power and the government was again dominated by a series of military leaders. In 1968 the Ba`th Party, with the help of conservative military officers, staged a successful coup and proceeded to consolidate its power.

The ideology of Ba`thism has been used to legitimize the government's arbitrary rule and total domination of society. The Iraqi Ba`th Party, formally founded in 1952 as a branch of the Syrian Party, calls for the creation of a single secular Arab state (al-Khalil, 1989). In brief, the ideology insists that the Arab world, artificially divided first by the Ottomans and subsequently by imperialism and Zionism, must be reunited so that the "Arab nation" can fulfill its "eternal mission" (Ghareeb, 1981; Farouk-Sluglett and Sluglett, 1991). By definition, those who opposed the Ba`th Party or questioned its authority were "enemies of the Arab nation" (Farouk-Sluglett and Sluglett, 1991). The domination of the Ba`th Party, which for all practical purposes behaves as a "state within a state," was accomplished in a series of stages. From 1968 to 1973, the Ba`th Party institutionalized its rule by creating a vast network of Ba`th organizations. The next four years were devoted to consolidating rule by eliminating all opposition. Finally, since 1979, Ba`th leader Saddam Hussein has held absolute power over the party and the state.

Institutionalizing Ba`th Rule, 1968-1973

The constitution made the Revolutionary Command Council (RCC), which consisted of a small group of top Ba`th officials, "the supreme body in the state." The RCC was empowered to unilaterally promulgate laws and decrees, mobilize the army, approve the budget, ratify treaties, and declare war and peace. The constitution also provided for the establishment of a National Assembly, which had only limited power (Middle East Watch, 1990). General Ahmad Hassan al-Bakr was president of the RCC and of the state until 1979.

The party institutionalized its power within the state by dominating the RCC. In 1969, the RCC was enlarged to 15 members and all those appointed were Ba`thist (Marr, 1985). Once the Ba`th Party's power within the government was secured, the party unleashed a campaign of terror against opponents of the Ba`th, marked by frequent public executions (Zaher, 1989). From 1969 to 1973, the Ba`th leadership worked to consolidate its power within all state organizations, beginning with the military. Military officers of questionable loyalty were replaced by Ba`thists or Ba`th sympathizers. The government then turned its attention to the education system, the judiciary, and media. The party established its authority over these institutions by banning non-Ba`thists from employment in the Ministries of Defense, Interior, Foreign Affairs, Education, Culture, and Information (Zaher, 1989). Furthermore, those who opposed "Ba`thization" faced arrest, torture, and "disappearance."

During this period, the Ba`th Party designed a hierarchical organization meant to capture the loyalty of every Iraqi citizen (Marr, 1985). This organization, fully operational by 1974, was based on a party cell or circle (*halaqah*) in each neighborhood, consisting of between three and seven members who met to carry out party directives. Several cells made up the party division (*firqah*), which operated in small urban villages. Professional and occupation units similar to the divisions were located in offices, factories, schools, and other organizations. Two to five divisions formed the core of the section (*shu`bah*), which had jurisdiction over a territory the size of a large county. At least two sections formed a branch (*far`*), operated at the provincial level. Finally, there was a regional command, elected by the party's congress, that operated at the national level. This extensive system of control was soon accompanied by a professional Ba`th security apparatus.

Consolidation of Ba`th Rule, 1974-1978

In the mid-1970s, Saddam Hussein emerged as the regime's strongman. In 1974, Hussein was responsible for the consolidation of the Ba`th Party through a series of repressive measures and the establishment of the security apparatus, controlled by members of Hussein's clan (Takrit) (Chalabi, 1991). From 1974 to 1978, repressive laws were used to eliminate any suspected opponents of the Ba`th government. A series of death penalties made public insult of the president or top institutions of the state or party punishable by life imprisonment or death (Middle East Watch, 1990). In 1978, membership in any other political party became a capital offense for members or former members of the armed forces, which included all adult men, since conscription was universal (Farouk-Sluglett and Sluglett, 1991).

A system of terror buttressed the consolidation of Ba`th power. In 1974, the entire policing system was overhauled and three main agencies were formed to ensure the supremacy of Ba`th rule: (1) the Amn, or State Internal Security; (2) Mukhabarat, or General Intelligence Department, designed to watch over other policing networks; and (3) Estikhbarat, or military intelligence, said to operate only abroad (al-Khalil, 1989). The security agencies operated openly, detaining citizens at will, making arrests without warrant, and routinely torturing and frequently murdering detainees (Middle East Watch, 1990). At the base of the security system was a network of informers who had the obligation to keep surveillance over their neighbors (Bartram, 1991).

The security systems were headed by Hussein's family members and close friends. The internal security machine was run by Hussein's half-brother, Barzan Ibrahim, until 1983. His cousin, who also was his brother-in-law, was in charge of the defense portfolio (Dawisho, 1986). By the time Hussein assumed the presidency in 1979, he had destroyed all possible threats to his personal authority and had achieved a position of clear dominance over the security apparatus.

The use of torture became widespread as a means to obtain confessions or to force the victims to renounce their convictions and pledge themselves to the ruling Ba`th Party (Zaher, 1989). Confession rituals, public hangings, corpse displays, and executions became institutionalized practices in Iraq, designed to breed and sustain widespread fear (al-Khalil, 1989). The security forces and agencies, which had full discretion in carrying out arrests and executions, were known to use collective punishment against the population. For instance, when persons wanted for political or security crimes could not be found, family members were frequently arrested, and in some instances, tortured and murdered (Middle East Watch, 1990).

Saddam Hussein and Absolute Authority, 1979-present

In 1979, Saddam Hussein became president of the RCC and the state. He began his rule by having 21 senior Ba'th officials, including members of the RCC and senior ministers, summarily executed (Zaher, 1989). The purges were designed to transfer bonds of loyalty away from the party and to Hussein. The Hussein government soon turned its attention to neighboring Iran, as the Ayatollah Khomeini was installed as head of the revolutionary government. That same year, Hussein began the deportation of the Shi`a community. Eventually some 300,000 Shi`as were forced out of Iraq into Iran (Miller and Mylroie, 1990). On September 20, 1980, Iraqi planes and ground forces attacked Iranian territory, igniting eight years of hostilities.

Throughout the 1980s, Hussein was able to retain absolute authority by eliminating any and all perceived threats. For example, following the conclusion of the war with Iran, Hussein had hundreds of officers and top generals who had become public figures arrested and in many cases executed (Miller and Mylroie, 1990). Each year, thousands of political prisoners were arbitrarily arrested and detained and hundreds of extrajudicial executions were reported. Torture continued to be routinely used by the security forces and large numbers of people simply "disappeared" (Amnesty International, 1989a). By the time of the Halabja massacre, Hussein had eliminated all political rivals and ensured his personal authority by surrounding himself with loyal family members of his Takrit clan and long-standing associates.

Civil War

Kurdish nationalist movements have battled the Baghdad government periodically since 1922. In the 1980s, the Kurdish rebel fronts posed a major challenge to the Iraqi regime. But once the war with Iran was concluded, the Iraqi government effectively decimated the Kurdish front. The government's war against the Kurds included strategies of "Arabization," mass deportations, "villagization," scorched earth campaigns, and finally, the use of chemical weapons against the civilian population.

Kurdish Insurrection

The first major rebel organization, the Kurdish Democratic Party (KDP), led by Mustafa Barzani, was formed in 1946. The KDP led the Kurdish nationalist movement for nearly three decades. In 1974, the Iraqi government enacted the Law for Autonomy in the Area of Kurdistan, which provided an autonomous area with an elected legislative council. But the KDP objected to the law, mostly because it excluded important Kurdish provinces, such as Kirkuk, the home of

Iraq's richest oil fields. The lack of consensus led to an outbreak of new hostilities between the KDP and Iraqi government. One year later, the KDP was crushed by waves of arrests, deportations, summary executions, assassinations, and public hangings (al-Khalil, 1989).

The humiliating defeat of the KDP led to the splintering of the organization into the KDP-Provisional Command and the Patriotic Union of Kurdistan (PUK), led by Jalal Talabani. Each of the parties controlled large areas of Kurdistan, roughly corresponding to tribal divisions. The KDP controlled the northern Kurmanji areas and PUK the Sorani-speaking areas. In the mid-1980s, the various Kurdish movements pursued their own agenda, often at the expense of one another. For instance, KDP forces joined the Iranians for the 1983 offensive in Iraqi Kurdistan, while the PUK fought to repel the Iranian/KDP forces (Bulloch and Morris, 1992). To further complicate matters, the PUK was engaged in a struggle with smaller left-wing parties in order to establish its supremacy within its area of control. Two years later, the Iranians stepped up their support of the Iraqi Kurds and successfully acquired the support of both the KDP and PUK (Entessar, 1989).

The Iran-Iraq war changed the nature of the Kurdish nationalist movement. On the one hand, Kurdish forces were able to expand their operations against the Iraqi government, thanks to an influx of aid from Iran and its allies. On the other hand, the Iraqi government was amenable to a peaceful solution of the Kurdish "problem" so that it could focus its war efforts against its neighbor. In 1983, secret negotiations between Talabani and the Iraqi government led to a cease-fire. But months later, as Western military support poured into Iraq, Baghdad broke the cease-fire. The PUK exacted its revenge against Saddam by attacking army units stationed in territory it controlled. In return, Hussein launched fresh waves of arbitrary arrests, torture, and executions (Bulloch and Morris, 1992). The secret negotiations and ensuing outbreak of hostilities reversed the level of support for the two major Kurdish insurrection movements, and the KDP once again became the dominant force (McDowall, 1992).

In May 1986, the *peshmergas* launched a new offensive. By the spring of the following year, the Kurds were in control of a vast area of northern Iraq. In 1987, the KDP, PUK, and three smaller parties united their forces under the banner of the Iraqi Kurdistan Front (IKF). This new front, complemented by Iranian forces, captured a number of Kurdish towns, culminating in the capture of Halabja in March 1988. But as the war with Iran was winding down, the Iraqi government turned its attention to the Kurdish insurrection. By autumn 1988, the IKF, abandoned by Iran and the rest of the world, found itself virtually defenseless (McDowall, 1992).

The Government's War Against the Kurds

Iraq's relationship with the Kurds has always been unstable. The government's Autonomy Law, promulgated in 1974 over the objection of the main Kurdish party, acknowledged the existence of the Kurdish people as a distinct national group within Iraq possessing their own language and culture. The law granted a number of national rights to the Kurds and offered them the opportunity to run their own affairs locally through autonomous government organs. At the same time, however, the law limited Kurdish control over natural resources and placed the security apparatus under Baghdad control. Clearly, the Iraqi government considered the Kurdish area and its people to be an indivisible part of Iraq (Ghareeb, 1981). The Kurdish rejection of the Autonomy Law led to a new round of hostilities.

The government's "Arabization" strategy began with a ban on the Kurdish press and all Kurdish political, social, and vocational organizations. In 1974 and 1975, the Iraqi regime escalated the forced removal of Kurds from the Autonomous Region. This plan, first initiated in 1963 with the forced removal of Kurds from the oil-rich fields of Kirkuk, involved removing thousands of Kurds from their homes (Zaher, 1989; Saeedpour, 1992). The removal of Kurds served two purposes. First, the forced removal of Kurds, accompanied by a "villagization" plan, ensured government control over the population. Second, the mass deportations and subsequent resettlement by Arab peasants essentially turned strategic Kurdish-dominated areas into Arab majorities.

The Iraqi government first undertook the mass deportations of Kurds inhabiting the frontier zones. Upon their removal, the government created a "security belt" six miles wide, along a line running from the Iranian to the Syrian frontiers (Sherzad, 1992). Entire populations were transferred to government "strategic villages," which were little more than concentration camps. The government also established numerous "cluster villages," designed for easy surveillance of the houses (Entessar, 1992). In 1977, the government expanded its "resettlement" policy, sending tens of thousands of Kurds to "strategic villages" in the desert (Middle East Watch, 1990).

While Kurds were removed from the Autonomous Region, the government invoked a new land reform program. Under this program, the government confiscated land from Kurdish landholders and then offered loans and credits with favorable terms to Arab peasants to purchase parcels of the confiscated land. The creation of Arab majorities was combined with the administrative division of the Autonomous Region. The Ba`th government simply redrew administrative boundaries, leaving predominantly Kurdish areas out of the Autonomous Region (Entessar, 1992).

The mass deportation of Kurds and their transfer to government-controlled villages did not occur without government repression and terror. In 1974, Iraqi planes systematically napalmed and bombed Kurdish villages, forcing hundreds of thousands of Kurds to seek refuge in the mountains (al-Khalil, 1989). In March 1974, two Kurdish towns of about 25,000 and 20,000 inhabitants were razed to the ground (Miller and Mylroie, 1990). From 1975 to 1978, more than 350,000 people were deported from Kurdistan and 240 villages were burned down (Zaher, 1989).

The Iran-Iraq war was accompanied by the escalation of the Iraqi assault on the Kurds. In 1983 alone, 8,000 Kurds "disappeared" (Human Rights Watch, 1991). The regime continued to arrest, torture, and summarily execute large numbers of Kurds suspected of opposition. In 1985, the Iraqi government intensified its campaign of systematically razing Kurdish towns and villages and sending their inhabitants to "strategic villages." Within the next two years, 781 villages in the Sorani region alone were destroyed (Saeedpour, 1992).

In the mid-1980s, Iraq began to use chemical weapons against both the Iranians and the Kurds. In a United Nations report published in 1986, Iraq was shown to have increased its use of chemical weapons over the previous two years (Entessar, 1989; Muhsin, Harding and Hazelton, 1989). The Iraqi use of chemical weapons was accelerated in 1987, and especially 1988. In June 1987, Iraqi jets dropped chemical bombs in the marshlands of southern Iraq, where thousands of Iraqi war resisters had taken refuge. In 1988, as the war with Iran was nearing an end, the regime began to use chemical weapons and cluster bombs against civilian targets suspected of supporting the Kurdish movement (Whittleton, Muhsin, and Hazelton, 1989). In April alone, the entire population of Sheik Wasan was killed or injured by poison gas; seven villages in the Sulaimaniya province were attacked with mustard gas; and several villages in the Balisan Valley were bombarded with chemical weapons. The attacks left more than 300 dead and wounded, mainly children and women (Saeedpour, 1992). The chemical attacks culminated with the Halabja massacre, which left thousands dead.

The government's war against the Kurds was carried out in a brutal manner. The decimation of Kurdistan can be summarized in statistics. By June 1988, 3,479 of the 5,000 Kurdish villages had been destroyed, 825 schools were closed, and 2,247 mosques and churches were burned to the ground (Saeedpour, 1992). In the 1980s, more than 50,000 Kurds were believed to have "disappeared," while over 800,000 Kurds were deported to camps near the Saudi and Jordanian borders (Bradshaw, 1991; Sherzad, 1992).

PERPETRATORS, VICTIMS, AND MOTIVES

Iraqi military forces, acting on order from the Ba'th regime, carried out the chemical bombardment of Halabja. The victims of the massacre were Kurdish inhabitants of the city who were unable to flee the poison gas. While retribution certainly played a role in the massacre, the government's ulterior motive appears to be that of pacifying, and possibly destroying, the Kurdish population.

Perpetrators

Saddam Hussein had absolute power in Iraq. His control of the military and all state institutions was beyond question. The escalation of chemical weapons use in Kurdistan occurred after March 1987, when the RCC passed a decree giving the governor of Kurdistan, Saddam's cousin, Ali Hassan al-Majid, unlimited powers to "preserve security and order and ensure stability" (Whittleton, Muhsin, and Hazelton, 1989).[2] In the year leading up to the Halabja massacre, the Iraqis had launched chemical attacks on 21 separate days (Bulloch and Morris, 1992). Clearly, the Halabja massacre was not an isolated incident.

Under al-Majid, an atmosphere of terror permeated Iraqi Kurdistan. The governor instituted revenge killings by ordering the public execution of a young Kurd each time a member of the regime died at the hands of the *peshmerga*. He also ordered the deportation of all civilians from areas that were only partially under government control and razed these villages to the ground (Bulloch and Morris, 1992). Chemical weapons were systematically used under his authority, and therefore it is highly probable that al-Majid and his staff directed the chemical bombardments of Halabja. Even in this case, however, the Ba`th regime and Saddam Hussein directed the war against the Kurds and were ultimately responsible for the actions committed by their agents.

Victims

The chemical bombardment of Halabja was an act of indiscriminate violence. The majority of the over 5,000 killed and 7,000 chemically injured at Halabja were women, children, and the elderly (People for a Just Peace, 1988). These people were not killed because of any act they committed, but simply because they were Kurds. Thus, the Halabja massacre was genocidal in nature, targeting an entire nationalist group, regardless of any other factor.

If the Kurds were guilty of any crime, it was the "crime" of being a Kurd. Iraqi troops and security agents have long engaged in collective punishment. Throughout Iraq, citizens were arrested and tortured for acts committed by their family members. In Kurdistan, collective punishment was carried out in dramatic fashion. Under this scheme, all Kurds were assumed to support the nationalist cause, and therefore all Kurds were legitimate targets.

Motives

Why did the Iraqis use chemical weapons against the Kurdish population? A clear motive is impossible to discern, since the Iraqi government repeatedly denied its use of chemical weapons. The most obvious motive for the Halabja massacre would appear to be retribution. The Kurdish rebels and Iranian forces had just captured the city. The chemical bombardment enabled the Iraqi troops to reclaim the city, as well as punish the Kurds for their insurrection (Bulloch and Morris, 1992). The fact that the bombs were dropped in the residential districts, ensuring heavy loss of life, seems to bear out the retribution motive.

While retribution may have played a significant role in the Halabja massacre, the broader context suggests that the use of chemical weapons served the purpose of depopulating Kurdish areas and forcing survivors into government-controlled villages. The creation of "Saddamite Halabja," surrounded by military posts, serves witness to this phenomenon. According to some, the systematic use of chemical weapons constituted the final phase of an Iraqi policy designed to bring an end to the Kurdish nationalist movement (Saeedpour, 1992). Thus, the government used chemical weapons as part of its overall strategy of repression and terror—all designed to establish control over the Kurdish "nation" and maintain the current political system, dominated by Hussein and the Ba`th Party.

AFTERMATH

The Iraqi government refused to accept responsibility for the Halabja massacre, despite pressure from the United Nations. Meanwhile, the Iraqi regime moved to annihilate the Kurdish population. Two years after the conclusion of the war with Iran, Hussein moved his forces into Kuwait, starting a new round of brutality and war.

Investigation and Accountability

Iraq had no system of checks and balances. The judiciary was completely dependent on the executive, who appointed and dismissed judges and controlled the police agencies (Middle East Watch, 1990). There was no recourse for citizens who had been victimized by the state. Loyalty to Hussein was the only criterion by which people were judged. In Halabja, as in all other acts of aggression, the government simply continued its repressive strategy. There was no independent institution that could hold top government officials accountable for the crimes carried out in their names.

While the Halabja massacre had no internal repercussions for the legitimacy or strength of the Ba`th Party, an international protest required the government to respond to allegations concerning the massacre. Immediately following the massacre, Iran filed a vigorous protest with the United Nations, requesting a UN investigation. Iran, which still maintained control of the city, also invited the international media and humanitarian organizations to Halabja to view the bodies and to interview survivors (Middle East Watch, 1990). In response, the Iraqi government accused Iran of the massacre. In a statement delivered to the United Nations, an Iraqi government official claimed, "With respect to the town of Halabja, it was occupied during these operations by Iranian troops which used various weapons, including chemical weapons, against its Iraqi civilian inhabitants" (Amnesty International, 1989a). The Iraqi attempt to shift responsibility for the massacre onto Iran was foiled by Iraq's continued use of chemical weapons against the Kurds after the end of the war.

In mid-September, the UN Secretary General asked permission of Iraq and Turkey (where many of the refugees had fled) to send a team of experts to investigate charges that Iraq had used poison gas against the Kurds. Both governments promptly rejected the secretary general's request. In Baghdad, Iraqi Defense Minister Adnan Khairallah commented that "the Kurds are Iraqis and it is an internal issue"; furthermore, there was "no justification" for the United Nations or any international party to infringe upon Iraq's sovereignty by independently investigating conditions in Kurdish areas of Iraq (Middle East Watch, 1990: 81).

In an effort to weaken international criticism, the Iraqi government invited a group of 24 Western journalists to visit the Kurdish areas. As expected, the journalists found no physical evidence of chemical weapons use while on their carefully supervised helicopter tour (Middle East Watch, 1990). The Iraqi government, which has never allowed independent verification of charges of human rights violations, continues to deny having used chemical weapons against its Kurdish citizens (Middle East Watch, 1990).

Government Practices and Policies

Between March and August 1988, more than 10,000 Kurdish men, women, and children were killed by the Iraqi government's use of chemical weapons (Atarodi, 1991). On August 20, a cease-fire ended the Iran-Iraq war. The cease-fire enabled the Ba`th government to turn its weapons against the Kurds. From August 25 to September 1, Iraqi planes used chemicals to attack 76 Kurdish villages along the Turkish border (Bulloch and Morris, 1992; Saeedpour, 1992). The depopulated areas were declared free-fire zones in which the Iraqi army followed a policy of shoot-to-kill (Middle East Watch, 1990). More than a half-million Kurds living along the frontier with Iran were resettled in "strategic hamlets" (Marr, 1991). Meanwhile, the leadership of the Kurdish movement went into exile abroad.

In August 1990, Iraq invaded Kuwait, resulting in the outbreak of war between Iraq and UN forces led by the United States. After months of Iraqi occupation, Kuwait was liberated on February 26, 1991. The embarrassing military defeat was a crushing blow to Saddam Hussein. In March, Hussein faced a major uprising and lost control of major cities and towns in northern and southern Iraq. The Kurdish guerrillas managed to liberate 95 percent of Iraqi Kurdistan (Bulloch and

Morris, 1992). The uprising was followed by a wave of government repression, this time targeted against both the Kurds and the Shi`a population.

In northern Iraq, government forces detained an estimated 5,000 Kurdish men and boys from the Kirkuk area, most of whom were released in April. Hundreds, possibly thousands, of people "disappeared" in the custody of the Iraqi authorities, including Kurds and Shi`a Arabs detained at the time of the uprising. Hundreds more were extrajudicially executed by government forces (Amnesty International, 1992a). The Shi`a community was particularly targeted for reprisal. By 1992, Shi`a mosques, schools, and other institutions had been closed, confiscated, or demolished, and entire areas of historic significance to Shi`a culture were destroyed by the authorities (Human Rights Watch, 1992).

In mid-April 1991, the United States and allied forces were deployed in northern Iraq to establish havens for the Kurdish population. In October, Hussein imposed a tight economic embargo on the Kurdish region. The area, protected by Western allies, became a semi-independent zone, under the authority of the principal Kurdish parties. The Kurds were able to rebuild their infrastructure and create a self-governing political entity.

The Kurdish enclave survived through 1992, although it faced increasing signs of hostility from its neighbors (Iran, Turkey, and Syria). Elections were held in May. The PUK, led by Talabani, pressed for self-determination, leaving open the possibility of eventual independence. The PUK was opposed by Barzani's KDP, which favored some type of autonomy, to be negotiated with Baghdad. The outcome was a virtual dead heat and a coalition government was formed by the two parties. In September, a new security force, known as the *asaysh* (Kurdish for "security"), was created, commanded by former PUK and KDP *peshmerga* leaders (Human Rights Watch, 1992). In October, members of the Kurdish National Council approved a motion calling for the creation of a federated state within a democratic pluralistic Iraq. In 1993, a new Kurdish government was announced.

Outside the Kurdish enclave, the Iraqi government continued to engage in massive human rights abuses, from the indiscriminate bombing of rebel positions to the arbitrary arrest and execution of suspected opponents. Large parts of the country were subjected to blockades that prevented food, fuel, and medicines from reaching the population. Iraq's security agents reestablished a strong grip on the country, and throughout the year, there were reports of punitive military operations (Human Rights Watch, 1992).

DISCUSSION

What was the government's rationale for bombing the Kurdish town of Halabja? In its immediate context, the massacre might be considered an act of war, designed to recapture Halabja after it was overrun by Iranian and Kurdish forces. However, the armed forces could have accomplished this feat through less deadly means.

Instead, the chemical bombardment of Halabja and other Kurdish villages was an integral element of the state's terrorist strategy. The regime utilized a policy of mass destruction, forcing the exodus of survivors to government-controlled villages or across the border. The overall design of this strategy was to destroy the unique culture of the Kurdish population, and supplant it with Ba`th ideology and Arab culture.

What factors influence the character of terror in Iraq? Primarily, terror serves an ideological purpose. The Ba`th regime, and Saddam Hussein in particular, control all institutions in society, and use education and the media to serve the interests of the party. Critics of the regime are purged and/or executed, torture is commonplace, and the security forces have full discretion in carrying out arrests and executions. In Kurdistan, the strategies of terror take on an added dimension, as the Ba`th regime not only seeks to assert its authority but also attempts to "Arabize" the population.

Has terror achieved its goals? On the one hand, the regime has successfully used terrorism to eliminate all political rivals and maintain Ba`th authority. On the other hand, the Kurdish insurrection continues, although the Kurds are aided by international measures, which give them some protection from the Hussein regime. In all likelihood, the state's genocidal policy, if fully implemented, could very well decimate the Kurds.

Iraq's experience with state terrorism seems to indicate that a strong leadership with clear direction may have considerable success with terrorist strategies. If strong leadership is a prerequisite, how will the use of terror by relatively weak, democratic governments affect the level of opposition and dissent? In the next chapter, the character of terror in Sudan is reviewed. In Sudan, a fragile democratic government was opposed by an ethnic-based insurgency.

NOTES

1. The Arab Sunni minority accounts for 20 percent of the population; the Arab Shi`a constitute 50 percent; and the Kurds make up the remaining 30 percent of the population (Atarodi, 1991).

2. In 1990, al-Majid was appointed governor of occupied Kuwait.

7

Sudan: Wau Massacre

Sudan had a democratic but unstable government. The government, dominated by northern Arabs, was challenged by an ethnic-based insurgency that sought to gain full economic and political rights for the southern population. The government promoted ethnic hostilities by defending Islamic law and forming tribal militias. In this context, government and tribal forces carried out the Wau massacre of members of the Dinka ethnic group. State terrorism failed to eliminate the rebels, however; the return to military rule brought a high level of terror to the country and forced the insurgency on the defensive.

THE MASSACRE

By the beginning of 1987, civil war had spread through almost all of the Bahr al-Ghazal region. For most of the year, the capital city, Wau, was the base for the province's military commander, Major General Abu Gurun. On August 11 and 12, 1987, the army and Fertit militia sealed off Hillet Dinka, a housing area northeast of the center of town, following a missile attack on a military transport plane believed to have been launched from the area. The search of the poor regions of Wau raged into a government massacre.

In the course of their operations, troops allegedly opened fire on civilians, killing at least 90 people. All people without identification were shot by the army/militia forces, and many houses were burned or looted. Hundreds of Dinkas were brought to the riverside, machine-gunned, and dumped into the river. Dinka boys, aged six to ten, were reportedly forced to kill their families with spears (*Cultural Survival Quarterly*, 1988). At least 60 civilian prisoners were killed at Grinti army barracks in Wau. These victims died from carbon monoxide poisoning after soldiers piped the poisonous gas from their vehicles into the cell (Amnesty International, 1988b). Hundreds of others were machine-gunned or crushed to death by military vehicles. Hundreds more were detained; many were subsequently killed in detention (Amnesty International, 1989h). Several hundred other Dinkas were killed by the army and militia in Wau from September 6 to 11, after a shootout between the army and Dinka police officers who had reportedly tried to prevent the killings of Dinkas (Amnesty International, 1989h). A partial list of missing or killed Dinkas totaled 1,132 (*Cultural Survival Quarterly*, 1988).

HISTORICAL CONTEXT

Sudan is one of the world's most culturally diverse countries, with more than 300 ethnic groups speaking at least 100 languages (Hubbell, 1990). The Dinka-Nuer group is the largest ethnic group in the whole of Sudan. In general, Sudan's population is divided between the northern Arabic and Muslim population and the mostly Christian and animist black peoples of the south. Northern domination has taken the form of both economic exploitation of the severely underdeveloped south and the "Arabization" and "Islamization" of society. The Christian and animist population of the southern Sudan is largely composed of black Africans, as opposed to the people of northern Sudan, who are predominantly Arabic and Muslim (House, 1989).

Government

Sudanese government and the conflicts between the northern and southern regions are for the most part an artifact of British colonialism. Following independence in 1956, Sudanese government was dominated by weak coalition governments and military regimes. In 1969, Major General Gaafar Mohamed Nimeiri established his authority over the government. In the early 1980s, Nimeiri imposed an Islamic state and provoked the outbreak of civil war. In 1985, Nimeiri was ousted by a military coup, which restored democratic rule.

The Influence of British Colonialism

The British ruled Sudan from 1898 to 1956. Administratively, the British treated southern Sudan and parts of western Sudan as an internal colony. Under the Closed Districts Ordinance (1922), the entry into and exit from the southern regions were practically denied to anyone other than the colonial administrators. This system of separate administration created gross inequality between the southern and northern regions of Sudan (Akol, 1987).

The British created a political and economic structure dominated by northern elites. The power elite became centered around two families: the El Mahdi family (the spiritual and political leaders of the Arsar sect), and the El Mirghani family (the leaders of the Khatinia sect). The families, utilizing the free labor available in those areas, created enormous wealth as well as religious and political power for themselves. That power base has remained more or less intact up until the present day (Malwal, 1991).

After independence, the north advanced a colonial policy in which southern Sudan was viewed as a natural resource for northern exploitation (Burton, 1991). The "Arabized" northern Sudanese commanded the government, commerce, trade, finance, politics, the civil service, and the armed forces (Prah, 1989). The south, with valuable resources of water, its potential sources of oil, and a large labor reserve, was regarded as a land of opportunity for northern Sudanese. Religion played an integral role in the colonial policies of the north as membership in the state was equated with being Muslim, and "civilization" with "religion" (Johnson, 1988).

For southerners, independence from Britain meant a continuation of policies intended to suppress their national and cultural rights (Prah, 1989). Southern leaders first attempted to delay independence, and later proposed a federal system of government for the entire country. When this option was decisively rebuffed in 1958, secession began to appear as the only alternative (Johnson, 1988). A civil war soon broke out, with the south being led by the Southern Sudan Liberation Movement (SSLM), better known as Anyanya ("scorpion"), and its military arm, whose objective was the establishment of an independent state (Deng, 1990).

The Nimeiri Regime

In 1969, Major General Gaafar Mohamed Nimeiri became prime minister and two years later, Sudan's first president. Nimeiri consolidated his position by dissolving the Revolutionary Council and establishing the Sudanese Socialist Union (SSU) as the only recognized political party. In 1972, the Addis Ababa agreement ended the civil war. The agreement granted recognition to the pluralistic nature of Sudanese society and proclaimed the south's right to legislate in accordance with its customs. Free elections to the Southern Regional Assembly were decreed, and the assembly was empowered to elect its own president (Warburg, 1991).

In 1977, President Nimeiri pursued a policy of "national reconciliation," which effectively returned opposition parties and organizations to political prominence, including the Muslim Brotherhood. The reconciliation and Nimeiri's placement of Islamic fundamentalists into powerful positions within the government soon changed the landscape of Sudanese politics. In addition, the discovery of oil in the south led to further exploitation as Nimeiri maneuvered to retreat from the Addis Ababa agreement.

In the late 1970s and early 1980s, Nimeiri began to give the Islamic Charter, linked to the international Muslim Brotherhood, widespread power and influence. The Islamic Charter later became known as the National Islamic Front (NIF). Its members had leading positions in the judiciary, and with the appointment of Dr. Hassan El Turabi to the post of attorney general, the fundamentalists began to work for the eventual total abrogation of the south's regional autonomy (Malwal, 1991). Its influence also spread in the teachers union and the medical profession. Its efforts particularly focused on the south, where the NIF had a long-term strategy to convert the population so that a unified Muslim consciousness would prevail throughout Sudan. The NIF election program argued that Islam was the official religion of the state and Arabic the official language (Lesch, 1986).

In 1980, Nimeiri dissolved the Southern Regional Assembly and its government (Warburg, 1991). Nimeiri further broke the Addis Ababa agreement by dividing the south into three regions (Bahr al-Ghazal, Equatoria, and Upper Nile) with reduced constitutional powers. In 1983, in alliance with the Muslim Brotherhood, the president imposed the so-called September Laws which called for the implementation of harsh Islamic law (*sharia*). These actions indicated the government's desire to transform the south into the image of northern culture and identity (Burton, 1991).

Under *sharia*, the subjects of an Islamic state are strictly classified in terms of religion or belief. Only male Muslims have full legal capacity and complete access to any public office in the state (Arzt, 1990; An-na'im, 1992). The new laws, which relegated the non-Muslim population to the status of second class citizens, were immediately carried out with the application of the *hudud* punishments, as 150 men were condemned to public execution and amputation (Chand, 1989; Woodward, 1990).[1]

On April 30, 1984, Nimeiri declared a state of emergency and imposed martial law. He transformed the judiciary into a system of emergency courts. After six months, he dismissed the Supreme Court and appointed in its place the judges of the emergency courts. By the middle of June 1984, 871 people had been tried under martial law (Khalid, 1985). But by 1985, Nimeiri's authority was in doubt and the power of the Muslim Brotherhood became a significant threat. In response, Nimeiri turned on the Brotherhood, arresting its leadership (Woodward, 1990).

Coalition Government

In 1985 a military coup ousted the Nimeiri regime, replacing him with General Abdul Rahman Swar al-Dahab, who headed the Transitional Military Council (TMC). The TMC announced that it would hand over power after a general election scheduled for April 1986 (Salih, 1990). The TMC and the Sudan People's Liberation Army (SPLA) met in March 1986 to sign the Koka Dam Declaration, which called for a "new Sudan that would be free from racism, tribalism, sectarianism and all causes of discrimination and disparity" (Woodward, 1990: 204). The declaration outlined steps to be taken to facilitate peace talks and to initiate a constitutional conference aimed at resolving the major political disagreements among the Sudanese. Despite the declaration, *sharia* still lay at the base of the conflict, and the TMC refused to revoke the law, claiming the newly elected civilian government must take responsibility for the future of *sharia*.

The April 1986 elections, the first multiparty elections since 1968, brought Sadiq al-Mahdi of the Umma Party and a coalition government to power. The new government embarked on some impressive reforms. The presidential power of the State Security Courts was abolished, thus ensuring that trials of political prisoners would in the future be held before criminal courts. The State Security Act, which provided for detention without charge or trial for three-month periods, was also abolished. However, administrative detention without charge or trial for an indefinite period was still permitted. The government continued the state of emergency through 1986.

In the crucial area of *sharia*, al-Mahdi was able to suspend some of the harsher sentences, like amputations and stoning to death for adultery, but refused to abrogate the law. The continuation of *sharia* was certainly influenced by the fundamentalists' threat to declare any Muslim leader who abrogated the law subject to assassination (Nduru, 1991). The two major coalition partners, the Umma and the Democratic Unionist Party (DUP), proved unable to address the crucial problems facing Sudan, such as the deteriorating economy and civil war. On July 25, a state of emergency was declared for a one-year period on economic and security grounds. New emergency regulations were used to ban demonstrations and strikes and to detain people for prolonged periods without charge or trial. Meanwhile, the ineffectiveness of the government coalition led al-Mahdi to dismiss the government. Between August 22, 1987, and May 15, 1988, Sudan was virtually without a government.

From 1986 to 1989, Sadiq al-Mahdi led six different coalition governments. Each coalition government was characterized by rivalries, factionalism, and corruption. From independence onward, the government and political parties, drawn from the traditional sectarian families who thrive on parochialism, proved to be ineffective as agents of national integration (Assam, 1989; Malwal, 1991). The majority of Sudanese view party politics, and government, as corrupt. Political parties buy votes in their election campaigns and favor sons and relatives of the traditional leaders (Assam 1989). Under Sadiq al-Mahdi, the coalition governments were weak, and the pursuit of power by the leaders appeared to be more important than what was achieved once in office (Shawky, 1988; Bechtold, 1990; Salih, 1990). The inability of the coalition governments to address the issue of *sharia* and major SPLA attacks shattered any prospects for a peace settlement.

Civil War

In 1983, civil war again broke out in southern Sudan. The issues underlying the outbreak of hostilities included the dominance of the Arab north over the south, the implementation of *sharia*, the nature of regional government, the annexation of oil-rich areas to the northern territory, and the transfer of the Southern Military Command to the north (Akol 1987; Chand, 1989). The rebel forces managed to capture large areas of the south while the military resorted to tribal militias as a means to fight the guerrillas. Both sides were accused of using food as a weapon.

Guerrilla Opposition

In 1983, the SPLA, led by a former Anyanya officer, Lieutenant John Garang, was created from a corps of mutineers from the army, and hundreds of police, prison officials, and game wardens. The SPLA quickly became a very capable guerrilla army. The SPLA does not advocate secession but the establishment of a secular democratic state and the end of what it sees as Arab and Muslim hegemony (Voll 1990; Deng, 1991). The numerous southern factions and the SPLA reject any suggested solution that does not abolish *sharia* law throughout the whole country (Johnson, 1988; Salih, 1990).

At its inception in 1983, the SPLA was predominantly a Dinka movement. The rank and file has since expanded to include other groups, but the Dinka are still over-represented at the senior levels. On the SPLA's political front, the Sudan People's Liberation Movement (SPLM) began to develop as an organization that could appeal to northerners as well as southerners (Woodward, 1990). The SPLM soon attracted some of the ablest of the younger generation of educated southern Sudanese. The SPLM showed more unity of purpose than any of the other southern political parties (Johnson, 1988).

The SPLA, assisted by Ethiopia, Libya, and Cuba, has periodically pursued negotiations with the government. The possibility of ending the conflict peacefully was greatest in 1986, following the Koka Dam Declaration. But the SPLA's attacks, in particular, its shooting down of two civilian airplanes in August 1986 and again in May 1987, ensured the continuation of civil war.

In 1986, the SPLA controlled large areas of the south outside of main towns. Its strategy included the use of violence against civilians and the use of food as a weapon. In particular, Fertit villages and refugee camps were especially targeted for SPLA attacks. The guerrillas also attempted to prevent food from reaching government-held towns, including Wau (Mawson, 1991). Throughout 1987, the war ravished the southern countryside, with local communities bearing the brunt of the violence from the SPLA, the army, and armed militias.

The Military's War

The government chose to fight the war against the guerrillas by relying on tribal militias. The militias, which were given weapons but no pay, first appeared in 1983. The militias came into prominence in 1985 under the guidance of Major General Fedulla Burma, who occupied a major seat in the coalition government.

The government-backed militias, often referred to as "friendly forces," were involved in combat with the SPLA and have targeted civilians suspected of being supporters of the SPLA (Amnesty International, 1989h). Although the tribal militias were formed to battle the SPLA, in reality, they have often been used to further the economic gain of a certain tribe, resulting in indiscriminate violence aimed at traditional enemies (Mawson, 1991). Militias have been responsible for the deliberate killing of tens of thousands of civilians while hundreds of thousands of people have fled to the towns and cities of northern Sudan, the town of Wau, and the refugee camps of Ethiopia (Mawson, 1991).

An example of the militias and their behavior is the Murahaleen ("armed nomad"), a militia formed among the Rizeigat and Misseriya communities, and primarily used to raid cattle from the Dinka of northern Bahr al-Ghazal. The militia has also been involved in highly publicized massacres of Dinka. For instance, on March 28, 1987, members of the Rizeigat ethnic group and Murahaleen attacked Dinkas seeking police protection in Ad-Daien. Several hundred Dinkas were killed, most of whom were burned alive in locked railway carriages or at the railway police station. Four months later, two university lecturers from Khartoum published a paper on the incident, declaring that government policy was "at the root" of the massacre and accuseing the government of having "squarely introduced the Rizeigat ethnic group into its war with the SPLA" (Mahmud and Baldo, 1987: 19). Other tribal militias have been formed among the Mundari in Equatoria and the Nuer in the Upper Nile. The Nuer, traditional enemies of the Dinka, created a militia known as the Anyanya II. The government also began to encourage the Arab tribes of Baqqara to raid southward, thus bringing in accusations of slave-raiding (Woodward, 1990; Fluehr-Lobban, 1991).

In late 1985, the military and militias began major assaults against the Dinkas of northern Bahr al-Ghazal, one of the most densely populated areas in all of Sudan. Through 1986 and 1987, the cycle of violence culminated in a series of massacres of displaced Dinkas and a breakdown of relief efforts. At least 100,000 people were forced to flee Bahr al-Ghazal for the north in search of food (Duffield, 1990). These actions by government and SPLA forces were directly responsible for the widespread starvation in southern Sudan. Furthermore, the use of tribal militias promoted traditional hostilities and turned the war into a civilian battlefield between various communities.

PERPETRATORS, VICTIMS, AND MOTIVES

The Wau massacre was carried out by army and militia troops. The victims were Dinkas, most of whom lived in the poor areas of the city. The motive was retribution for a guerrilla attack. In a broader sense, the massacre was part of an overall strategy that aimed to divide the southern tribal population, thus ensuring northern domination of the state.

Perpetrators

The army in Bahr al-Ghazal consisted mostly of troops from northern Sudan, Equatoria, and the Fertit tribe. The tribal identity of the troops demonstrates the ethnic component of the civil war. The Fertit militia, known as Jesh al-Salaam ("Army of Peace"), was formed in 1986 after the SPLA engaged in attacks on villages of the Fertit peoples around Wau. The militia received support from the armed forces, and throughout 1987, hundreds of Dinka and Luo civilians in and around Wau were abducted and murdered by Jesh al-Salaam members, sometimes acting with army personnel (Amnesty International, 1989h). Many of the corpses subsequently found were severely mutilated.

The Fertit militia was opposed by death squads consisting of members of the Dinka and Luo communities. Some of the death squads reportedly incorporated personnel from the police, the Wildlife Department, and the Prisons Service. These squads were implicated in killings of Fertit civilians and militia members (Amnesty International, 1989h). Thus, the conflict in Wau was based on ethnic hostilities. Each community felt the need to defend itself from the other. Yet, it was the government that manipulated ethnicity by arming one community and engaging in operations against the other community. The Fertit militia was just one of many tribal militias that acted in accordance with military policy. Hence, the military and government were ultimately responsible for the Wau massacre.

Victims

Members of the Dinka ethnic group were the primary victims of the Wau massacre. In fact, Dinka civilians are frequently targeted by military and militia forces, simply because of their ethnic identity. Government forces operate on the assumption that, since the SPLA primarily is a Dinka organization, all Dinkas naturally support the rebel army. Therefore, Dinkas must be held accountable and punished for rebel activity.

Motives

The motives behind the massacre are more complex than they first appear. There is a long history of communal violence between the Fertit and Dinka communities. The Fertit communities felt they were excluded from the new regional government in Wau, and tensions between the two groups grew

(Woodward, 1990). In particular, the Fertit people were highly suspect of the police, the Department of Prisons, the Department of Wildlife, and the regional authorities. The Fertit felt these institutions were unduly dominated by members of the Dinka and Luo peoples. In turn, the members of these institutions and the Dinka and Luo communities had poor relations with the Fertit militia and the army (Amnesty International, 1989h). Thus, for the Fertit militia, the massacre may have been an attempt to end Dinka dominance of Wau and shift the balance of power to the Fertit. It is even more likely that the Fertit engaged in the killings for the very simple reason of retribution.

The Fertit militia did not act alone, and the army had no concerns about the political struggle within Wau. It was the army that directed the massacre, not the militia. The armed forces represented the northern government, dominated by Islamic Arabs who have traditionally viewed the south and its population as a natural resource to be exploited. The military's war, which included the use of food as a weapon, suggests that the motive behind such acts of terror was to eliminate the SPLA's primary base of support, the Dinkas. By encouraging tribal attacks between communities, the government hoped the SPLA would be consumed with factional fighting, and the Arab regime would gain control of southern resources.

AFTERMATH

The government refused to acknowledge the Wau massacre in particular and the military's role in human rights violations in general. The coalition government proved weak and in 1989, a military coup brought a new dimension of government terror. The military joined forces with the NIF to create arguably one of the most repressive regimes in Africa. The government legitimized the tribal militias and continued its offensives against the SPLA and Dinka population.

Investigation and Accountability

Sudan had no internal mechanism to monitor human rights violations. Its judiciary had very little, if any, independence from the executive. Furthermore, the government had turned the judiciary into a tool of Islamic fundamentalism. While the legal system was not equipped to deal with abuses committed by government forces, the civilian government did have the legislative ability to investigate massacres and other severe violations. In the case of the Wau massacre, there was no investigation whatsoever. This reflected the incompetence and corruption of the coalition governments and their willingness to ignore army atrocities committed in the south.

At the international level, the Sudanese government pointed to the tribal nature of the war as a way to distance itself from outside criticism. Indeed, the government regularly dismissed massacres and killings as "tribal fighting" (Amnesty International, 1989h). The attempt to blame tribes for violence in the south was accompanied by denials and accusations. In a general comment to the United Nations, the Observer for Sudan pleaded that "organizations and Governments would pay no heed to the lies and misleading propaganda that had been circulating since the democratic transformation in the Sudan" (U.N. Doc. E/CN.4/1989/SR.49/Add.1).

Government Practices and Policies

One month after the massacre, Wau was effectively divided into two towns. The east was controlled by police, mostly Dinkas; the west was run by the Fertit militia. Civilians from the rival ethnic groups were slaughtered indiscriminately by the armed factions (Amnesty International, 1989h). In 1988, the situation in Wau was relatively calmer but the killings of civilians continued. Killings in Wau continued in 1989, despite a cease-fire between the government and the SPLA. For instance, on July 19, at least 34 civilian detainees were extrajudicially executed by government soldiers (Amnesty International, 1989h).

A new "government of national unity" finally materialized and took office in 1988. The NIF joined the new government and was able to control much of the agenda and policy direction. In May, the government adopted a more hardline approach to the war, with the aim of achieving a decisive military victory (Salih, 1990). But in a surprise initiative in November, Mohammed Osman el-Mirghani, the leader of the DUP, signed an agreement in Addis Ababa with the SPLA leadership that called for a cease-fire, the freezing of *sharia*, the lifting of the state of emergency, and the abolition of all political and military pacts with other countries. The NIF condemned the agreement, reiterated its former position that it would oppose any move to freeze or abolish the *sharia*, and organized a massive rally in order to exert pressure on the government. When the other parties refused to back the agreement, the DUP retaliated by withdrawing its ministers and support, thereby contributing to the downfall of yet another coalition (Salih, 1990). A new coalition was formed in which the Cabinet included representatives of all political parties except the NIF.

On June 30, 1989, Sudanese democracy ended in a military coup that brought to power Omar Hassan Ahmad al-Bashir and the National Salvation Revolution Command Council (NSRCC). Immediately following the coup, the government declared a state of emergency. Under this emergency, prisoners were held without charge or trial, the showing of any political opposition to the regime was illegal, and the authorities were empowered to arrest and detain anyone suspected of being a danger to political or economic security. Under the decree, detainees had no right to know why they were detained, no right to challenge their detention before the courts, and no recourse to periodic judicial review of their cases (Amnesty International, 1992e). Under the state of emergency, the government also banned all non-religious organizations and trade unions, dissolved the Constituent Assembly, suspended the constitution, and purged suspected opponents (Amnesty International, 1990b). The military government joined forces with the NIF, led by Dr. Hassan al-Turabi, and appointed Islamic militants to senior positions throughout the government (Hubbell, 1990). In addition, several secret security forces were established, the most dreaded and powerful of which was a group controlled and headed by a fundamentalist and former lecturer in the University of Khartoum (Nduru, 1991). Most observers believe the NIF merely used the army as a vehicle for a broader plan to take over the government (Robison, 1992).

There was considerable opposition to the new government's policies from elements in the army and from civilians. Several purges of the army were undertaken, through forced retirement, arrest, and imprisonment, and recently, 28 officers accused of plotting a coup were executed (Hunwick, 1992). Civilian protests since October 1989 have led to the arrest and detention without trial of hundreds of trade unionists, doctors, academics, artists, and lawyers as well as the dismissal of about 1,000 public servants (Hunwick, 1992).

The new government was quick to indicate its continuing support for the general policy of using militias. In November 1989, a Popular Defense Act was promulgated, creating Popular Defense Committees. These committees in essence were made up of militia forces, thus legitimizing their actions (Mawson, 1991). The Popular Defense Committees stepped up their activity, and in early 1990, massacres of hundreds of villagers in western Sudan were reported (Voll, 1990). In 1990, the armed forces and tribal militias continued to engage in extrajudicial executions of prisoners and unarmed civilians (Amnesty International, 1990b).

In December 1989 and January 1990, several hundred trade unionists were arrested. Many were taken to unofficial detention centers known as "ghost houses" and subjected to torture (Human Rights Watch, 1991). In 1990, the government imprisoned hundreds of non-violent government opponents, resumed the use of torture in detention centers in the capital, and increased the number of floggings of criminal offenders. Justice was meted out in special Revolutionary Security Courts, staffed by active-duty military officers, in which no defense counsel was allowed, rules for admitting evidence were arbitrary, and rights of appeal were limited (Human Rights Watch, 1991). Despite an amnesty declared in April 1991, in which nearly 300 political prisoners were released, detention and torture remained routine in Khartoum and the other major cities of northern Sudan (Human Rights Watch, 1992). Several hundred detainees were kept in ghost houses. Their families were not informed of their whereabouts. The government denied their very existence and the prisoners received no visitors.

In 1991, the government introduced a new penal code allegedly founded upon Islamic principles. Significant sections of the code that relate to treason and other offenses against the state reduced non-Muslims to second-class citizens. Apostasy, the renunciation of Islam, became a capital offense (Amnesty International, 1992a). The government also embarked on a program intended to transform the major universities into centers of exclusively Islamic learning, following the doctrines of the Muslim Brothers (Human Rights Watch, 1992).

In August 1991, two leading commanders split from the mainstream SPLA of Colonel John Garang, accusing him of holding more than 40 political detainees, forcibly recruiting children as soldiers, and ruling the organization in a highly authoritarian manner. The split in the SPLA led to some of the worst human rights abuses that the south has witnessed since the outbreak of war. On September 28, the SPLA fractured further when Garang's senior commander broke away (Human Rights Watch, 1992). In November 1991, forces loyal to the breakaway faction of the SPLA, led by SPLA commanders in Upper Nile and popularly known as the Nasir Group, arbitrarily killed over 2,000 civilians in southern Upper Nile (Amnesty International, 1992e). Furthermore, the rebel forces were weakened by the change of government in Ethiopia which meant they could no longer operate from bases there.

During 1992, Sudan suffered from an extraordinary range of human rights abuses committed on a huge scale. The military government headed by General al-Bashir remained firmly in power and resolutely committed to the transformation of Sudan into an Islamic state, by whatever means necessary. In March, the government launched its largest offensive yet against the SPLA. The offensive proved successful, and by July a string of important SPLA-held towns had fallen to government attack. The offensive produced numerous abuses of human rights, including arbitrary killings of civilians. The cumulative effect of the war and human rights abuses in the south has been to bring the region to the brink of a major humanitarian disaster (Human Rights Watch, 1992).

In 1993, peace talks between the government and various factions of the rebel forces commenced. A cease-fire was declared in March. In May, the government and rebel factions accepted the concept of a unified federal state, with the implementation of *sharia* in the northern states but not in the south. As of this writing, peace had not been fully restored in Sudan.

DISCUSSION

Why did government forces resort to the massacre of Dinkas? The massacre demonstrated the military's tendency to engage in collective punishment by holding the Dinka population accountable for acts committed by rebel forces. But the participation of a tribal militia in the massacre displays another side of the conflict. In Sudan, ethnic and religious cleavages are associated with economic and political opportunities. In the city of Wau, conflict became communalized, with the minority Fertit group forming a tribal militia and the emergence of death squads composed of members of the dominant Dinka and Luo community. In this context, the massacre was carried out not only for retribution, but signaled an attempt to change the distribution of power in Wau.

What factors account for the character of terror in Sudan? The government used terror to assert the dominance of the Islamic regime and impose its cultural mores on other ethnic groups. The imposition of *sharia* demonstrates this motive. The major strategy of terror can be described as indiscriminate enforcement terror, which especially targets members of the minority population living in the southern regions. The character of terror also was influenced by the government's reliance on tribal militias. In brief, the military manipulated ethnic hostilities to carry out the war, and consequently, terror took on an added element. Tribal militias turned their weapons against traditional enemies as a means to further economic gain.

Did state terrorism succeed in eliminating the ethnic-based insurgency? The rebels, who also relied on terrorist tactics against the civilian population, made significant advances against government troops. However, a military coup ended the Sudanese experiment with democracy and established a brutal military regime. The new government consolidated its power through purges, mass arrests, the banning of all non-religious organizations, and the systematic abuse of human rights. The government, benefiting from divisions in the rebel organization, successfully captured rebel-held territory and prompted peace talks.

The Sudanese case suggests that ethnic hostilities can be manipulated to the advantage of the ruling group. But can democracy survive in a society polarized along ethnic lines? The next chapter discusses state terrorism in India, where a heterogeneous state with a strong tradition of democracy is challenged by ethnic and religious-based insurgencies.

NOTE

1. Criminal offenses under *sharia* are divided into three classes: *hudud, qisas,* and *ta'zir.* *Hudud* are the most severe of the offenses and include theft, highway robbery, drinking wine, fornication, and according to some, apostasy by a Muslim, and rebellion. *Hudud* crimes require stiff punishment, such as amputation of the right hand for theft and stoning to death for a married person accused of fornication (An-na'im, 1992).

8

India: Meerut/Maliana Massacre

India is a secular democracy dominated by the Congress Party. The state is divided along ethnic and religious lines, and several insurgencies battle the government in an effort to establish independent states. The government, which advances the interests of upper-class Hindus, has encouraged communal hostilities by endorsing fundamentalist religious groups. In the context of Hindu-Muslim riots, regional police carried out the massacre of Muslims in Meerut and Maliana. The government's terrorist strategies failed to deter the insurgencies and resulted in the intensification of communal violence.

THE MASSACRE

In mid-April 1987, widespread communal violence between Hindus and Muslims broke out in the city of Meerut, Uttar Pradesh. Riots broke out again in May after large numbers of Muslims were indiscriminately arrested. From May 19 through 23, the entire town of Meerut was under a curfew. On May 22, the Hindi-dominated Provincial Armed Constabulary (PAC) rounded up several hundred Muslim men in the Hashimpura area of Meerut. Most of the arrested were taken to police stations or jail but around 100 men were driven to the Upper Ganga canal (Engineer, 1987a). Once at the canal, the PAC lined up the men, shot them one by one, and threw their bodies in the water (Engineer, 1987a; Amnesty International, 1988c, 1988e). The floating bodies were discovered after a few days, and two survivors chronicled the massacre (Engineer, 1988). *The Times of India* commented: "Here is a clear case of an organ of the state going out with cold-blooded calculation to raid and round up a whole group of citizens, whisk them away, shoot them while in custody and then throw their bodies into the river" (Chakravartly, 1987). The following day, the PAC arrived in the village of Maliana, under the pretext that Muslims from Meerut were hiding in the area. The

PAC went on a rampage, deliberately shooting unarmed men, women, and children and burning some of the victims alive in their own houses. Eighty bodies were found in the area, believed to be those of victims of these killings (Amnesty International, 1988e).

An exact count of the number of dead as the result of the Meerut/Maliana massacre is not known, although most experts agree that dozens of people were killed. According to official figures, from May 19 to May 23, 117 people were killed, 159 persons injured, and 623 houses, 344 shops, and 14 factories were looted, burned, and destroyed (Engineer, 1989). Another report notes that in the first three or four days of the riot, 51 Hindus were killed, and from May 21 to May 25, at least 295 Muslims were killed, almost all by or under the active supervision of the police and the PAC (Balagopal, 1987). Violence, including bomb explosions and isolated incidents of killing and stabbing, continued until June 15 (Engineer, 1989).

HISTORICAL CONTEXT

India is one of the most heterogenous states in the world. It contains every major religion in the world, and there are thousands of caste divisions among the many Hindu linguistic divisions. It is also a very poor state, and half of the population is impoverished and illiterate (Amnesty International, 1992d). Throughout the 1980s, the Indian government faced ethnic- and religious-based struggles. Demands for increased autonomy or separation were made in various parts of India, including Punjab, West Bengal, Bihar and several parts of northeast India. Political violence and armed opposition were widespread in these states, particularly in Punjab, where armed Sikh groups advocated Khalistan, a separate Sikh state. Much of the conflict has its origins in British colonialism and the partition of India.

British Colonialism and the Partition

India was under British rule for centuries. For the purposes of governance, the British imperial authority divided the country into British India, consisting of directly administered provinces, and Princely India, made up of roughly 560 feudal states and territories (Khan, 1989). For the most part, political divisions were made along religious lines. In this manner, the British transformed religious cleavages into political cleavages (Khan, 1989). Although independence was declared in 1947, the government inherited boundaries and divisions based on the religious composition of the nation.

Another factor significant to understanding the nature of conflict in India is the partition. In 1930, the Muslim League demanded creation of a Muslim state wherever Muslims were in the majority. The league supported Britain during the war, and afterward Britain agreed to the formation of Pakistan as a separate dominion. The partition resulted in a serious problem of discrimination and hostility against the Muslims who remained in India and whose loyalty was now in question (Hussain, 1989).

Half of India's Muslims live in three states: Bihar, Uttar Pradesh, and West Bengal. Muslims in these states were most affected by the partition. For one thing, the exodus to Pakistan greatly diminished the Muslim middle and professional classes. As a result, there were hardly any Muslims left in the defense services, in police, in universities, law courts, and in the General Secretariat in Delhi (Hasan, 1991). The exodus reduced the Muslim population from 25 percent before the partition to less than 10 percent in 1951, and left the remaining population facing dim economic prospects (Shakir, 1986; M. Hasan, 1991). In addition, the Hindi-dominated state governments adopted a hostile attitude toward the Muslim population. This was especially noticeable in Uttar Pradesh, where the administration ordered the sealing of Muslim shops and made it known that Muslims would not be employed in government or recruited in the police. Furthermore, the chief minister discouraged the teaching of Urdu, a language spoken mostly by Muslims, and in 1951, Hindi was declared the sole official language of the state (M. Hasan, 1991).

Government

The Congress Party, founded in 1885, has dominated India's political scene since independence. In 1966, Indira Gandhi became prime minister and ruled almost continuously until her assassination in 1984. She was succeeded by her son, Rajiv. The Congress government has, for the most part, responded to growing crises throughout the country by resorting to repressive legislation. In recent times, as the Congress Party's popularity waned, it turned to the divisive politics of religion as a way to capture votes. The outcome of these strategies has been the polarization of society along sectarian lines and escalating violence.

Repressive Legislation

India is a federal republic, in which the 25 state governments are responsible for public order, police, and the administration of justice and prisons. Among the first repressive acts that came into effect after independence were a series of state-level laws that enabled the government to designate any area as "disturbed" and confer extraordinary powers on the police or security forces (Mukhoty, 1990). An example of state repressive legislation is the Jammu and Kashmir Public Safety Act, which permits preventive detention and has resulted in the detention of political prisoners without trial for engaging in alleged "anti-nationalist" activities (Amnesty International, 1988e).

At the national level, the Congress government enacted the National Security Act (NSA) in 1980. Under the NSA, people could be detained without charge or trial for loosely defined security reasons for up to one year (two years in Punjab). In 1983, the Armed Forces Special Powers Act was promulgated. In force in Assam, Jammu and Kashmir, and Punjab, the act widens army powers of arrest and grants the security forces immunity from prosecution for "anything done or purported to be done" under the act (Amnesty International, 1992d). In August 1984, the Congress government promulgated the Terrorist Affected Areas (Special Courts) Ordinance. Under this decree, trials were to be held *in camera*, the burden of proof was shifted to the accused upon certain minimal findings, and appeals to the Supreme Court were possible only within a 30-day period. By the end of 1984, several thousand people were reportedly awaiting trial before three Special Courts (Amnesty International, 1985).

Indian politics reached a major crisis in 1984. In June, the Indian army killed as many as 1,000 people at the Golden Temple in Amritsar, the holiest shrine of the Sikh religion and the base for terrorist raids. The sacrilege to the Golden Temple brought a spasm of mutinies and desertions by Sikh officers and soldiers in the army. On October 31, Indira Gandhi was assassinated by two men identified by police as Sikh members of her security guard. In the riots following the assassination, approximately 3,000 Sikhs were killed (Amnesty International, 1985). The ruling Congress Party chose her son, Rajiv Gandhi, to succeed her as prime minister.

The new government continued the trend toward repressive legislation as a way to deal with insurgency. In 1985, following a series of bomb explosions in New Delhi and neighboring states, the government passed one of the most repressive laws in Indian history, the Terrorist and Disruptive Activities (Prevention) Act (TADA). The legislation effectively institutionalized state violence by arbitrarily labeling certain kinds of offenses as "terrorist" and giving even lower-rank police officials considerable discretion in capturing suspects (Mukhoty, 1990). The law mandated the death penalty for "terrorist" acts that resulted in death. It also made "disruptive" activities, broadly defined, punishable by three years to life imprisonment. In 1987, both the NSA and TADA were amended. The NSA, as it applied to Punjab, allows detainees to be held for an extended period of six months before being brought before an Advisory Board. The TADA, which shifts the burden of proof to the accused, was also strengthened to allow detention in judicial custody without formal charge or trial up to a year (Amnesty International, 1988e; Mathur, 1992).

India's repressive legislation was accompanied by the detention of political activists, widespread reports of torture, staged (or "encounter") killings, and more recently, "disappearances" (Amnesty International, 1988e; 1989a; Mukhoty, 1990). In 1987, several thousand political detainees were held without charge or trial under special anti-terrorist laws and preventive detention legislation (Amnesty International, 1988e). In addition, there were reports of deliberate police killings in areas where landless laborers were involved in disputes with landowners. In these cases, evidence suggests that local politicians and police have worked in close collaboration with private armies, or *senas*, hired by landowners (Amnesty International, 1988e).

The government's resort to repressive legislation failed to solve the conflicts and eroded the rule of law. The enormous discretion given to members of the security forces led to widespread and severe abuses. Their immunity from prosecution and the court's permission to try certain prisoners without the usual legal safeguards effectively legitimized government repression.

Divisive Politics

At the national level, Congress Party supporters represented a variety of social classes, occupational groups, religions, and languages. But regionally, the electoral support of the party was quite homogeneous, composed of factions of elites who cooperate in the pursuit of office (Chhibber and Petrocik, 1990). In the 1980s, the Congress Party shifted its orientation from being an all-inclusive party to a party of communal interests.

In 1975, India veered toward authoritarian rule. The turn of events occurred when a judge found Indira Gandhi's landslide victory in the 1971 elections invalid because civil servants had illegally aided her campaign. Amid demands for her resignation, Indira Gandhi declared a state of emergency and ordered mass arrests of her critics. In 1977, the Congress Party, which had ruled India for 30 years without interruption, was defeated at the polls by the Janata Party. Gandhi's defeat brought significant changes to the party system and the strategies of mobilization. In the 1977 elections, the Congress Party lost the support of the Muslim constituency, leading Indira Gandhi to turn to the Hindu vote. From the late 1970s, the Congress Party moved toward the right and began discreetly promoting the cause of Hindu religious groups (Engineer, 1989; Z. Hasan, 1991). Gandhi, campaigning around themes of Hindu hegemony, was able to recoup most of her losses in the northern Hindi-speaking states and in 1980, regained control of the central government (Brass, 1985; Z. Hasan, 1991).

The 1984 parliamentary elections produced a stunning majority for the Congress Party, under its new leader, Rajiv Gandhi. The election campaign was marked by a noticeable shift in attitudes of Congress Party candidates toward the minorities. The campaign focused nearly exclusively on the dangers to the country posed by internal and external enemies and on the need for Indians, meaning Hindus, to close ranks to save the country. Some Congress Party candidates went so far as to group the Muslims together with the Sikhs as internal threats, supported by external agents and foreign countries (Brass, 1985).

The rise of communal politics benefited the right-wing parties. In particular, the Bharatiya Janata Party (BJP), which promoted Hindu "nationalism," improved its position dramatically in the 1984 elections. At the same time, there was a national resurgence of religious movements and an increase in violence between the Hindu and Muslim communities. In the 1986 by-elections, the Congress Party continued its strategy of direct appeals to the majority community, while abandoning larger social issues, such as poverty (Z. Hasan, 1991). However, this strategy did not generate large-scale support for the party and it again turned to the Muslim vote.

In 1986, the Congress Party government passed the Muslim Women's (Protection of Rights on Divorce) Bill, which sought to establish the supremacy of Muslim Personal Law (Datta, 1991). By voting this act, the Congress Party government gave in to the Muslim fundamentalist demand to overrule the Supreme Court verdict that a divorced woman should be paid alimony by her former husband (Elst, 1990). The bill was an obvious attempt to woo the Muslim vote by appeasing Muslim fundamentalists (Z. Hasan, 1991). However, it was met with a massive outcry. The controversy generated by the bill forced the Congress Party into a defensive position, and the party shifted the blame on to the Muslim community.

Following the outrage caused by the Muslim Women's Bill, the Congress Party set out to placate the Hindu fundamentalist movement, in particular, the Vishwa Hindu Parishad (VHP), an organization devoted to "liberating" scores of Hindu places of worship (Engineer, 1989). For years, the most volatile symbol of Hindu-Muslim relations was the Ram Janambhoomi/Babri Masjid controversy. In brief, the controversy revolved around a mosque in Ayodha, Uttar Pradesh. The Babri mosque, an Islamic monument, was built over the ruins of a temple where Hindus believe the warrior-god Rama was born. The VHP led the campaign to "liberate" the temple, organizing massive pledge-taking rallies to "protect" Ram Janambhoomi (Bhatnagar, 1987; *Economic and Political Weekly*, 1987). The site had been off limits to both communities since a 1949 court order. But in 1986, the Congress Party government allowed the lock on the mosque to be removed and handed the structure to Hindu worshippers (Datta, 1991). The government's communal politics further polarized Hindu-Muslim relations in Uttar Pradesh and was a major force behind the Meerut/Maliana massacre.

Communal Violence

The most intractable problem of the Indian polity and society is communalism, or "the belief that a group of people who follow a particular religion have, as a result, common social, political and economic interests" (Chandra, 1987: 1). Communalism is an ideology in which political allegiance to a religious community is considered primary (Khan, 1989). Despite its religious nature, the real basis of communalism is the struggle over political and economic power between various communities (Puri, 1987; Saiyed, 1988; Banu, 1989). For example, competition among trading communities has been an historic cause of riots in Uttar Pradesh. By using political connections strengthened through religious memberships, one community would try to weaken the other for more profits (Candor, 1988).

The government's interpretation of secularism is partly responsible for fueling the animosity between the Hindu and Muslim communities. Secularism can be interpreted as indifference or neutrality to religion, or as equal respect for all religions (Shakir, 1986). In the case of India, secularism has come to mean equal treatment of all religions and has resulted in special legislation for each religion (Ghosh, 1987). In particular, the Muslim Personal Law and Uniform Civil Code is a communally sensitive issue. The majority of Hindus hold that family laws for all religious communities should be the same, while the majority of Muslims believe that a separate body of Muslim family laws is a necessary part of their freedom of religion and their right to preserve their distinct culture (Ansari, 1990). In practice, Hindus must strictly observe monogamy, while Muslims are allowed to follow personal law, which gives men the right to take four wives and divorce their wives at will. Personal law also excludes Muslims from family planning programs (Ter-Grigoryan, 1983; Ghosh, 1987).

The government itself took a communal posture. As previously noted, communalism has been used to promote political mobilization (Saiyed, 1988). To the politicians, communalism served the function of diverting attention from the pervasive poverty (Candor, 1988; Engineer, 1989). Instead of blaming their condition on the faulty policies of the government, the masses tended to accuse the other community for their troubles (Candor, 1988). In the end, communalism effectively divided the Indian populace, thus serving the interests of the ruling classes, who were able to ensure their own domination (Shakir, 1986; Hussain, 1989).

Communalism thrives on the Hindu community's perception that Muslims and other minorities receive favored treatment from the state (Malik and Vajpeyi, 1989; Sisson, 1990; Gargan, 1992). In the mid-1980s, there was a resurgence of Hindu communalism, linked both to the terrorist violence against Hindus in the Punjab and Kashmir and to the 1984 assassination of Indira Gandhi (Girdner and Siddiqui, 1990; Mukhoty, 1990). The rising popularity of the VHP and electoral success of the BJP were evidence of this trend. In actuality, Muslims held relatively few positions of power and influence in Indian society (Ansari, 1990). From their point of view, the police, administration, and electoral system, heavily favoring upper-class Hindus, had little credibility (Puri, 1987). Indeed, communal riots strengthened the Muslim perception that government officials and police were abetting violence against them (Sisson, 1990).

The number and intensity of Hindu-Muslim riots have been increasing since the 1970s (Hussain, 1989). The riots, which tended to occur in cities where the Muslims had some degree of economic influence, were typically sparked off by an incident associated with religious festivals and customs (Ahmad, 1980; Sudhir, 1980; Rajgopal, 1987; Engineer, 1988; Saiyed, 1988; Hussain, 1989). Police brutalities were regular features of communal riots. The police and state agencies invariably participated in widespread arson, looting, and killing of Muslims, while the regional and central governments repeatedly failed to punish civil servants and police participating in riots (Hussain, 1989; Mukhoty, 1990).

Since the 1978 Aligarh riots, Muslims have increasingly viewed the police and state paramilitary forces as instruments of torture and repression (Ansari, 1990). In 1982, the PAC killed numerous unarmed Muslims during riots in Meerut (Engineer, 1988). In the 1984 Bhiwandi-Bombay and Assam riots, the majority of the more than 3,500 deaths were caused by police shootings (Engineer, 1987b). In Uttar Pradesh alone, between February 1986 and early 1988, there were nearly 60 riots, resulting in at least 200 deaths (Z. Hasan, 1991). In the aftermath of communal riots, it was almost certain that the overwhelming majority of those arrested, killed, or injured would be Muslims, and state security personnel accused of connivance would not be brought to justice (Ansari, 1991).

PERPETRATORS, VICTIMS, AND MOTIVES

The perpetrators of the Meerut/Maliana massacre were members of the provincial police force. The victims were Muslims, who were killed indiscriminately. The motive would appear to be punishment as well as intimidation. In a broader context, the massacre served the function of upholding Hindu domination of the state.

Perpetrators

The Provincial Armed Constabulary (PAC) had a history of human rights violations. It was blamed for worsening the situation during the 1978 Aligarh riots, for massacring more than 150 people at places of worship in Moradabad in 1980, and for instigating communal violence in Meerut in 1982. In 1984, at least two petitions were filed in the Supreme Court for the disbandment of the PAC (Noorani, 1987; Amnesty International, 1988e). The PAC, like the Uttar Pradesh administration, reflected the dominance of Hindus. Muslims made up just 2 percent of its members (Bhatnagar, 1987; *Economic and Political Weekly*, 1987).

Was the massacre the outcome of poorly trained soldiers acting on their own, or was it officially condoned? Although it is doubtful that the killings were actually ordered by high-level officials, it seems clear that the massacre required a certain degree of planning and coordination. The PAC had an unwritten policy of treating the Muslim population in an arbitrary fashion. Of the 4,000 arrests during the riots, the vast majority were Muslims, including scores of children (Bhatnagar,

1987). The killings in Maliana seemed especially deliberate and planned, since violence was not reported from the area and the PAC's presence was not required. The Meerut/Maliana massacre was not an isolated incident, but part of an overall repressive strategy that targeted the Muslim community. The state government had repeatedly failed to make the PAC accountable for its abuses, and has neglected to make the force more representative of the population it serves. Although the Uttar Pradesh administration ultimately was responsible for the actions of the PAC, the Indian central government also was responsible for encouraging communal violence by bowing to pressures both from Hindu and Muslim fundamentalists.

Victims

Those killed in the Meerut/Maliana massacre were Muslims. Their guilt or innocence of any crime was never an issue. Rather, the men who were killed at the Upper Ganga canal were picked up and arrested for one reason: They were Muslims. In Maliana, the killings were carried out in an entirely indiscriminate manner, with no regard for the gender or age of the victim. The Meerut/Maliana massacre was a genocidal massacre, targeted against a particular ethno-religious group regardless of any other factor.

The massacre and victimization of Muslims was not uncommon. For the most part, the massacre was a product of communalism. The riots involved crimes committed by members of both Muslim and Hindu communities. But the government and police forces systematically disregarded crimes committed by Hindus, and instead directed all their enforcement powers against the Muslims. In the Meerut riots, Hindu mobs openly indulged in looting, burning, and killing, yet the vast majority of those arrested were Muslims (Engineer, 1988). Typically, the Hindu officials assume that Muslims are to blame for instigating the riots, and therefore need to be reprimanded for their crime. Even if this were the case, the PAC victimized members of the Muslim community because of their identity, not their role in the riots.

Motives

Why did the PAC massacre Muslims? Certainly, the killings were not in self-defense, and the PAC could have terminated its action at the arrest and detention stage. Since the PAC and Uttar Pradesh government have not accepted responsibility for the massacre, it is difficult to document a motive. However, given the context, it would seem that the massacre was carried out as a way to punish and intimidate the Muslim population.

The most obvious motive for the massacre was retribution. Without a doubt, the riots involved Muslim attacks against members of the Hindu community. In an effort to "teach them a lesson," the PAC sought out Muslims and killed them. But aside from retribution, the context suggests the role of wider political and economic forces. Meerut's Muslim community, which accounts for about 45 percent of the population, had substantially increased its economic power and political aspirations, enough to pose a threat to Hindu domination of the local political and economic structure (Engineer, 1988). For the Hindus, the obvious goal was to maintain or enhance their dominant position in society. Repression is one way to assert authority and power. It is entirely plausible that the massacre was carried out as part of an overall repressive policy designed to keep Muslims "in their place." The massacre certainly had the effect of ensuring Hindu hegemony.

AFTERMATH

Official investigations followed the Meerut/Maliana massacre, although the inquiries were limited in scope. Communal politics continued at the federal and regional levels, with significant gains by Hindu fundamentalist parties. Violence continued, and in 1992, Hindu extremists tore down the Babri mosque, triggering a new round of Hindu-Muslim riots.

Investigation and Accountability

The initial response of the government to the massacres at Meerut and Maliana was one of denial, followed by attempts to cover up the crime. In a desperate attempt to find someone else to blame, an Indian embassy official explained the allegations by stating that "police uniforms were stolen and used as a disguise by anti-social elements" (Amnesty International, 1988c). Meanwhile, the Uttar Pradesh administration, led by Chief Minister V. B. Singh, claimed that the Muslims were the real aggressors, implying that the PAC's behavior was justified (Akbar, 1988; Saxena, 1988). Singh did suspend the PAC's commandant, Tripathi, but after one day he was reinstated for fear of revolt in the PAC (Bhatnagar, 1987).

The facts surrounding the massacre were a cause of contention. There was a great deal of official silence concerning the event. Details of the massacre were difficult to verify, as the government banned Muslim leaders from the area, failed to issue curfew passes to reporters, and did not acknowledge the incident in the day's official briefing (Yusuf, 1987; Vyas and Mukhopadhyay, 1988). In an attempt to downplay the massacre, Union Home Minister Buta Singh told the National Integration Council that only ten persons were killed in Maliana (Vyas and Mukhopadhyay, 1988). The Indian government, despite granting compensation to the relatives of the Meerut victims, has never acknowledged that its security forces were responsible for the massacre (Noorani, 1989).

Days after the massacre, a High Court judge was appointed to conduct an inquiry into the incident in Maliana. After one year, the inquiry reportedly held just two hearings (Amnesty International, 1988e). Apparently, no findings were ever published and as of this date, no charges are known to have been brought against any persons responsible for the Maliana killings.

In June, the Uttar Pradesh government formed a committee, chaired by Gian Prakash, to investigate the events in Meerut. The committee was assigned the task of studying the causes of violence in Meerut between May 18 and 22 and of making recommendations on preventing further incidents. The committee was to focus on the underlying causes of the riot, not the PAC's behavior during the riot. The committee's report, which was never officially published, found that Muslim leaders, who deliberately provoked, instigated, and organized the Muslim community to turn violent, were responsible for the riots. The report also noted the role of the Ram Janambhoomi/Babri Masjid controversy in creating a climate of communal hatred (Balagopal, 1987). In regard to the PAC, the committee only concluded that the use of force "appears to have been excessive" and recommended that special courts be set up to prosecute those responsible for the killings in Meerut (Amnesty International, 1988e). No members of the PAC were ever charged for crimes associated with the Meerut massacre.

Government Policies and Practices

Throughout the latter part of the 1980s, the government continued to face armed insurrection groups. Political violence increased in Punjab and in May 1987, Punjab was placed under direct rule from Delhi. In March 1988, parliament passed the 59th Amendment to the constitution, which suspended the right to life and empowered the security forces to shoot people at will in Punjab. The amendment was repealed in December 1989.

The November 1989 elections led to a period of political instability. The Congress Party was forced into opposition for the second time since independence, and the Janata Dal Party, led by V.P. Singh, formed a minority government. After one year, Singh's government was forced to resign and a breakaway faction from the Janata Dal Party, the Janata Dal (Socialist) Party led by Chandra Shekhar, formed a new minority government heavily dependent on the support of the Congress Party. It in turn resigned in early 1991.

A major issue contributing to the downfall of the two governments was the intensification of communal violence. In 1989, terror in Punjab reportedly claimed more than 1,700 lives, Muslim militancy rose in Kashmir, and the Ram Janambhoomi/Babri Masjid controversy intensified (Sisson, 1990). In 1990, BJP leader Lal Krishna Advani led a march to Ayodhya to begin work on the temple. About a dozen people were killed when the government forcefully stopped the march. A new round of riots broke out, claiming more than 1,000 lives over a three-month period (Hundley, 1992). In December 1990, communal violence was reported in six districts in Uttar Pradesh, including the city of Meerut.

In May 1991, Rajiv Gandhi was assassinated, allegedly by Tamil militants from Sri Lanka. In the June elections, the Congress Party won the largest number of seats and the new Congress Party leader, Narasimha Rao, became prime minister, heading a coalition with the National Front Alliance. The Hindu nationalist BJP formed the official opposition and won control of the state assemblies in four northern states, including Uttar Pradesh. The BJP's electoral success signaled a new era of communal politics and communal violence.

On December 6, 1992, Hindu extremists tore down the Babri mosque, triggering yet another round of communal riots. The rioting left more than 1,200 dead, most of whom were Muslim demonstrators killed by the Hindu police (Hundley, 1992). The BJP was blamed for instigating the incident and the government's response included the dismissal of the BJP-run government of Uttar Pradesh. The BJP leader in parliament, Lal Krishna Advani, resigned his post and was placed under arrest along with his senior colleagues for allegedly encouraging mob violence. The government arrested some 2,600 right-wing Hindu leaders.

In January 1993, the president promulgated an ordinance with immediate effect acquiring the land in and around the Ram Janambhoomi/Babri Masjid complex. Six leaders of the BJP, including Advani, were released unconditionally. In May, the president's rule was extended for six months in Uttar Pradesh and three other states.

DISCUSSION

What led to the government massacres in Meerut and Maliana? The killings, committed by the Hindu-dominated police force, reflect the ethnic and religious nature of conflict in India. The massacres occurred in the context of Hindu-Muslim riots in the city of Meerut. The police, assuming that Muslims instigated the event and were involved in crimes against Hindus, directed their force against members of the Muslim community. Although the massacres mostly were carried out for retributive purposes, local conditions suggest that an economic motive underlies the government's use of force. In particular, the economic success of the Muslims in Meerut posed a threat to Hindu control of the local political and economic structures. In this context, the massacre served the function of affirming the domination of Hindus.

What is the character of state terror in India? The government primarily uses terrorist strategies in its struggle to eliminate ethnic-based terrorist insurgencies. Repressive legislation has been accompanied by reports of arbitrary arrests, torture, extrajudicial executions, and "disappearances." Although these strategies tend to be restricted to certain parts of the country, regional governments have engaged in massacres and terrorist strategies against minority communities. At the federal level, the government has fueled ethnic tensions by supporting extremist Hindu and Muslim demands. Consequently, as the level of violence increases, government forces have expanded their use of terror. The overall strategies of terror and the identity of the victims are suggestive of the ruling party's desire to maintain the domination of upper-class Hindus.

Is state terrorism a successful strategy? The insurgencies continue to use terrorist tactics against the government and do not show any signs of weakening. In terms of communal violence, the continued use of state terror against Muslims and the rise in power of Hindu nationalist groups has resulted in an increase in the level of communal violence. By all accounts, state terrorism has not brought security to the state.

India's experience indicates that state terrorism may intensify the level of insurgent activity and communal violence. But India is a very heterogenous society in which ethnic, religious, and caste divisions abound. Can state terror be used more effectively in relatively homogeneous states? The remaining cases are devoted to the character of state terror in Latin America, a region characterized by relatively few ethnic divisions. The next chapter focuses on Guatemala, where a democratic government is challenged by an indigenous-based insurgency.

9

Guatemala: El Aguacate Massacre

Guatemala has a democratic form of government, although the military has considerable influence. The government is opposed by an indigenous-based insurgency that seeks to reform the inequitable social system. The government has attempted to establish control over the indigenous population through a policy of terror. In this context, government forces carried out a massacre at El Aguacate. The government has continued to practice state terrorism, but the prospects of a negotiated settlement to the conflict are encouraging.

THE MASSACRE

A great deal of controversy surrounds the November 24, 1988, massacre of El Aguacate residents. However, independent investigations into the massacre document the following scenario.[1] On November 22, Carlos Humberto Guerra Callejos failed to return to the village after journeying into the mountains. On November 24, a search party of 30 men went into the mountains to look for Guerra Callejos. According to most reports, 19 of the men were captured by the army soldiers and taken to the military base in Chimaltenango (Military Zone No. 302), where they were submitted to interrogation and torture, and eventually killed. Local villagers saw the kidnapped men in the custody of the army, and two soldiers told relatives of the missing men that they were being held at the military base (Guatemala Human Rights Commission/USA, 1989a).

On November 25, the army found the body of Guerra Callejos buried in a shallow grave. The following day led to the discovery of 21 other bodies, buried in shallow holes. All of the bodies showed signs of torture and each body had a bullet hole in the back. Nineteen of the bodies were identified as members of the search party; however, two bodies could not be identified and were buried as "XX."[2] The two unidentified bodies are presumably the two soldiers who confirmed the presence of the captured men on the military base. Father Méndez Doninelli, director of the Center for the Investigation, Study, and Promotion of Human Rights (CIEPRODH), said, "The facts show that the victims were detained by members of the army, taken to the military base at Chimaltenango, submitted to interrogation and torture, and then murdered" (Doninelli, 1989).

HISTORICAL CONTEXT

Guatemala is a society divided by race. Between 50 percent and 70 percent of the population are of pure Mayan Indian descent, while the remainder are *ladino*, or of mixed European and Indian descent (Painter, 1987). The Indian population is diverse, with over 22 different languages and over 250 ways of dress (Barry and Preusch, 1986). Although Indians form a majority, they have been relegated to the margins of society, isolated in terms of language and politics. Economically, the nation's agro-export system depends on cheap Indian labor for its profits, and practically all Indians live in poverty with little or no land (Barry, 1991; Carr, 1991).

The relegation of Indians to the margins of society is coupled with a high degree of socioeconomic inequality. For instance, Guatemala has the most unequal ratio of land distribution in Latin America (Painter, 1987; Larmer, 1989b). While the vast majority of the population lives in poverty, a few hundred families of large landowners, bankers, businessmen, and military officers control the entire economic structure (Van den Berghe, 1990). The reactionary and intransigent ruling class has traditionally formed a partnership with the military to defend the existing structure of socioeconomic privilege (Carr, 1991).

Government

In 1954, a CIA-directed military coup resulted in the repeal of agrarian reform, the destruction of trade union and peasant movements, and the institutionalization of the right wing and the military in national politics (Barry and Preusch, 1986). Over the next three decades, the military successfully institutionalized its rule to become the dominant force in society. For the most part, the military's superior position was gained through the use of indiscriminate terror against the Guatemala population. In 1963, a coup d'etat by Colonel Enrique Peralta Azurdia signaled the beginning of the systematic use of state terrorism. By the mid-1960s, the repression of trade union and popular leaders, the concealment of political prisoners, extrajudicial executions, and death squad killings became routine. From 1970 to 1974, approximately 20,000 people died or "disappeared" under the administration of Arana Osorio (Guatemala Human Rights Commission/USA,

1989b). Military rule and repressive government prevailed throughout the early 1980s. Finally, the 1985 elections brought the return of democracy to Guatemala.

In January 1986, Marco Vinicio Cerezo Arévalo became the first civilian president in nearly 20 years. Unions and popular organizations, suppressed under the military regimes, once again began to operate openly. Cerezo's administration was expected to bring the rule of law back to a state that had arbitrarily terrorized its citizens. But Cerezo's domestic policies, contingent on the approval of the military and elite, did not significantly alter the political landscape.

Domestic Reforms

President Cerezo entered office with promises of enforcing respect for human rights. But Cerezo's first act was to adhere to an amnesty decree by the outgoing military government, thereby ensuring that no military personnel would be prosecuted for crimes committed between March 1982 and January 14, 1986. Although the new administration dismissed previous human rights abuses, it had the opportunity to establish a system that could protect human rights in the future. The constitution of 1985 created numerous governmental human rights organizations, and President Cerezo announced several other bodies to inquire into human rights violations. But it soon became clear that these organizations were not functioning; some never actually operated and others failed to carry out genuine investigations into the abuses reported to them. For instance, a great deal of hope rested with the first Human Rights Ombudsman named by Congress, but he led the office into insignificance and disrepute (Amnesty International, 1989d).

In other areas of human rights, Cerezo's actions were nothing more than cosmetic. "G-2," or army intelligence, was the hub of all military action and responsible for coordinating the system of repression that prevailed throughout the country. Instead of reorganizing or placing limits on the organization, Cerezo simply renamed it "D-2," although most people still refer to it as "G-2." In 1986, he disbanded the Department for Technical Investigations (DIT), a judicial police unit implicated in political violence. A year later he replaced it with the Special Investigations and Narcotics Brigade (BIEN), renamed the Department for Criminal Investigations in 1988. Similarly, the Civil Defense patrols were renamed Voluntary Civil Defense Committees, although participation remained forced in many areas. For all practical purposes, the organization and structure of these agencies remained intact.

On the socioeconomic front, Cerezo initiated some reforms, including a bold tax reform in 1987, the first in at least three decades. At the end of the year, the government held the first conversations with the guerrilla front since the war began in the 1960s. In March 1988, Cerezo agreed to a Social Pact with labor unions, committing the government to social and land reform and endorsing the need for a new investigation of "disappearances" and other human rights violations.

Cerezo's conciliatory attempts were met with hostility from the oligarchy and military. In May 1988, a group of officers attempted to overthrow the civilian government. Reportedly, Cerezo was allowed to remain in office only after substantial concessions, including the cancellation of dialogue with the rebels; cessation of all efforts to forge a police force independent of army control; cancellation of agrarian reforms; and limitations on the growth of human rights, and peasant and union organizations (Americas Watch, 1988a). A month later, the government reneged on all the agreements in the March Social Pact. This was followed by the creation of the System of Civil Protection (SIPROCI), which centralized the actions of all police and security forces.[3] The attempted military coup was followed by a resurgence in abductions, "disappearances," and extrajudicial executions.

Military Power

The military's strength rests on its political and legal autonomy, and its economic influence. Political autonomy is achieved by military control of its own assignments, promotions, and, to a large degree, its budget (Millett, 1991). Legal autonomy is guaranteed by the military control of the National Police, which remains a mere appendage of Guatemalan Army Intelligence (Anderson, 1989). Top officers have amassed large fortunes, becoming members of the oligarchy themselves. The army owns more than 40 state enterprises, including its own national bank (Carr, 1991). The military's assertion of supreme power lies in its belief in the National Security Doctrine, which proclaims that one must wage war in order to prevent war (Schirmer, 1989). Under the doctrine, the army considers itself to be the only national institution capable of imposing patriotic unity on the Guatemalan society (Carr, 1991).

The militarization of civil society has effectively limited the power of civilian government, and in particular, the criminal justice system. Human rights abuses by members of the armed forces have typically been ignored by the judiciary, which has chosen not to prosecute members of the military. Notably, the Supreme Court has given the military courts jurisdiction over cases in which military officers have allegedly violated human rights (Washington Office on Latin America, 1988). In a telling statement, the United Nations Commission on Human Rights reported that the judiciary had been stripped of its "credibility, independence and autonomy" (Amnesty International, 1989d: 33).

In this context, it is army intelligence that is considered by many to be "the unelected government of Guatemala" (Manuel and Stover, 1991; Nairn and Simon, 1986). G-2, which tracks and eliminates "subversive" enemies, continues to operate out of the National Palace and G-2 officers occupy key command posts under the civilian administration. The civilian government is in a position of vulnerability, unable and unwilling to assert its authority.

Civil War

The civil war in Guatemala is an ethnic-based war. While the guerrilla leadership is composed entirely of *ladinos*, the combatants are mostly from the Indian community (Barry, 1992). The insurgents have fought Guatemalan governments since the early 1960s. The government's war against the rebels included scorched earth tactics, "model villages," mass relocations, and civil patrols.

Guerrilla Opposition

The early guerrilla movement was forced into exile in 1969, where it formed the Rebel Armed Forces (FAR). In the early 1970s, two new guerrilla groups emerged, the Guerrilla Army of the Poor (EGP) and the Organization of People in Arms (ORPA). Both adopted the strategy of "prolonged people's war." In February 1982, the various guerrilla armies formed a united military front, the Guatemalan National Revolutionary Unity (URNG).

The URNG embraced Marxism-Leninism, as well as liberation theology and social democratic tendencies (Barry, 1992). The coalition of armies hoped to achieve equality between Indians and *ladinos*, the distribution of property of the very rich, agrarian reform, and the elimination of repression (Barry and Preusch, 1986). In the late 1970s and early 1980s, the guerrillas successfully mobilized rural support through strategies that emphasized popular education and the political formation of peasant communities. Despite significant levels of rural support, the URNG's effectiveness was limited by its lack of a well-defined political platform and the absence of a popular movement ally (Barry, 1992).

In the early 1980s, the guerrilla forces were decimated by the military's scorched earth campaign, which virtually destroyed the guerrillas' rural base of support (Barry, 1991). In the mid-1980s, the guerrillas were not considered a significant threat to the government. In 1987, the army launched an "end of the year offensive," designed to wipe the guerrillas out of the isolated northwestern highlands once and for all (Larmer, 1988). The offensive failed to break the URNG. Meanwhile, the war escalated as the guerrillas struggled to gain a negotiating position and the army fought to prove that dialogue was unnecessary (Hood and Bazzy, 1988). In 1988, the URNG launched its first joint offensives involving all four guerrilla armies, and the number of operations doubled in 1989 (Barry, 1991). By 1990, the guerrilla had forces active in 12 departments and the country's two largest cities.

The Military's War

In the 1980s, the government's war was carried out in three stages: (1) total war, 1978-82; (2) militarization of society, 1983-85; and (3) democratic politics as an extension of war, 1986 to the present. A pervasive feature of the military campaigns throughout this period was the indiscriminate use of terror. The military drew a wide net of victims, eventually affecting every sector of society.

Total War, 1978-1982. In the late 1970s, the guerrilla movement posed a serious challenge to the military regime of General Romeo Lucas García. While the guerrillas scored significant victories, popular organizations and protest movements asserted their demands for fundamental reforms. The government's response was total war. In January 1980, government forces burned the Spanish embassy, occupied by 39 protesters. Later in the year, 41 labor activists belonging to the National Confederation of Workers (CNT) "disappeared." Popular movements and their supporters, including trade unions, the Catholic Church, rural activists, journalists, students, and professors, were effectively silenced by 1981 (Barry, 1992).

The destruction of popular organizations was followed by a scorched earth campaign in the highlands, unleashed in October 1981. In June 1982, a coup replaced Lucas García with General Efraín Ríos Montt, an avid Christian evangelist. Ríos Montt, who regarded the counterinsurgency campaign as a holy crusade against atheism and communism, continued the scorched earth strategy. In the end, 440 villages were destroyed, 50,000 to 75,000 people were killed, and as many as 150,000 Guatemalans became refugees (Krueger and Enge, 1985).

The Ríos Montt government added a developmental approach to the military effort. In 1982, the National Security and Development Plan (PNSD) outlined the military's strategy. The plan declared that the war was to be fought on the socioeconomic front, adding that "the minds of the population are the principal objective" (Barry, 1991: 221). The development strategy was carried out through civic action projects, "model villages," re-education and psychological operations, food distribution, development projects, and the encouragement of evangelical proselytizing. The overall goal was to undermine the Indian community and assert the dominance of "the national identity" (Barry, 1992).

The innovative "Beans and Bullets" program was a good example of this development approach. Under this program, food distribution was used as a pacification tool, with food given to those who cooperated with the military. The "bullets" part of the program consisted of the civil patrols, established as the cornerstone of the rural counterinsurgency campaign in late 1981 and 1982. The patrols, in which participation was required of teen-aged boys and men, served two purposes. First, the patrols, sent out ahead of the military to engage the guerrillas, were a cheap way to fight the war. Second, the patrols were ordered to report population movements within their villages, thus providing surveillance for the military (Davis, 1985). By 1984, the civil patrols incorporated nearly one million men and included virtually all Indian males (*ladinos* were almost always exempted) in the western highlands between the ages of 16 and 60 (Smith, 1990; Manuel and Stover, 1991).

Militarization of Society, 1983-1985. In August 1983, Ríos Montt was replaced in a military coup by General Oscar Mejía Víctores. The new military regime expanded Ríos Montt's development strategy with the Plan of Assistance to the Areas of Conflict (PAAC), an elaborate program designed to consolidate military power in the rural areas. Three main features of this program were "model villages," "development poles," and the Inter-Institutional Coordinating System (IICS). The "model villages" were designed as a means to control the peasant population, who were forcibly relocated from the highlands to the villages. Once in the village, the army had total domination over the population. All activities were to be reported to and authorized by the army. The villages were referred to as "concentration camps, under the control of an army of occupation" (Comite pro Justicia y Paz de Guatemala, 1986). The "model villages" formed the core of the "development poles." In these areas, peasants were obliged to join civil defense patrols, perform unpaid labor on public works projects, and cultivate cash crops for export (Oxfam America, 1985). Between October 1983 and December 1984, the Inter-Institutional Coordinating System was established. This system required that all rural development projects of government and outside organizations coordinate their efforts through the departmental military zone commanders (Simon, 1987). The IICS resulted in the establishment of a military structure superior to that of the civilian administration (Jonas, 1991).

Democratic Politics as an Extension of War, 1986 to the present. By the mid-1980s, the military regime laid the groundwork for a national security civilian government. The move to democracy was influenced by a deteriorating economic environment and international criticism. On the domestic front, the military regime was confronted with inflation, the deterioration of living standards, and increased strikes and protests. In the international arena, criticism of the regime's human rights practices threatened the continuation of military support. The establishment of a civilian government was viewed as a means to gain international support, while enabling the military to wash its hands of the domestic problems (Washington Office on Latin America, 1988). As previously noted, the democratization of the country did not involve a real transfer of power to the civilians (Anderson and Simon, 1988; Jonas, 1991).

Human rights violations continued as the civilian government consistently failed to assert its authority over the military and proved unwilling to investigate abuses (Washington Office on Latin America, 1989; Lawyers Committee for Human Rights, 1990). Although the level of human rights violations never approached that of the early 1980s, the security forces continued to kill, torture, and "disappear" their perceived opponents with impunity (Manuel and Stover, 1991). Abuses involving the Voluntary Civil Patrols continued, as peasants who refused to join the patrols or accused the patrols of human rights violations were threatened, "disappeared," or killed (Amnesty International, 1989d). The military continued to forcibly relocate civilians from guerrilla-held areas, eventually transferring them to the "model villages" and bringing in peasants from other regions to repopulate the area (Guatemalan Church in Exile, 1988). Trade unionists, academics, students, clergy, human rights workers, and peasants were particularly targeted by the police and military agents, who operated both in uniform and in plain clothes as members of death squads (Amnesty International, 1989d, 1989e). From January 1986 to January 1989, at least 222 "disappearances" were reported (Amnesty International, 1989d).

PERPETRATORS, VICTIMS, AND MOTIVES

The El Aguacate massacre was allegedly committed by government troops. The victims were male residents of an Indian village. Circumstances surrounding the massacre suggest that the killings were carried out as a warning to those who engage in subversive activity. The overall pattern of repression indicates the government's desire to maintain the current political and social order by establishing a system of control over the Indian population.

Perpetrators

The alleged perpetrators of the massacre were soldiers from the Chimaltenango military base. If the reported facts are accurate, the victims were tortured and killed at the military base, suggesting that base commanders were involved in the decision to kill the men. Furthermore, the torture and interrogation of the men indicates that the massacre was premeditated. Unfortunately, the secrecy and suspicions surrounding the massacre do not enable us to identify the individual(s) responsible for ordering the killings, or how that decision was reached.

Although the individual perpetrators of the El Aguacate massacre are not known, responsibility for the systematic violation of human rights falls with the military hierarchy. Despite the common occurrence of torture, extrajudicial executions, and "disappearances," the military does not sanction its soldiers for these crimes. In fact, G-2 has been shown to order political assassinations. But ultimately, the civilian government is to be held accountable for human rights violations committed under its authority.

Victims

The victims of the El Aguacate massacre were Indian men who had traveled into the mountains in search of a neighbor. The massacre was clearly carried out in an indiscriminate manner, as the capture of the men was not predicated on any presumption of guilt. It would seem that the victims were mostly targeted because of their status as Indians. Also, the fact that there were no women or children in the search party suggests that the army may have originally considered the group of men to be members of the guerrilla army.

The military engages in a policy of collective punishment, in which all members of the Indian community are considered guilty of being subversive simply because of their ethnic identity. The El Aguacate massacre was typical of the pattern of repression in Guatemala. The rural Indian population, labor organizers, political activists, and students are the primary targets of torture, "disappearances," and assassinations. Most massacres occur in the countryside, where the Indian population has been targeted for wholesale murder.

Motives

The military never admitted its involvement in the El Aguacate massacre, so a motive can only be deduced by examining the context of the event and subsequent military acts. In the aftermath of a series of earthquakes, the army-controlled National Emergency Committee (CNE) established six military camps within ten miles of the village of El Aguacate. In addition, the military was especially active in the area as a result of an increase in guerrilla and subversive activity. Of particular concern was the presence of a peasant movement demanding the dissolution of the civil patrols (Reed, 1989).

While these events outline the reasons for military presence in the area of El Aguacate, subsequent military actions suggest a motive behind the massacre. In the days following the massacre, air force helicopters dropped thousands of fliers on nearby villages, exhorting the people to join the "voluntary civil-defense committees" (Webster, 1990). Thus, it would appear the massacre was a means to threaten those in the Indian community who refused to accept the government's civil patrol program.

In a broader sense, the massacre was part of an overall strategy intended to control the Indian population. Key elements of this strategy included "model villages," "development poles," and civil patrols. The ultimate motive would seem to be the continuation of the inequitable social structure, which heavily favors the army and economic elites.

AFTERMATH

The El Aguacate massacre gave the government the opportunity to assert civilian law over the military. The media, internal human rights organizations, and Congress called on President Cerezo to authorize an official investigation. Instead, the government collaborated with the army to portray the massacre as the work of guerrillas. The massacre did not result in any changes in government policies or practices. Despite the inauguration of a new civilian president, the security forces continued to engage in the systematic violation of human rights and the government moved toward authoritarian rule.

Investigation and Accountability

According to the army's version of the massacre, the victims had been strangled to death by members of a guerrilla group, the Revolutionary Organization of the People in Arms (ORPA) (Larmer, 1989a). Although the army could not produce evidence to support its claim and forensic evidence showed inconsistencies in its story, President Cerezo fully supported their version of events.[4] When the Guatemalan Congress called for an investigation, the president said that the surviving villagers "accuse the guerrillas of committing this bloody act, and therefore we should not continue making conjectures" (Amnesty International, 1989e: 4).

Despite Cerezo's affirmation of the army version of the massacre, Human Rights Attorney Gonzalo Menéndez investigated the event. The criminal investigation was repeatedly obstructed by military and civilian officers. For instance, the investigating attorney was unable to speak to key witnesses, and the forensic doctor who performed the autopsies refused to turn over the report. In January 1989, one of the Human Rights Attorney's assistants, Arturo Martínez Gálvez, announced his resignation, charging that documentation had been withheld from him concerning the massacre and that "there has been no interest in investigating the high level of human rights violations that occur in our country" (Network in Solidarity with the People of Guatemala, 1989a).[5] No charges were filed.

The inability of the legal system to act in the case of El Aguacate led to an independent investigation carried out by the Center for the Investigation, Study, and Promotion of Human Rights. CIEPRODH is one of a number of independent organizations in Guatemala that carry out investigations and document cases of "disappearance," torture, and political execution. The center definitively concluded that the army was responsible for the massacre. The day before the press conference announcing the findings, the CIEPRODH's Guatemala City office was attacked by unknown assailants. In a verbal attack, the army discredited the organization by accusing it of pursuing "propagandistic goals for personal achievement" (Network in Solidarity with the People of Guatemala, 1989a).[6]

Despite the evidence uncovered by independent investigators, the civilian government, in conjunction with the armed forces, used its version of the El Aguacate massacre as a public relations tool. In brief, the massacre became a propaganda gimmick to show the world that the Guatemala government was dealing with "terrorists" and thus deserving of foreign aid (Larmer, 1989a).

Immediately after the massacre, the government coordinated a "tour of survivors" in which two "survivors" of the massacre, accompanied by four military officers, were sent to the United States to give their testimony to Washington politicians. But later evidence showed that the "survivors" never witnessed the massacre, and in fact, one of them (Oscar Orlando Callejas Tobar) was identified as a former member of G-2 (Stix, 1989).[7]

The tour of "survivors" was part of an overall plan by the Guatemala government to gain international approval and aid. This plan was given further support by the Civil Protection System's (SIPROCI) report, *Human Rights in Guatemala*, which was distributed at the 45th session of the United Nations Commission on Human Rights. The document claimed that the majority of "missing" persons had "returned" and that some of the major reasons for "disappearances" included accidents, emigrations, family problems, kidnappings, alcoholism, mental disorder, and journeys within and outside the country (Guatemala Human Rights Commission/USA, 1989a).

While the government carefully covered up the massacre, the surviving residents of El Aguacate were subjected to army harassment. In particular, those who cooperated with independent investigators and journalists were forcibly taken to the Chimaltenango military base and questioned (Guatemala Human Rights Commission/USA, 1989a). Although the military did provide some financial compensation to the widows, this compensation was contingent on their adherence to the army version of the massacre (Webster, 1990). In June 1991, eight Guatemalan peasants initiated legal proceedings in the United States against former Minister of Defense Héctor Gramajo for the alleged military massacre at El Aguacate.

Government Policies and Practices

In the late 1980s, the human rights situation continued to deteriorate. Torture, political killings, and "disappearances" claimed hundreds of lives, mostly Indian peasants, students, labor leaders and local political figures. In addition to official military repression, death squad activity re-emerged with the appearance of groups such as the Righteous Jaguar (JJ) and the Soldiers for the Salvation of Central America (Carr, 1991). Between January and July 1989 alone, there were 367 extrajudicial executions and 140 forced or involuntary "disappearances" (Comite pro Justicia y Paz de Guatemala, 1989). In the first nine months of 1990, the Human Rights Attorney reported 276 political murders and 145 "disappearances" (Millett, 1991). In December, a major massacre occurred at Santiago Atitlán when soldiers fired into a crowd of people peacefully protesting army abuses, killing 13 Indians and wounding 12 others (Human Rights Watch, 1991).

In January 1991, Jorge Serrano Elías, an evangelical businessman, was inaugurated president of Guatemala. The new administration oversaw some positive developments in the area of human rights. In particular, the government held negotiations with the URNG, and in a rare event, a military court sentenced an officer to 16 years in prison for the Santiago Atitlán massacre. But these positive developments were countered by a renewed campaign of death threats against the leaders of unions, human rights groups, and members of the left, as well as a series of high-profile assassinations that appeared to have political motives. In the first few months of 1991, the Human Rights Ombudsman reported 180 extrajudicial executions and 46 "disappearances" (Manuel and Stover, 1991).

Throughout 1992, the human rights situation remained bleak, with selective assassinations, "disappearances," and torture by the security forces a persistent feature of the landscape. Although negotiations between the government and the URNG were still bogged down in mid-1993, some positive accords were struck. For instance, a partial accord was reached on the issue of civil patrols, which called on the Human Rights Ombudsman to verify on a case-by-case basis whether the patrollers were serving voluntarily. The government and representatives of more than 40,000 refugees also reached an agreement on conditions for their return. While these developments suggested an optimistic future, the militarization of civil society continued at a steady pace. In March, the Hunapú Task Force was inaugurated. The Task Force, a combined military and police patrol aimed at combating urban crime, was involved in a series of violent abuses in 1992. Another sign of the continued military domination of Guatemala was the new drive to recruit former military personnel into the National Police.

In May 1993, President Jorge Serrano opted to govern by decree. He immediately placed the attorney general and the president of the Supreme Court under house arrest. Serrano then dissolved the National Congress, Supreme Court, and the Justice Department. The coup followed weeks of public protests of a government austerity program that had raised prices for essential goods. In addition, the human rights movement and labor unions and students were particularly active. A week before the coup, an organized protest drew 10,000 people to the capital (Bernstein, 1993). Among the laws suspended were the rights to demonstrate, to receive a fair hearing if arrested, to strike, and the right of a free press.

The "self-coup" failed, and on June 6, Ramiro de León Carpio, a former human rights ombudsman with considerable popularity, was inaugurated as president. In a gesture of goodwill, leaders of the URNG announced a cease-fire. At the time of this writing, a negotiated settlement to the conflict in Guatemala had not been reached.

DISCUSSION

Why did soldiers commit the massacre at El Aguacate? In the immediate context, it would appear that the massacre was intended as a warning to the local

Indian community, which had protested against the government's civil patrol program. But in the broader context, the massacre was part of an overall strategy of terror that included indiscriminate enforcement terror, the "model village" program, civil patrols, and population replacements. These strategies of terror indicate a cultural motive, as they resulted in the destruction of indigenous culture and the promotion of *ladino* culture.

What factors influence the character of terror? State terror in Guatemala targeted a large sector of the population. In addition to the use of terror against the indigenous population, the government targeted members of leftist organizations, especially students, labor leaders, and political figures. "Subversives" were subjected to arbitrary arrest, torture, extrajudicial execution, and "disappearance." Covert forces, or death squads, also played a significant role in the elimination of economic and political targets. State terrorism has primarily been motivated by economics, in particular, the desire of economic and military elites to maintain their extreme domination of society.

Is state terrorism an effective strategy? The guerrillas continue to press their demands, despite being weakened by genocidal policies. While extreme levels of state terror weakened the insurgency, guerrilla forces continue to be active. Furthermore, negotiations have increased the possibility that the rebel organization will gain legitimate political status. State terrorism may have upheld the prominent role of economic elites and the military; however, terror strategies have failed to deter the opposition.

The Guatemala case demonstrates the use of terrorist strategies in the context of an indigenous-based insurgency. But is the character and outcome of terror influenced by the level of violence used by the insurgency? The next case study focuses on Peru, where a democratic government is opposed by a revolutionary and extremely violent indigenous-based insurgency.

NOTES

1. Independent investigations were conducted by the Guatemala Human Rights Commission/USA, the Center for the Investigation, Study, and Promotion of Human Rights (CIEPRODH), the Campesino Committee of the Highlands (CCA), and independent journalists and filmmakers.

2. The Guatemalan Embassy listed 21 victims in a press announcement; other press reports mention 22 or 23 victims (Stix, 1989).

3. SIPROCI did little to check the crime wave but proved effective in breaking strikes and removing workers from occupied workplaces (Barry, 1992).

4. The army claimed the victims were strangled rather than shot, but each body had a bullet hole in the back (Larmer, 1989a).

5. Originally cited in the Guatemalan newspaper *Prensa Libre*.

6. Originally cited in the Guatemalan newspaper *Prensa Libre*.

7. According to documents by the Campesino Committee in Defense of the highlands (CCDA), a Chimaltenango-based organization, Orlando Callejas participated in massacres between 1980 and 1983.

10

Peru: Cayara Massacre

Peru has a democratic political structure that features a wide spectrum of parties. The government is challenged by a revolutionary and extremely violent indigenous-based insurgency. The military has waged a campaign of terror against the indigenous population. In this context, government troops engaged in a massacre in the village of Cayara. State terrorism has not deterred guerrilla activity, although the resort to authoritarian rule and the capture of revolution leaders have damaged the insurgency.

THE MASSACRE

On May 14, 1988, an army of over 100 soldiers, many of their faces disguised in black paint and ski masks, converged on the town of Cayara in the department of Ayacucho (*ICCHRLA Newsletter*, 1989). The soldiers reportedly shot the first person they encountered and then assassinated five men who were working in the village church. The army troops assembled the villagers in the main square and waited for the men to return from work in the nearby fields. According to numerous witnesses, the soldiers then forced 18 men and boys to lie down in the cornfield, put branches of prickly pear cactus on their backs and stomped on them. Afterwards, the soldiers hacked their victims to death with machetes, picks, and scythes (Day, 1988). Following the massacre, the soldiers buried the bodies in several mass graves (Americas Watch, 1988c; Amnesty International, 1988f).

The actual number of victims of the Cayara massacre is unknown, but reports conclusively indicate at least 28 deaths (including several boys, the headmaster of the local school, and members of the local council) and the "disappearance" of 41 others (Americas Watch, 1988c; Chiang, 1990). Another source cites the number of deaths to be closer to 100 (*Miami Herald*, 1988).[1] Four days later, the army returned to Cayara and established a permanent base in the schoolhouse. General

Valdivia, chief of the Political-Military Command of Ayacucho, inquired about several Cayara residents, presumably sought as "subversives." Some of these persons were arrested and have since "disappeared"; the corpses of three were found in early August (Americas Watch, 1992a).

HISTORICAL CONTEXT

The basic cleavage in Peru is between the coastal country, centered in Lima and dominated by the Hispanic culture, and the rural country, populated by Indians who speak the indigenous language and have their own distinct culture. Traditionally, there has been little interaction between the coastal centers of political power and wealth and the population of the jungles and highlands (Brown, 1990). With few exceptions, Peruvian governments have not responded to the needs of the rural population, and have continued to ignore the issue of land tenure, which has embittered the rural Indian population (Brown, 1990; Woy-Hazleton and Hazleton, 1990; Mauceri, 1991).

Government

From 1968 to 1980, Peru was dominated by military regimes. But unlike most of Latin America's experience with military rule, the regime of General Juan Velasco Alvaredo (1968-75) was known for its progressive and sometimes radical policies. The Velasco regime promulgated a major agrarian reform, addressed the problems of urban migrants, expanded the state's role in the economy, and created industrial communities whose workers had a voice in the management of firms (Bourque and Warren, 1989; Pion-Berlin, 1989). These reforms led to a politically mobilized middle and lower class, and democratic values became entrenched at the mass level (C. McClintock, 1989).

The leftist Velasco regime was followed by the military rule of General Francisco Morales Bermúdez. During this period, selective political repression became the norm. Organized labor was particularly targeted and subjected to curfews and states of emergencies. Thousands of workers were arrested, constitutional guarantees were suspended, and civilian trials were transferred to military courts (Pion-Berlin, 1989). While selective repression was institutionalized, the military government successfully undertook measures that enabled the return of civilian rule. The 1979 constitution established universal adult suffrage for the first time, and the 1980 elections brought political parties back into the system of government (Crabtree, 1992).

In 1980, Belaúnde Terry, the previous civilian president and the candidate of the conservative parties that have traditionally ruled Peru, was elected president. Belaúnde's administration inherited a crumbling economy, general strikes protesting austerity measures, and charges of widespread corruption. On the eve of President Belaúnde's election, a fierce guerrilla organization, Sendero Luminoso ("Shining Path"), launched its "people's war" in the heavily Indian department of Ayacucho. Belaúnde dealt with Sendero attacks, as well as labor strikes, by imposing temporary states of emergency and ceding ever increasing amounts of political responsibility to the military (Crabtree, 1992).

At first, Belaúnde placed responsibility for counterinsurgency in the hands of the Civil Guard, a branch of the police force. But in 1982, responsibility was transferred to the armed forces, under the overall direction of the Minister of Defense. In 1983, as more provinces were placed under emergency regulation, a systematic pattern of torture, "disappearances," and extrajudicial executions emerged. In June 1985, Congress passed Law 24,150. Under this law, military control over the emergency zones was formalized. In practice, each emergency zone was placed under a political-military command that had the authority to carry out detentions without notifying civilian authorities. Furthermore, the law placed members of the security forces under military jurisdiction, bypassing the civilian legal system. By the end of Belaúnde's five-year term, the country was in the midst of an acute social and economic crisis.

In July 1985, Alan García Pérez, a candidate of the center-left American Popular Revolutionary Alliance party (APRA), assumed the presidency of Peru. García began his administration by stating his commitment to human rights, lifting the state of emergency in Ayacucho, and rejecting a purely military solution to the guerrilla war. He created a Peace Commission to look into methods of providing lasting peace and led a campaign against police corruption and military repression. Notably, the president fired three top generals for resisting his order to punish soldiers who had massacred peasants.

In June 1986, the Peruvian military quelled riots in three Lima prisons by killing 250 prisoners. Although García gave the orders for this action, he was quick to distance himself from the political consequences (Crabtree, 1992). As Sendero continued to expand its operations, the human rights situation deteriorated. García's development plans were never implemented and efforts to rein in the soldiers failed. The president increasingly resorted to the strategy used by his predecessor—declaring a state of emergency. By the end of 1988, Peruvians were being governed under a state of emergency in eight departments and part of a ninth.

While the state of emergency was expanded to more and more territory, the government moved increasingly toward repressive legislation. In the Anti-Terrorist Law (Decree 46), the crime of "terrorism," defined in vague terms, was widely used by the security forces in zones of emergency to arrest opposition political activists, labor unionists, and peasant leaders not associated with Sendero (Brown, 1990). In March 1987, Law 24,651, which increased the maximum penalty for acts of terrorism, was enacted. Three months later, Law 24,700 established special tribunals to try people accused of terrorism. The enactment of these laws effectively transferred many of the duties and responsibilities of the civilian government and its judiciary to the military.

García's endorsement of a military solution to Sendero damaged the civilian judicial system. In addition to being chronically underfinanced, the courts did not receive cooperation from the military, and safety was a primary concern for judges and prosecutors. In areas under a state of emergency, judges and prosecutors had so little assurance of security that many were forced to leave (Brown, 1990). Those rare cases where the courts have pursued allegations of military abuse have been paralyzed by military denials and the government's lack of will to oversee military actions in the emergency zones (Brown, 1990). Furthermore, the judiciary itself enabled the military to remain largely unaccountable by repeatedly handing down controversial rulings favoring military jurisdiction over civilian. Under military courts, military personnel were simply not convicted of charges stemming from torture, rape, or extrajudicial executions in the emergency zones (Amnesty International, 1989f).

As the war with Sendero raged, García encountered considerable problems within his own administration. In July 1987, he expropriated the nation's ten private banks, six finance companies, and 17 insurance companies. The announcement of the measure came as a surprise to both the public and high-ranking members of his party (Graham, 1992). The surprise announcement and García's tendency to surround himself with technocrats rather than APRA members led to a political crisis within his own party (Crabtree, 1992). García also faced problems maintaining an amiable relationship with the military. The 1987 creation of a Defense Ministry, which would maintain control over the various branches of the armed forces, was strongly opposed by most high-level officers, as it promised to erode the autonomy of the three branches (Graham, 1992). By 1988, the García administration's effectiveness was seriously questioned, and as the Sendero campaign expanded, civilian authority correspondingly deteriorated.

Civil War

A Maoist-oriented guerrilla movement, Sendero Luminoso began its war against the government in 1980. Throughout the decade, Sendero systematically expanded the territory under its control. The armed forces have responded to this movement by combining military offensives with pacification tools aimed at establishing control over the rural Indian community.

Guerrilla Opposition

Sendero Luminoso is the major guerrilla movement in Peru, although a lesser-known urban movement, the Movimento Revolucionario Túpac Amaru (MRTA), made its debut in mid-1984. Sendero Luminoso is the conception of Dr. Abimael Guzmán Reynose, who nurtured his philosophy and trained his followers within the confines of the University of Huamanga, a remote provincial university in Ayacucho. In the 1960s and 1970s, Guzmán sent out student cadres into the Indian communities to provide direct services and benefits that had been consistently neglected by the central government (Woy-Hazleton and Hazleton, 1990). Guzmán promised an unrelenting war to establish a primitive agrarian communist society. According to the movement, revolution would occur over a number of stages: (1) agitation and armed propaganda; (2) sabotage against Peru's socioeconomic system; (3) the generalization of the people's war; (4) the conquest and expansion of the revolution's support base and the strengthening of the guerrilla army; and (5) general civil war, the siege of the cities, and the final collapse of state power (Masterson, 1991).

In 1980, Sendero launched the armed phase of the revolution. By the end of 1982, it was apparent that the insurgency was growing rapidly (Mauceri, 1991). Regional support for Sendero seemed tied to a generalized anger at the neglect of the region by the central government, which had no concerns for the Indian community (C. McClintock, 1983, 1984; Palmer, 1986; Bourque and Warren, 1989; Mauceri, 1991). It was no coincidence that Sendero was launched from the department of Ayacucho, one of the poorest regions in Peru (Dietz, 1990). The guerrilla movement's support and combatants consisted mainly of rural indigenous peasants.

Sendero Luminoso quickly gained control over much of the southern highlands. Once in control, Sendero brutally redistributed wealth, imposed "people's justice," set up schools for purposes of indoctrination, and blocked all but subsistence economic activity (Woy-Hazleton and Hazleton, 1990; Spalding, 1992). Residents living under Sendero rule were forced to live by a strict code under which they swore allegiance to Sendero. The organization enforced its position through brutality, including the murder of entire families, threats against citizens who participated in elections, selective murders of local officials and parliamentary candidates, and bombings (Brown, 1990). Sendero financed itself mainly through a tax on the drug traffic, offering peasant growers fair prices and shelter from violence in return (Spalding, 1992).

The 1986 prison massacres changed the nature of the Sendero movement. While the massacres decimated an important group of Senderista leaders, it generated a backlash of sympathy for the guerrillas among students and the revolutionary left (Woy-Hazleton and Hazleton, 1990). In 1987, Sendero took advantage of its expanded base of support in the cities and adopted a new urban strategy in the capital. Sendero was able to establish legal front groups, infiltrate competing organizations, and even stage open political rallies (Werlich, 1991). Thus, by all appearances, Sendero had reached the final stage of its revolutionary agenda.

The Military's War

From 1980 to 1982, Sendero violence was treated as a problem of common delinquency and police units were sent out to tackle the problem. While the police units were able to recapture some of the territory lost to Sendero, their methods proved particularly corrupt. Police-inflicted abuses, beatings, and deaths were commonly reported from the conflict areas (Harding, 1987; Dietz, 1990; Crabtree, 1992). Perhaps appropriately, rural support for Sendero became obvious during this period (Bourque and Warren, 1989).

In December 1982, the Belaúnde administration transferred the control of counterinsurgency strategy from the police to the armed forces. At the same time, the government created the Ayacucho Emergency Zone, thereby suspending a number of constitutional rights. Under the state of emergency, the security forces could carry out arrests without warrants, and the rights to public assembly and freedom of movement were suspended. The armed forces took advantage of their new role by engaging in a consistent policy of torture, "disappearances," and extrajudicial executions in the emergency zones. By the end of Belaúnde's term in 1985, the war against Sendero Luminoso had taken about 8,000 lives, mainly those of innocent civilians (Werlich, 1991).

In addition to the use of indiscriminate terror, the military's war against Sendero included the implementation of pacification strategies designed to establish control over the indigenous population. Pacification of the "dissident" communities hinged on mass relocations, "strategic hamlets," and civil patrols. Mass relocations, the first line of defense, were used to eliminate Sendero strongholds in the mountains, where the population was relatively isolated from the outside world. In this scheme, people living in the highest altitudes were forcibly moved into the valleys, where the government had constructed special camps, or "strategic hamlets" (Crabtree, 1992). Once in these government-controlled villages, the population was mostly dependent on the military for its economic survival.

The cornerstone of the military's campaign was the civil patrols, or *rondas campesinas*, which were first created in 1982. Indigenous peasants were obliged to participate in the *rondas*, although they received little training or weapons and in many cases were forced to provide unpaid labor (Americas Watch, 1992a). The *rondas*, which provided the military with a cheap way to implement the war, became primary targets for Sendero attacks (Brown, 1990; Mauceri, 1991; Spalding, 1992). At the same time, the *rondas* were more often used to solve private disputes between peasant communities than to protect them from insurgent forces. Among the problems with the civil patrol strategy, as cited in a special Peru Senate commission report, were the following: Communities that did not bow to pressure to form patrols were often victimized by the army and other patrollers; the militarization of communities severely undermined traditional communal authority; and the patrols generated intercommunal conflict (Americas Watch, 1992a).

In the emergency zones, repression was institutionalized. To a great extent, the military relied on secrecy to carry out its mission. Soldiers were often disguised with knitted masks or camouflage paint, there was no system of numbered badges, and officers were as a rule identified only by "war names" (Amnesty International, 1989b, 1989f). Although these tactics offered a great deal of protection for the soldiers, they ensured that no soldier would be held accountable for abuses against civilians, which were carried out on a systematic basis by these same forces.

Civilians in the emergency zones were routinely arrested without warrant. Once in custody, military zone commanders denied all access by civilian authorities and all information on those held captive. In practice, prisoners were often held for prolonged periods in secret military custody, only to become victims of torture or execution (Amnesty International, 1989f). For the most part, many of those detained simply "disappeared." This type of military behavior was all too common in the emergency zones, which in 1989 included nearly half the national territory and over half the population (Amnesty International, 1989f). From 1982 to 1989, over 3,000 prisoners held in government custody "disappeared," and official statistics put the death toll at 15,000, a high proportion of whom were victims of extrajudicial execution by government forces (Amnesty International, 1989f). The military's campaign of using "terror to fight terror" gave it one of the most abysmal human rights records in the world (*Latin American Regional Reports Andean Group*, 1989; Andreas and Sharpe, 1992).

Since 1988, the military's approach to insurgency has been increasingly fragmented, with a strengthened role for local military commanders and a growing reliance on *rondas*. The increased reliance on *rondas* coincided with the growing tolerance of the APRA government for "private" responses to insurgents (Mauceri, 1991). In 1987 and 1988, right-wing death squads appeared on the scene. Of the four or five squads, the Comando Democrátic Rodrigo Franco was the most prominent, having so far initiated 35 attacks and murdered nine people who, it claims, were Senderistas or their sympathizers (Woy-Hazleton and Hazleton, 1990). This organization was widely believed to have links to Augustín Mantilla, who became minister of the interior in 1989, and to elements of the armed forces and police (Graham, 1992). Death squad killings since mid-1988 have increasingly targeted individuals of high social status who were well known for their critical stance toward the government (Amnesty International, 1989f).

If there was a constant in the military's conduct of the war, it was its support of the National Security Doctrine, which perceived the "enemy from within" to be "communism," of which Sendero was but one manifestation (Crabtree, 1992). But the actual implementation of this ideology was left in the hands of regional political-military commanders, who had total autonomy in carrying out the war (Americas Watch, 1987). This regional approach resulted in abrupt shifts of strategy, especially between "internal war" philosophies and "developmental" approaches.

The Ayacucho Military Command provides an example of the degree of autonomy and types of approaches taken by the regional commands. The political-military commander of Ayacucho at the time of the Cayara massacre, General José Valdivia Duenas, adopted an "internal war" approach to Sendero. He instituted a curfew, prohibited the Red Cross from operating in the region, and oversaw a worsening human rights situation that included massacres. His successor, General Howard Rodríguez, turned to a "developmentalist" approach, which included lifting most repressive measures and the adoption of civic action programs, such as food distribution (Mauceri, 1991). Although neither approach prevented the expansion of the guerrilla movement, it demonstrates the degree of authority given to regional military commanders.

PERPETRATORS, VICTIMS, AND MOTIVES

The Cayara massacre was allegedly carried out by soldiers under the leadership of General José Valdivia Dueñas.[2] The victims were men and boys from an Indian village. The immediate motive would appear to be retribution for an earlier Sendero ambush of an army patrol. The broader context suggests that the massacre was part of an overall government strategy designed to destroy the insurgents' rural support base through severe repression and pacification techniques.

Perpetrators

Regular government troops were the alleged perpetrators of the Cayara massacre, which would appear to be part of General Valdivia's "internal war" strategy for fighting Sendero. Under this strategy, troops regularly engaged in the arbitrary detentions, tortures, killings, and "disappearances" of the mostly Indian civilian population. Simply put, the massacre was not an isolated incident of military brutality.

The Cayara massacre appears to have been a premeditated act. The soldiers spent considerable time waiting for their targets to return from the fields. Furthermore, the victims were subjected to physical cruelty and an especially vicious death. These facts suggest that the perpetrators were acting under orders of a higher command and their behavior was consistent with military policy.

Victims

Those killed in the Cayara massacre were men and boys from the Indian community. They were not "chosen" for murder because of their beliefs or actions, but rather because of their ascribed status as Indians. Apparently, the troops felt that the men and boys, rather than the women, were more likely to be Sendero members or at least supporters. The ethnic identity of the victims shows the genocidal nature of military operations.

In the emergency zones, the military regularly supports the notion of collective responsibility. Under this notion, an entire population or community is held responsible for the actions of guerrillas. Since the guerrilla combatants were primarily Indian, it was the Indian community that was presumed "guilty" and especially targeted by the military. Referring to the Cayara massacre, General Valdivia stated that the armed forces had acted on "the assumption that all the residents in the area have been organized, indoctrinated and also obliged to participate in the various 'forms of struggle' favoured by *Sendero Luminoso* from the 1970s until the present" (Amnesty International, 1991b: 3).

Motives

The day before the massacre, the army suffered the loss of a captain and three soldiers in a battle with a guerrilla contingent. Evidence suggests that the soldiers, suspecting that the local population of Cayara had collaborated with the guerrilla group in the attack, killed the residents under a plan of operations called "Persecution" (Amnesty International, 1989b, 1989f). Certainly, retribution for the Sendero ambush seems likely, especially since massacres and "disappearances" have been periodically reported in the aftermath of a guerrilla attack, and the great majority of victims are indigenous peasant farmers from remote mountain areas (Amnesty International, 1989f).

Retribution may have been the primary motive behind the Cayara massacre, but it does not adequately explain the nature of human rights violations in the rural areas. Massacres were just one element in the military's arsenal. "Disappearances," torture, and other acts of physical violence were obvious weapons used by the armed forces. But other elements, in particular, the mass relocation of peasants from the highland into government-controlled villages and their coerced participation in civil patrols, were aimed at destroying the indigenous culture, and in so doing, establishing government control over a "naturally subversive" Indian population.

AFTERMATH

The Cayara massacre was followed by both a criminal investigation and legislative inquiry. The criminal investigation was met with military obstruction, and the case eventually was dropped. The legislative inquiry, fraught with political overtones, resulted in several different reports with contradictory conclusions. In the realm of government policies and practices, the García regime continued its trend toward legitimizing repression. In 1990, a new president assumed office and began an era of rule by authoritarian measures.

Investigation and Accountability

The Cayara massacre was met with a public outcry demanding that the military explain its behavior. Military officials responded by first denying that a massacre had taken place. In an official communique, the army stated that the denunciations were "unfounded" and that its sole purpose was to prevent the forces of order from continuing "to arrest the subversive delinquents, authors of the ambush of an army patrol" (*ICCHRLA Newsletter*, 1989). But the media's thorough documentation of the event forced the government on the defensive. The army finally acknowledged the killings but declared that soldiers chased rebels toward Cayara and killed an undetermined number of "subversives" in a military sweep following an ambush (*Miami Herald*, 1988). A spokesman from the army later claimed that 18 of the victims were all terrorists attempting to escape from a military patrol (Day, 1988).

While the army turned to denials and justifications, President García ordered a probe into the massacre. The attorney general's office began an immediate investigation, under the direction of State Prosecutor Carlos Escobar Piñeda, who had previous success in investigating army abuses as the special prosecutor for the Investigation of Disappearances in the department of Ayacucho. Prosecutor Escobar's investigation was met with violence and the destruction of evidence. For more than one week after the massacre, the army denied access to all investigators, medical experts, and journalists who tried to visit the scene. When Escobar finally reached Cayara, he found empty graves. Witnesses reported a massive army coverup. Soldiers allegedly spent the week after the massacre removing bodies by helicopters and horseback, clearing all evidence from the bloodstained church, and installing Peruvian flags atop the town's adobe houses (Day, 1988). When some bodies were rediscovered in a common grave in August, they again disappeared before investigators were able to transport them to a lab for autopsies (*Latinamerica Press*, 1988b).

Meanwhile, witnesses to the massacre became new victims. On June 29, two of the witnesses cooperating with Escobar were arrested by the army and "disappeared" (Americas Watch, 1992a). In December, three more witnesses, including the mayor of Cayara, were shot to death at an army roadblock (Americas Watch, 1992a). No less than 33 eyewitnesses came forward to testify that members of the armed forces murdered the villagers and later stole the bodies to conceal the evidence (*Latinamerica Press*, 1988a). More than one year later, at least nine witnesses who provided key testimony about the massacre became the victims of "disappearance" or killing (U.N. Doc. E/CN.4/1990/22). Clearly, anyone who spoke out against army abuses soon became targeted for retribution.

After a five-month probe, Escobar reported that military soldiers had been responsible for killing 28 unarmed peasants, and placed the blame on the commander of the army, General Valdivia Dueñas (Chiang, 1990). After his key witness was murdered in September, Escobar went public with his accusations against the military. Within days of receiving the final report on Cayara, which recommended the prosecution of General Valdivia and other officers, the Peru government closed Escobar's office (*ICCHRLA Newsletter*, 1989). In October, the case was transferred to a provincial prosecutor, who made no progress. In January 1990, the case was definitely closed and no charges were brought before either the civilian or the military courts for crimes committed at Cayara (Amnesty International, 1989f; Brown, 1990). In January 1991, it was announced that the case had been heard by the Supreme Council of Military Justice, which had ordered it suspended. Meanwhile, Escobar faced threats on his life, and in November 1990, the prosecutor and his three children sought refuge in the United States (Chiang, 1990).

In the legislature, two Special Commissions of Inquiry, chaired by APRA members Senator Carlos Enrique Melgar and Representative Jorge Sanchez Farfan, were appointed to investigate the massacre. Members of the Melgar Commission traveled to Cayara a month after the massacre and met principally with the military authorities, deliberately avoiding direct contact with witnesses to the massacre and relatives of the victims (Americas Watch, 1988c; *ICCHRLA Newsletter*, 1989). From all appearances, Senator Melgar's hidden agenda was to clear the army's name. The senator spent much of his time questioning Escobar's credentials and demanding that the prosecutor turn over confidential information. A few days after Escobar acceded to a request from Melgar for the names of witnesses, five persons "disappeared" in Cayara after their arrest by the army. Among the "disappeared" was a key witness to Escobar's investigation, and three of the others were his parents and sister (Americas Watch, 1988c).

The majority report of the Melgar Commission was issued in May 1989. It was signed by the APRA members of the commission only. The report concluded "categorically that there was no abuse on the part of military personnel in Cayara" and proposed that legal action be initiated against Prosecutor Escobar for misconduct of the investigation (Brown, 1990: 47). Furthermore, the report claimed that Military-Political Commander General Valdivia was neither the intellectual nor the material author of any criminal act, but rather was a victim of a subversive campaign to undermine his authority, and that he should be congratulated for his efficient work in the zone (Amnesty International, 1989f).

In addition to the majority report, the commission produced three minority reports: one by Senator Navarro Grau, a political independent, who did not consider it possible to determine whether the army had been responsible for any crime in Cayara, and two by opposition Senators Mohme and Diez Canseco. The latter reports concluded that the massacre was "indisputably" the responsibility of General Valdivia and the soldiers who carried out the killings. Further, the reports stated that "everything leads to the supposition that facing the public denunciation of the massacre, the Political-Military Command of Ayacucho took a decision to make the evidence disappear" (Brown, 1990: 48).

In sum, Peru's Congress turned the investigation of the massacre into a political whitewash, with the ruling party claiming the military had been simply victimized by "subversive" allegations. Meanwhile, the government failed to protect or support Prosecutor Escobar, forcing him to flee the country in fear for his life. The massacre and ensuing official response demonstrated the government's role in justifying and legitimizing the military's campaign of terror.

Government Practices and Policies

The García government defined 1989 as the year of an all-out effort against Sendero. During 1989, more than 300 Peruvians "disappeared" after detention, death squads were believed responsible for over 150 assassinations, and at the time of the national elections, the death toll in the ten-year guerrilla war approached 21,000 people (Brown, 1990; Pendzich, 1990; Werlich, 1991). Meanwhile, Sendero's goal for 1989 and 1990 was to sabotage the November municipal and April general elections. The guerrillas launched an especially intense campaign in the five weeks before the municipal elections. In what became known as "Red October," more than 360 persons were killed, including 28 government officials, 11 mayors and vice mayors, two district lieutenant governors, and one governor (Woy-Hazleton and Hazleton, 1992). But during this period, it became evident that Sendero was having difficulty expanding its movement. It was in this context that there was persistent speculation of serious divisions in Sendero, in particular between the leadership and the various organizations within Sendero's orbit (Crabtree, 1992).

At the time of the April elections, Peru was pushed to the edge of bankruptcy, and inflation surpassed 2,700 percent in 1989 (Brown, 1990). Meanwhile, García's authority was undermined by persistent rumors of a military coup, the glaring mismanagement of the judicial system and prisons, and the growing violence in Lima (Bourque and Warren, 1989; Graham, 1992). The result was an electoral loss for the APRA party and the 1990 inauguration of Alberto Keinya Fujimori as president of Peru.

President Fujimori moved increasingly toward authoritarian rule. The military was given full control of the emergency zones and civilian institutions were further stripped of their authority. Fujimori's authoritarian style soon clashed with Congress, which overturned Fujimori's decree to ensure that all military personnel in emergency zones would be judged in military courts regardless of their crimes or circumstances, virtually guaranteeing impunity for the armed forces (Mauceri, 1991). A new era of authoritarian rule began in April 1992, when President Fujimori dissolved Congress, suspended the judiciary, jailed members of the opposition, and assumed dictatorial powers (Hayes, 1992). Fujimori then fired 13 members of the Supreme Court, the leadership of the Public Ministry, and over 100 judges and prosecutors. In May, Fujimori promulgated Decree 25,475, an "anti-terrorist" law that authorized prosecution of anyone who "provokes anxiety" or "affects international relations" by any means. In August, Decree Law 25,744 was promulgated, under which the police need the permission of only a military court to carry out "preventative detention" of suspects and hold them incommunicado indefinitely (Human Rights Watch, 1992).

Fujimori's ascension to supreme leader was greeted with a new chapter in the war. On May 22, Sendero detonated the first of several car bombs in the capital, all aimed at civilian targets. But four months later, military forces made the astounding capture of Sendero leader Abimael Guzmán and 50 of his top followers. Guzmán's capture and subsequent sentencing to life imprisonment were used to justify Fujimori's tough anti-terrorism strategy, which had compiled a record of at least 169 extrajudicial executions and eight massacres in less than two years (Amnesty International, 1992c; Schmidt-Lynch, 1992).

Fujimori called for elections to be held November 22, a date he established unilaterally. In the election, boycotted by APRA and other major parties, Fujimori's New Majority–Change 90 coalition won a slim majority of seats in the Congress. In order to draft a new constitution and develop a new legislative system, the Democratic Constituent Congress (CCD) was formed. But under a decree by President Fujimori, the CCD had no authority to overturn executive actions. In essence, Fujimori had become the law.

Fujimori restored democracy to Peru by 1993. But in May, a human rights scandal implicating top levels of the Peruvian army split Congress. The scandal was over the 1992 "disappearance" of nine students and a professor from La Cantuta University. Opposition lawmakers charged the government with attempting a coverup and threatened to quit Congress. The military's involvement was cited by a high-ranking general who fled to Argentina after charging the presidential security adviser with running a death squad responsible for the La Cantuta "disappearances" (Schmidt-Lynch, 1993). At the time of this writing, the stability of Peru's democracy was clearly in doubt.

DISCUSSION

What factors account for the Cayara massacre? The massacre was committed by government soldiers, who carried out the killings in retribution for a Sendero attack. The identity of the victims demonstrates the ethnic component of the war, and the military's assumption that the Indian population, as a whole, is collectively responsible for guerrilla activity. But the massacre was part of a broader scheme that incorporated "villagization" strategies, civil patrols, and indiscriminate enforcement terror in an attempt to establish control over the indigenous population. These strategies undermined traditional authority and indicate a cultural motive of the terror as it applied to the indigenous population.

What is the character of terror in Peru? Massacres, arbitrary arrests, "disappearances," and torture are common in the emergency zones. But the government also selectively targets leftists, such as students and labor leaders. Furthermore, covert forces, in particular, death squads, have engaged in terrorist activity against economic and political targets. In general, the use of terrorist strategies against leftists indicates an economic motive, where terror is designed to maintain the dominant role of economic elites.

Did state terror eliminate the insurgency? The military resorted to extreme levels of terror in its war against the revolutionary movement. As the government expanded its scope of terror, the movement gained support. Recently, guerrilla activity has lessened, partially due to the capture of Sendero leaders and the emergence of authoritarian rule. However, state terrorism is unlikely to result in the full eradication of the insurgency.

The Peru case demonstrates the relative ineffectiveness of state terror in the context of ethnic-based insurgencies. Will state terror have a greater impact against class-based insurgencies? The next chapter reviews the character of terror in Colombia, where the democratic government is challenged by several regional class-based insurgencies.

NOTES

1. The original source is the Ayacucho Provincial Council, which used survivors' accounts to estimate the number of Cayara massacre victims.

2. General Valdivia was promoted in January 1992 to chief of the General Staff of the Armed Forces Joint Command, one of the most powerful posts in the country (Human Rights Watch, 1992).

II

Colombia: Segovia Massacre

Colombia is a democratic state dominated by economic elites. The government is challenged by several regional class-based insurgencies that seek to change the distribution of resources. The military has a close relationship with economic elites, and state terror has been directed toward members of the left. In this context, death squads, in conjunction with local police and military personnel, carried out a massacre in the town of Segovia. The government's use of terrorist strategies has failed to eliminate the insurgencies or deter support for leftist organizations.

THE MASSACRE

On November 11, 1988, 15 heavily armed men arrived in the gold mining town of Segovia.[1] The men, some of whom were reportedly in camouflage uniform and hooded, opened fire indiscriminately on people in the streets, bars, and cafes. Some of the gunmen intercepted two buses and killed numerous passengers with machine guns and grenades. Another group of assailants reportedly went from house to house with a list of names of political and union leaders, who were then shot (Amnesty International, 1989c). The gunmen were in Segovia nearly an hour before driving to a nearby town (La Cruzada) and murdering six more people. Forty-three persons, including at least three children, were killed in the massacre.

The massacre, believed to be committed by a death squad, The Realists, could not have been carried out without the cooperation of the military and police. Three routine checkpoints on the road into town had inexplicably been removed earlier that day, and the gunmen had to pass by the headquarters of a major army facility, the 42nd Infantry Battalion Bombaná. Facts also show that the regular garrisons of the police and military stood by while the gunmen moved freely through town. Furthermore, a preliminary judicial investigation established that "not only had the armed forces failed to intervene to protect the townspeople from attack but that army and police personnel, including the battalion commander, were directly responsible for the preparation of the attack on Segovia" (*Latin American Weekly Report*, 1988: 11).

HISTORICAL CONTEXT

Over half of all Colombians live in absolute poverty, and fewer than 10 percent of the landowners control more than 80 percent of the land (Pearce, 1990). In general, the high degree of socioeconomic inequality, and unequal land distribution in particular, has been an important cause of violence. In Colombia, violence is pervasive, coming from all sectors of society. Landlords and business people have formed alliances with the military to eliminate social movements (Fellner, 1986; Petras, 1988; Osterling, 1989). Guerrilla organizations have battled government forces throughout the 1980s. Death squads associated with the military, and in some cases, drug traffickers, have been responsible for a disproportionate amount of the violence. Private assassins also abound in this climate. In the past decade, the government has promoted a "dirty war," in which thousands of Colombians have been detained, tortured, and murdered.[2]

Government

The Colombian government has a history embedded in violence. It is a closed system that has traditionally represented the interests of the elite. For most of the 1980s, the government resorted to state of siege rule and repressive legislation. Consequently, while the government may be considered a stable democracy, the military retains a great deal of autonomy.

Elitist Democracy and the State of Siege

Colombia's government is best described as an "elitist democracy" (Dix, 1987a). It is a system dominated by two parties, Conservative and Liberal, which have traditionally represented the oligarchy (Dix, 1987a, 1987b; Hoskin, 1988). Third parties have almost no salience in Colombian politics. Both the Conservative and Liberal parties are shaped by clientelist relationships and thrive on family connections and powerful friendship cliques known as *roscas* (Osterling, 1989). Each party has several factions, ruled by a national boss, usually a congressman, who controls a political machine. In this system, favors and spoils are exchanged for political loyalty and votes (Osterling, 1989). Even local municipal leaders owe allegiance to the party boss who can grant government positions and promotions in exchange for loyalty (Pearce, 1990). The parties are not issue-oriented but rather, membership in a party is often inherited, and party leadership traditionally remains in the hands of the same families and their descendants (Osterling, 1989).

The current form of government has its origins in the years of political violence from 1947 to 1953, known as *La Violencia*, when the Liberal and Conservative parties fought a brutal war that left more than 200,000 people dead. During this period, Liberal landowners organized peasant armies that used "hit and run" tactics against the Conservative forces of the state (Pearce, 1990). The war officially terminated in 1957, when the two parties formed the National Front and agreed to take turns in the presidency every four years until 1986. Under the agreement, all national and local legislative seats, posts in the cabinet, the judiciary, and all levels of public administration were distributed between the two parties.

In the 1980s, the Conservative and Liberal governments increasingly relied on the military to maintain order. The military's strength and autonomy grew (Andreas and Sharpe, 1992). Under Liberal President Julio César Turbay Ayala (1978-82), whole sections of the country were placed under military rule. During this state of siege, the private armies evolved into death squads and paramilitary organizations aided the military in its campaign against the guerrillas (Watson, 1990). While the military and its associates began practices of "disappearances" and massacres, the government practically ensured military personnel immunity from prosecution. The national police were incorporated into the armed forces under the control of the Minister of Defense (Fellner, 1986). A controversial security statute also gave military courts jurisdiction over many "political" crimes. Military power reached its zenith during the Turbay administration.

Conservative President Belisario Betancur (1982-86) took a different approach to solving the conflict with the guerrillas. He ended the state of siege and in 1984, reached historic truce agreements with three of Colombia's four major guerrilla movements (Premo, 1988). But a new era of violence was touched off in November 1985, following the army's assault on the Palace of Justice, which the guerrilla group M-19 had taken over. The assault left 95 people dead, including 12 Supreme Court judges. The guerrillas stepped up their actions amid one of the worst economic recessions in Colombian history (Hoskin, 1988). Public antagonism toward Betancur's policies led to the overwhelming victory of Liberal Party candidate Virgilio Barco Vargas.

The Barco administration (1986-90) pursued seemingly inconsistent policies. On the one hand, Barco refurbished the civilian courts and spearheaded the restructuring of the political system. On the other hand, he expanded the military's power and ignored its abuses. Widespread violence escalated throughout this period, although most of the government's efforts focused on the violence associated with drug trafficking.

Barco's political reforms were an attempt to give the government more legitimacy and to make the traditional parties responsive to the population's needs. The reforms included the popular election of mayors, the government-opposition program, and proposals for a plebiscite and constituent assembly. The popular election of mayors, who in the past were appointed by political bosses, had the greatest potential for decentralizing the system and encouraging popular involvement. In March 1988, mayoral elections were held for the first time. Barco's government-opposition scheme proved harder to implement. Neither party was willing to transform itself from an elitist clique to a true government party, and there were no third parties that could fill the gap (Hoskin, 1988; Restrepo, 1992).

While Barco engaged in reforms designed to open the political system, he increasingly resorted to state of siege powers and repressive legislation. Under Barco's administration, official repression of the popular movement and of labor strikes became far more overt. For example, a guarantee of the right to strike could be overruled by the government in the interests of "national security." A general strike called for October 27, 1988, was treated as an act of "subversion." Legislation was introduced under the state of siege provisions declaring the strike illegal and allowing detentions for those who promoted or participated in illegal strikes (Pearce, 1990).

In January 1988, the president introduced a Statute for the Defense of Democracy, known as the anti-terrorist law. The statute defined a "terrorist" in such broad terms that arrests could be made if an individual was under suspicion or had participated in an act of civil disobedience that, in the judgment of the police, had provoked terror in the population or endangered lives or property (Pearce, 1990). By 1991, Barco had issued 61 legislative decrees under state of siege provisions (Pearce, 1990).

The government responded to intensified guerrilla activity by significantly increasing the military budget and ceding civilian authority to the armed forces. By virtue of the state of siege powers, President Barco designated certain zones of conflict to be special military areas, where extraordinary powers were placed in the hands of a military chief (Americas Watch, 1990a). Meanwhile, the government failed to acknowledge the involvement of the armed forces in death squads and presented the problems of violence in Colombia as the sole responsibility of the Medellín drug cartel (Human Rights Watch, 1991).

Military Autonomy

The military operates under the ideological framework of the National Security Doctrine (NSD). The armed forces believe the defense of national traditions and values falls uniquely to them. According to the NSD, the battle between the government and the guerrillas is synonymous with the global battle between the East and the West, between communism and capitalist democracy (Fellner, 1986). Under this ideology, the military has not felt obliged to operate under civilian rules and laws.

The military has been able to maintain its autonomy by declaring military jurisprudence over cases involving members of the armed forces. Under the

Military Penal Code, commanding officers act as trial judges, while operational chiefs, who in many cases have ordered, approved, or participated in the commission of abuses, are responsible for judging the conduct of their subordinates (Americas Watch, 1989). Lawyers for the victims and their families have no access to the proceedings and no way to monitor them. For the most part, the result is impunity for the perpetrators of human rights abuses.

Recently, the autonomy of the military has been challenged by the civilian courts. Between 1965 and 1987, civilians accused of insurgency-related crimes were tried by military courts. In 1987, the Supreme Court declared it unconstitutional for military courts to try civilians. The court has also struck down emergency decrees on the grounds that the extraordinary powers given to the executive would infringe on constitutional guarantees (Americas Watch, 1989). Despite these measures, virtually no one accused of human rights violations is ever tried by civil courts (Watson, 1990).

The criminal justice system has simply not been effective in bringing the military under the rule of law. For one thing, the system is plagued by threats, assassinations, corruption, and complicity. Almost three dozen judges were assassinated during the Barco years alone (Martz, 1991). The system is also overburdened, with the backlog of cases in 1989 estimated at more than 300,000 (Martz, 1991). But the primary reason accounting for military impunity is obstruction by the armed forces. The Public Order Courts have not received the military's cooperation when investigations into human rights violations led to officers. Even when judges have ordered the arrest of military officers, they have found it difficult to have their warrants executed (Americas Watch, 1990a). For instance, the attorney general's investigation of Death to Kidnappers (MAS), a death squad that appeared in 1981, led to accusations that 49 members on active military service belonged to the organization. The army command rallied to their defense and most of those officers accused of MAS involvement have been promoted, not investigated (*Latin American Weekly Report*, 1988).

"Dirty War"

Death squads, guerrilla groups, and private armies are casual features of Colombian society. The armed forces and their associated paramilitary armies and death squads account for the vast majority of casualties in this war. The targets of organized violence have not been the guerrillas, but members of legal popular organizations. The government's "dirty war" has cost the lives of an estimated 8,000 peasants, workers, opposition politicians, and left-wing activists between 1986 and the first four months of 1989 (Pearce, 1990).

Guerrilla Opposition

There are four major identifiable, independent, Marxist-oriented guerrilla groups: Revolutionary Armed Forces of Colombia (FARC), National Liberation Army (ELN), Popular Liberation Army (EPL), and April 19 Movement (M-19). Each group controls different regions of the country and uses different strategies. FARC is considered the largest and best organized of the guerrilla groups. It was formed in 1965 and is built on strong local bases of support, primarily in sparsely populated areas. The ELN, formed in 1964, is considered the most "terroristic" of the rebel groups and responsible for the largest number of violations of war (Washington Office on Latin America, 1989). It is best known for its extortion campaign against international oil companies, which includes dynamiting oil pipelines. The EPL, another guerrilla group formed in the 1960s, has its stronghold in the northwestern Urabá region. The M-19, formally constituted in 1974, has been concentrated in the cities.

The guerrillas' armed insurrection against the government was interspersed with negotiations and cease-fires. FARC was the first to reach an agreement with the government. As a vehicle for the reintroduction of the FARC guerrillas and their sympathizers into legal political life, the government legitimized the Unión Patriótica (UP), organized by the Communist Party in 1985 (Americas Watch, 1989). But the assassinations of guerrillas who joined the UP led members of FARC to abandon this option and continue their armed struggle. Since Barco took office in 1986, the various guerrilla groups have stepped up their operations, despite attempts at peace negotiations.

Military Counterinsurgency

The principal victims of the government's counterinsurgency have been the legal popular organizations and their activists, leading many to describe the government's military operations as a "dirty war" (Restrepo, 1992). The "dirty war" is carried out by an alliance between the drug barons, sectors of the army, businessmen, landowners, and political bosses (Pearce, 1990). This alliance, which seeks to eliminate suspected guerrillas and left-wing civilian activists, is responsible for the paramilitary death squads that claim the majority of victims of political violence (Pearce, 1990).

There are over 140 paramilitary death squads operating in Colombia (Amnesty International, 1989c; Youngers, 1989). Their success has been attributed to the pervasive "cooperation by middle-ranking military officers and police officials" (Americas Watch, 1989: 111). Officers in some regions of the country participate in death squad actions or assist in the crimes by providing intelligence, logistics, and legal impunity. Impunity characterizes the operations of both the army and the death squads, indicating, at the very least, that high-level officers have chosen to tolerate these crimes (Americas Watch, 1989). Most of the death squads function in areas with a strong military presence and aim at the same targets as the army; all of them are profoundly "anti-communist" (Pearce, 1990). Armed forces units that have been implicated in paramilitary death squad activities include the intelligence unit of the National Police (F-2), the army's intelligence unit (B-2), and the army's intelligence and counterintelligence unit (BINCI) (Amnesty International, 1989c).

Drug traffickers have formed active and violent death squads, sometimes with the cooperation of local military and police officials. Two of the death squads sponsored by drug traffickers that are especially violent are Death to Judges and Magistrates, which operates in the department of Antioquia, and Death to Kidnappers (MAS). Since 1982, over 120 judicial officials have been assassinated, the majority for investigating drug-related crimes (Andean Commission of Jurists, 1991).

Death squad activity has been supplemented with more conventional means of warfare. In 1987, Colombia experienced systematic killings of political leaders, human rights monitors, and leaders of grass-roots social movements. In 1988, the military resorted to scorched earth tactics and indiscriminate violence. In January, 8,000 peasants were forced to flee their homes in the Guayabero Region after indiscriminate artillery fire (Washington Office on Latin America, 1989). In mid-1988, the army conducted aerial strafing against guerrilla strongholds in Urabá. But the most disturbing new phenomenon was the massacre. In 1988, there were 82 massacres of four or more civilians, claiming a total of 674 lives (Washington Office on Latin America, 1989; Wirpsa, 1989). Massacres and political killings resulted in the deaths of 3,000 Colombians in 1988 (Americas Watch, 1989). Colombia's security forces were directly and indirectly involved in many of the massacres (Washington Office on Latin America, 1989).

PERPETRATORS, VICTIMS, AND MOTIVES

The perpetrators of the Segovia massacre were members of a death squad. Although the identity of the death squad participants was not known, the local military and police were implicated in the killings. The victims were residents of the town, most of whom were killed in indiscriminate attacks. It appears that the massacre was committed in an attempt to eliminate well-known activists of the UP and to intimidate other UP supporters.

Perpetrators

The gunmen were believed to be members of a death squad called The Realists. Local residents suspect The Realists were members of an older death squad, Death to Revolutionaries in the Northeast (MARN) (*Latin American Weekly Report*,

1988). MARN has claimed responsibility for the assassination of several left-wing political leaders, such as the mayor of Segovia's sister town, Remedios. While the killings were committed by a death squad, the army and police were directly involved in preparing the attack and allowing it to go forward.

Among the evidence cited to support the allegation of official involvement is the fact that on October 26, police and army troops simulated a guerrilla attack on the town and distributed pamphlets promising to "pacify" Segovia and accusing the UP of being "communist murderers" (Americas Watch, 1989). A similar attack took place on November 5. In October, the UP coordinator of Segovia sent a letter to the attorney general in protest of the harassment of the population by members of the Bombaná Battalion. The types of harassment noted include searches without warrant and physical attacks on the inhabitants (Pearce, 1990).

Other evidence relating to the killings was cited in the attorney general's report of December 1, 1988. The police did not react to the killings at the Johnny Kay Bar, site of the majority of the murders, although it is less than 100 meters from the Police Command Post (Washington Office on Latin America, 1989). Ten police agents crossed paths with the killers minutes before the shooting began and did not confront them, although they were toting machine guns (Washington Office on Latin America, 1989). The vehicles used by the killers drove right past the military base (Washington Office on Latin America, 1989). No radio alert was sent out to mobile units alongside the roadway on which the killers escaped (Washington Office on Latin America, 1989). On the day the killings took place, both the UP mayor and the UP councillor's bodyguards, provided by the Administrative Security Department (DAS), were removed, and as previously noted, three routine checkpoints on the road into town had been taken down earlier that day (Amnesty International, 1989c).

The Segovia massacre demonstrates the covert nature of government repression in Colombia. It would appear that death squads are used to cover up official involvement in political crimes against civilians. Without a doubt, death squads could not perform their deeds without military and police complicity. Yet it is nearly impossible to document who is involved in the squads and where the orders come from. Ultimate responsibility must lie with the military hierarchy and the civilian government, which have tolerated, if not encouraged, massacres and indiscriminate violence against the civilian population.

Victims

The victims of the massacre were residents of the town of Segovia. While most of those killed were the victims of indiscriminate attacks, individual political and union leaders were especially targeted for assassination. But in a sense, all of the victims were selected because of their perceived political beliefs. The Segovia massacre demonstrates the philosophy of collective punishment. Under this scheme, an entire town may be "guilty" because of its support of a "subversive" organization. The "subversive" organization in this case was the UP, which had won the Segovia mayoralty and six council positions in the March elections.

Although the UP disavowed its relationship with FARC in 1987, the military continued to associate it with the guerrillas and the Communist Party. The UP, which supports major social, economical, and political structural changes, has considerable support in the economically depressed and underpopulated regions (Osterling, 1989). Death squads have systematically selected UP members for assassination. Between 1985 and 1987, more than 500 UP members were assassinated by death squads, and over a thousand sympathizers "disappeared" (Watson, 1990). In 1988 alone, 154 UP activists were killed (Americas Watch, 1990a). Given this record, it was not unusual that Segovia residents were selected for murder.

Motives

The motives behind the massacre appear to be twofold. First, the intent of the gunmen was to eliminate certain well-known activists or sympathizers of the UP. Second, the indiscriminate killings aimed to intimidate other UP members and supporters, both in Segovia and other UP-government towns. The UP was targeted because of its perceived relationship with FARC and its endorsement of a socialist ideology that calls for economic reform.

An underlying motive behind the massacre may have been related to economics. The UP supported a nationwide general strike planned for the end of October 1988, in which the trade union active in the local gold mine planned on participating. The union was threatened with suspension if it joined the strike (Americas Watch, 1990a). It is entirely conceivable that economic motives, in particular, the desire to eliminate labor activism, played an important role in the decision to massacre the Segovia townspeople. In a broader sense, the government's motive behind the "dirty war" is to eliminate threats to the current distribution of economic and political power. Referring to the Segovia massacre, Attorney General Horacio Serpa Uribe noted: "All of these events bear all the characteristics of political crimes, committed to punish those belonging to certain parties or adhering to certain ideologies or to intimidate entire communities, to maintain a certain economic status quo or to prevent the rise of certain forms of political expression" (Pearce, 1990: 262).

AFTERMATH

The Segovia massacre resulted in a jurisdictional battle between the judiciary and military. In a landmark decision, the Supreme Court ordered two military officers to be tried under civilian law. Yet, the civilian case was limited in its scope and did not result in any convictions. Meanwhile, the government made several attempts to outlaw death squad activity. In the early part of the 1990s, the military increased its counterinsurgency operations and violence was rampant.

Investigation and Accountability

Public word of the Segovia massacre was met with army denial. General Raul Rojas, commander of the army 14th Brigade, blamed the Segovia massacre on FARC and ELN forces (Lambelin, 1988). Meanwhile, the president's behavior indicated the government's unwillingness to investigate the massacre. The president signed a decree depriving the attorney general of the authority to prosecute the military and the police involved in the massacre. Although the decree was subsequently revoked under public pressure, the "complicity of the Colombian Government" was noted by the mayor of Segovia (U.N. Doc. E/CN.4/1989).

The Office of the Attorney General conducted an inquiry into the Segovia massacre. The examining magistrate established that the commander of the Bombaná Battalion had personally prepared and arranged the printing of a leaflet containing threats against the residents of Segovia in the name of a so-called death squad (*Latin American Weekly Report*, 1988). The preliminary investigation also pointed to the involvement of the armed forces in preparing the attack on Segovia. In addition to the earlier intimidation attacks and the threats contained in the pamphlets, evidence suggested a definite coordinated activity between the military and the death squad (Kendall, 1989).

In January 1989, arrest warrants were issued by a civilian Public Order Court judge against three army officers, two police officers, and four civilians for their part in the killings in Segovia. The military courts immediately claimed jurisdiction to proceed with the criminal investigation against the armed forces personnel. In a landmark decision, the Supreme Court concluded that acts of terrorism are common-law crimes committed outside the line of duty and therefore fall outside military jurisdiction (Amnesty International, 1989c). However, the court added that each case must be examined individually to declare jurisprudence. The court's decision allowed two officers, Lieutenant Colonel Londoño and Lieutenant Edgardo Alfonso Navarros, both of the Bombaná Battalion, to be tried before civilian courts on the charge of disseminating pamphlets among the population with the intent to intimidate it. With respect to the others indicted, the court ruled that the charge against them, failing to defend Segovia from the attack, constituted the military offense of "cowardice," so they would be tried by military courts (Americas Watch, 1989).

Notably, none of the officers was charged with murder. The civilian case experienced numerous delays and was marked by threats on the judges and attorneys. In 1988, a judge who had gathered evidence on the massacre was murdered, and a year later, a former judge who was representing the relatives of the victims of the Segovia massacre was killed (Americas Watch, 1990a). Two years after the massacre, none of the accused officers had been brought to trial (Yarbro, 1990). As of 1992, the case still had not progressed.

The degree to which the civilian case was limited, by both the type of charges filed and the number of military and police personnel indicted, demonstrates the judiciary's inability to oversee military abuses. While the civilian courts pursued some type of action, the military courts apparently failed to pursue a case against those charged with "cowardice." The army punished the two officers charged with disseminating pamphlets with a 30-day suspension from active duty. Meanwhile, Lieutenant Colonel Hernando Navas Rubio, the army brigade intelligence commander at the time of the Segovia massacre, was named to head Colombia's prison system.[3]

Government Practices and Policies

In April 1989, President Virgilio Barco took an important step toward stopping paramilitary violence. Three decrees (813, 814 and 815) were issued which established a special force to carry out missions against paramilitary groups, and suspended the armed forces' authority to distribute weapons to civilians.[4] The government's new strategy was countered by the army's refusal to cooperate, and the persistent failure to investigate allegations of official involvement in the paramilitary sphere has made these decrees relatively ineffective (Americas Watch, 1990a).

In August 1989, the drug-financed assassination of presidential candidate Luis Carlos Galán signaled a new era of political violence. President Barco reacted with a major offensive against the Medellín drug cartel, the traffickers considered to be behind the murder. The cartel responded by declaring a "total war" against the state, killing hundreds of police officers, dozens of journalists and judges, and two presidential candidates. To combat the violence from the traffickers, the president promulgated Decree Law 1859, which empowered the armed forces to arrest and hold suspects incommunicado for up to seven working days in military installations. In August and September, the authorities arrested thousands of people under state of siege laws. Meanwhile, the Barco government signed a major peace agreement with M-19.

In 1990, César Gaviria Trujillo was inaugurated president and embarked on a diplomatic path to end the violence. In 1991, three more guerrilla groups demobilized after reaching peace agreements with the government: the EPL, the Revolutionary Workers' Party (PRT), and the indigenous group, Quintín Lame.

In July 1991, Colombia adopted a new constitution that would incorporate diverse and opposing forces into the political process and, it was hoped, produce a more participatory and pluralistic democracy (Andreas and Sharpe, 1992). But the new constitution put the military and police further from civilian control. The constitution reaffirms the jurisdiction of military courts over crimes committed by members of the armed forces and the National Police, and permits officers to employ the defense of obedience to superior orders to avoid responsibility for their abusive acts.

A major guerrilla offensive was launched at the beginning of 1991 and there was a renewed wave of killings and "disappearances" of UP members. UP leaders reported that in the first two months of the year, 50 party activists had either "disappeared" or been killed (Amnesty International, 1992a). In September, the procurator general released a special report on human rights covering January 1990 to April 1991. The report registered over 5,000 victims of abuses by the armed forces, including extrajudicial execution, torture, and "disappearance" (Amnesty International, 1992a).

In the wake of stalled peace talks in May 1992, guerrilla and military operations increased throughout the country. The guerrillas mounted another nationwide offensive in October. On November 8, the president declared a "state of internal commotion" after FARC guerrillas killed 26 policemen and staged a wave of bombing attacks in several cities. A new round of military offensives was led by army Mobile Brigades, elite counterinsurgency units made up of professional soldiers. The Mobile Brigade operates by isolating an area in which guerrillas are active, bombarding and strafing suspected bases from the air, and then sending in ground pursuit units. The operation has left civilians trapped in a war zone, subjected to attacks, detention, torture, rape, and executions. When the brigades leave, they establish fortified "self-defense" or paramilitary organizations, even though such organizations were supposedly outlawed in 1989 (Human Rights Watch, 1992).

By all accounts, 1992 was an exceptionally bloody year. In just the first eight months of 1992, there were 91 massacres carried out by state security forces, guerrillas, and paramilitary groups, causing 477 deaths (Human Rights Watch, 1992). The vast majority of political killings have been attributed to state agents and paramilitary groups acting in collusion with the security forces (Human Rights Watch, 1992). UP members continued to fall victim to government forces and death squads. At least 28 UP members were killed in 1992, bringing the total to 2,200 party members since 1985 (Human Rights Watch, 1992).

DISCUSSION

What led to the massacre of Segovia residents? The massacre was carried out to intimidate and harass members of the leftist UP Party. Segovia was chosen as the site of the massacre because of the city's governance, which was run by the UP. Local economic elites were especially embittered toward the UP's support of a national strike, while the military opposed the UP because of its status as a former guerrilla organization. These factors explain the coalition formed between death squads and local military and police units, which proved to be responsible for the massacre. The attacks on UP also demonstrate an ideological motive, in that the government considers the promotion of socialist ideology to be a threat to the state.

What is the character of terror? Covert forces, in the form of paramilitary death squads, play a significant role in the government's terrorist strategy. State terror is used to maintain the domination of economic elites, and common targets of terror include members of the UP, union activists, peasant leaders, and human rights monitors. The government has expanded the use of terror during states of siege, leading to indiscriminate enforcement terror, including massacres.

What is the outcome of state terrorism? Rebel armies have continued to wage war against government forces. At the same time, peace agreements have resulted in the disarmament of some of the guerrilla forces. Overall, the government has taken the initiative of opening its political system to diverse groups. However, state terrorism has not secured the position of economic and political elites.

This review of Colombia demonstrates that terrorism may not be a very effective strategy when the government is challenged by several regional class-based insurgencies. But will terror have the same outcome when the government is opposed by one well-organized rebel army? The next chapter focuses on El Salvador, where a democratic government was engaged in a class-based civil war.

NOTES

1. Segovia is a town of less than 10,000 in the department of Antioquia, about 160 miles north of Bogota.

2. "Dirty war" is a concept that was associated with Argentinian state terror of the late 1970s, where the military junta eliminated somewhere between 6,000 and 20,000 civilians and engaged in a systematic policy of "disappearances." It is used here to describe a system of terror that relies on secretive, decentralized, and often covert forces that target perceived political opponents. The concept tends to be used to describe the nature of terror in Latin American states (Sloan, 1984).

3. A warrant for his arrest was issued in connection with the 1992 prison escape of drug kingpin Pablo Escobar.

4. In May 1989, the Supreme Court declared unconstitutional the army's authorization to distribute weapons to civilians, thus turning the suspension dictated by Decree 815 into a permanent prohibition.

12

El Salvador: San Salvador Massacre

El Salvador is a democracy controlled by economic elites and the military. The government was opposed by a class-based insurgency that demanded reform of the political and economic systems. Throughout the conflict, the government relied on terrorist strategies, targeting members of leftist organizations. In this context, army troops carried out the massacre of six Jesuit priests and two others in the capital of San Salvador. The government failed to achieve military victory, and a negotiated settlement concluded the war.

THE MASSACRE

In early November 1989, rebel forces launched a major offensive in the capital. On November 12, the president declared a state of emergency in the country. At the same time, government radio denounced leftist politicians and called for the head of Father Ellacuría, an outspoken Jesuit priest (Bennett, 1990). On November 15, army troops and tanks were posted around Central American University (UCA), the campus residence of Father Ellacuría and several other Jesuit priests. In the early morning hours of November 16, approximately 30 men, allegedly members of the army's elite Atlacatl Battalion, pulled six priests, including Father Ellacuría, from their quarters and shot them at close range (Marquis, 1989). The priests' housekeeper and her 15-year-old daughter, found hiding in the residence, were subsequently killed by the soldiers. The massacre claimed a total of eight victims.

HISTORICAL CONTEXT

Civil war broke out in El Salvador in 1980. The war reflected the country's sharp class divisions and its tradition of militarization. El Salvador has a high degree of socioeconomic inequality, and much of the conflict derives from the demand for land and resentment at its monopolization in the hands of the "fourteen families" that are said to constitute the oligarchy (Needler, 1991).[1] It was essentially a class-based war between the government, which reflected the interests of the upper class, and the guerrillas, which fought in the interests of landless peasants and urban workers.

Government

Throughout the 1970s, fraudulent elections and military dictatorships dominated the political scene. In 1979, an army coup, intended to take a major share of power from the military-oligarchy partnership and transfer it to politicians, ushered in a new era of democracy. A decade later, the right-wing Nationalist Republican Alliance (ARENA) party gained control of the government. Although El Salvador's government remains in the hands of civilians, the military retains an enormous amount of power.

The Rise of ARENA

During the 1980s, constitutional government by elected civilians became institutionalized through five major elections and the peaceful transfer of power from one elected civilian to another in 1989. The decade began with a progressive military junta, which set out on a program of fundamental social and economic reforms, including a controversial land reform (Singer, 1990). The social reforms and the junta's attempts to restore respect for human rights provoked a great deal of hostility from the military-oligarchy alliance. In a final effort to implement the reforms, the junta gave the military leadership an ultimatum demanding that the armed forces recognize civilian control in the issuance of orders. The military rejected the ultimatum, and the government resigned in early 1980 (Needler, 1991).

A second junta was formed in which the civilian element was provided by the Christian Democratic Party. José Napoleon Duarte headed the junta and initiated major land reform, with limited success. But elections in 1982 led to the right-wing presidency of Alvaro Magaña, who immediately ended Duarte's land reform program. In 1984, elections resulted in the return of Duarte and the unexpected victory of his Christian Democratic Party. Despite the dominant role of the Christian Democrats, the right-wing parties, especially the ARENA party and the traditional army-backed party, exercised enough power to block Duarte's land reform.

Meanwhile, the guerrillas continued their attacks against the government, expanding their war to the urban areas. In 1986, Duarte initiated a new round of talks with the guerrillas, but the talks broke down in September. In October 1987, under the Central America Peace Plan, the government declared an amnesty. The amnesty allowed the release of 400 prisoners who had been implicated in political offenses. The releases were greeted with the re-emergence of some of the country's most notorious death squads. The armed forces high command expressed open opposition to the policies of President Duarte, especially the president's discussions with civilian leaders of the Democratic Revolutionary Front (FDR), on behalf of the guerrillas. By the time elections were held in March 1988, Duarte, who was seriously ill, oversaw an administration criticized for its incompetence and corruption (Acevedo, 1991).

In the 1988 elections, the right-wing ARENA, campaigning under the slogan "A change for the better," gained control of half the seats in the National Assembly. In 1989, the party captured the presidency and on June 1, Alfredo Cristiani took the oath of office. The appointment of a new Supreme Court gave ARENA control of all three branches of the government for the first time.

The success of the ARENA party was met with skepticism from many sectors of society. After all, ARENA, which brought together the oligarchy, rightists, conservative professionals, and military hard-liners around the themes of anti-communism and nationalism, had long been linked with death squad activity (Barry, 1991). Furthermore, Roberto D'Aubuisson, whom President Duarte named as the intellectual author of the assassination of Archbishop Romero, was the main force behind the party, and many believed he ran the administration from behind the scenes (Norton, 1991).

Military Power and Civilian Justice

The institutionalization of democratic elections and civilian governments did not lead to military capitulation to civilian law. For the most part, the fiercely anti-communist military is mostly independent of government regulation. The military has retained its autonomy by controlling all other security agencies and ensuring loyalty to the military through the *tanda* system. Under the *tanda* system, military officers are bound to loyalty to their graduating class, or *tanda*, from the Military School. The officers mutually assist one another in their advancement to high positions, regardless of merit or competence. In addition, the legal system has consistently failed to hold military personnel accountable for abuses committed while in uniform.

The military controls the Treasury Police, the National Guard, and the regular police. These agencies are themselves responsible for serious human rights violations, and the Treasury Police, in particular, have been responsible for death squad activity (Needler, 1991). The Special Investigations Unit (SIU), which is charged with investigating major crimes, is also an arm of the military. Hence, investigations into human rights abuses committed by the military are carried out by agencies that are under the control of the military (Amaya et al., 1987).

The military system of advancement was designed to build solidarity among members of the armed forces. Currently, the leadership of the military and government is dominated by a small group of men known as the *tandona* ("big class"). The *tandona* consists of the 45 members of the graduating military academy class of 1966. Members of the *tandona* include the former leader of ARENA (D'Aubuisson) and Armed Forces Chief of Staff Emilio Ponce. By 1989, the *tandona* had assumed control over ten of the 14 military zones, five of the seven military detachments, five of six prestigious brigades, the three police forces, and three of the military commands (Barry, 1991).

While the military remains a powerful force behind the government, the civilian criminal justice system has failed to bring the rule of law to El Salvador. The judiciary, despite adequate training and resources, ia a very weak institution, hampered by the intimidation of witnesses, victims, and judges, and the lack of cooperation of military and security forces. As previously noted, the partiality of the police has made investigations into military crimes nearly impossible, since the courts are dependent on the police for evidence. In the past, the civilian government and judiciary neglected to investigate human rights abuses committed by government personnel, with one exception—cases tied to the continuation of U.S. military aid (Amnesty International, 1990a).

Civil War

The Marxist-oriented Farabundo Martí National Liberation Front (FMLN) initiated its war against the government in 1980. In the early 1980s, rebel forces were met with the military's scorched earth strategy, which left thousands of civilians dead. Meanwhile, death squads effectively crushed the popular movements. In the latter phase of the war, the military relied on a policy of selective terrorism. In November 1989, as the war appeared to be nearing an end, the guerrillas launched an offensive, countered by a new round of military repression.

Guerrilla Opposition

Although the war in El Salvador broke out in 1980, the origins of the class conflict can be traced to the 1930s, when the military government responded to popular demands for basic political and economic rights by unleashing a ferocious attack that left an estimated 30,000 people dead (Barry, 1991). Among those killed was the Communist leader Augustín Farabundo Martí, whose name and cause were assumed by the FMLN. In the 1960s and 1970s, popular movements calling for land reform and decent wages resulted in military repression and the government's refusal to engage in any social reforms. Meanwhile, all political opposition was kept out of government, and by 1979, most popular organizations had clandestine components prepared to fight the government.

In 1980, the FMLN was created out of five guerilla armies: Popular Liberation Forces (FPL), People's Revolutionary Army (ERP), Armed Forces of National Resistance (FARN), Central American Revolutionary Workers Party (PRTC), and the Armed Forces of Liberation (FAL). Originally, these armies were covert organizations whose operations were largely limited to kidnapping members of the oligarchy and political organizing (Barry, 1991). The FMLN was primarily a Marxist-Leninist organization with a strong foundation in progressive Christianity. The thrust of political organizing was in rural areas. The FMLN also had strong roots in the unions, universities, and urban popular movements. The guerrillas hoped to gain agrarian reform and to guarantee the welfare of all Salvadorans by what the FMLN labeled "economic democracy" (Barry, 1991).

FMLN troops were divided into guerrilla units that fought in areas where they lived, regular units that moved throughout the country, and special forces that had significant combat experience. The troops were supplemented by militias, made up of active FMLN supporters and part-time combatants. The militias served as important links between the FMLN and the popular organizations (Barry, 1991). The FMLN, unable to compete with the military's aerial war and ground offensives, relied on landmines to inhibit army mobility and engaged in sabotage aimed at the country's economic and transportation infrastructure (Barry, 1991).

The FMLN was influenced by the Nicaraguan revolution that crushed the Somoza dictatorship. From 1980 to 1983, the El Salvador guerrillas launched several offensives in hopes of creating a popular insurrection that would topple the government. As military repression heightened, the FMLN launched a last all-out offensive in December 1981. The offensive had disappointing results, and for the next few years, the guerrillas and their supporters suffered at the hands of a fortified military.

In 1984, the government's campaign of aerial bombing forced the guerrillas to adopt a new strategy. Instead of large rebel units, the FMLN created smaller units, consisting of eight to 12 soldiers. Although the guerrillas engaged primarily in small-scale actions, they proved capable of reconcentrating their forces to wage impressive attacks, such as the assault on the military training center at La Unión in 1985, the June 1986 raid on the San Miguel garrison, and the devastating blow against the El Paraiso army garrison in April 1987 (Siegel and Hackel, 1988). In addition, the guerrillas switched their emphasis from establishing zones of control to creating a nationwide network of support. Although FMLN strength was weakened in the zones of control in the northern and eastern parts of the country, by 1986 the guerrillas had expanded the war geographically into all 14 provinces of the country, including San Salvador (Siegel and Hackel, 1988).

During the late 1980s, the FMLN had considerable success building an urban support network. It dramatically increased its urban military actions and launched attacks against military bases within San Salvador (Barry, 1991). At the same time, the FMLN began pressing for a negotiated settlement that would include some form of power-sharing. In January 1989, it announced an innovative proposal that demonstrated its new willingness to participate in the electoral arena (Barry, 1991). In return, the FMLN requested that the March elections be postponed until September. The proposal was rejected, and the FMLN began a new wave of killings of high-level government and military officials. As the March elections took place, the FMLN called on its supporters to abstain from voting, and no elections took place in the 22 local areas controlled by the guerrillas. In September, the FMLN agreed to end its sabotage campaign and declared a unilateral cease-fire during negotiations.

The government met the FMLN's unilateral cease-fire with a new round of arrests and attacks against members of popular organizations. On October 31, the headquarters of the National Federation of Salvadoran Workers (FENASTRA) was bombed, resulting in ten deaths and thirty people wounded. Two days later, the FMLN withdrew from the dialogue process, promising not to return until the security of popular organizations was assured (Goldston, 1990). In November, the FMLN launched a major offensive, controlling as many as 25 neighborhoods in San Salvador (*National Catholic Reporter*, 1989).

The Military's War

Throughout the civil war, the government relied on a strategy of terror to defeat the guerrillas. The military's main weapon was a brutal counterinsurgency strategy that was clearly aimed at non-combatants and, by the end of 1989, left over 40,000 civilians dead (Fish and Sganga, 1988; Barry, 1991). The government's "dirty war" was carried out in two stages: (1) indiscriminate terror, 1980 to 1983; and (2) selective terror, 1984 to present.

Indiscriminate Terror, 1980 to 1983. The El Salvador military began the decade in spectacular fashion. In January 1980, security forces fired on the largest demonstration in Salvadoran history, leaving dozens dead and hundreds injured. In March, the armed forces engaged in the high-profile assassination of Archbishop Romero and in December, three U.S. nuns and a layworker were massacred. These events touched off a military campaign of indiscriminate terror in the rural areas and the activation of paramilitary death squads.

On March 6, 1980, a state of siege suspended individual freedoms. Over the next three years, the military pursued a scorched earth strategy in the rural areas, designed to eliminate the FMLN's main base of support. In practice, the scorched earth strategy involved counterinsurgency sweeps that killed everyone in their path and virtually depopulated large areas of the countryside (Popkin, 1991). In addition to large periodic sweeps through guerrilla-controlled regions, the military maintained a conventional warfare strategy of indiscriminate air attacks (Siegel and Hackel, 1988). While these tactics decimated the rural civilian population and certainly affected the guerrilla ranks, they also led to international criticism.

The indiscriminate terror dealt the rural population was supplemented by death squad activity. Without a doubt, the death squads were paramilitary in nature, consisting of official personnel acting in plain clothes under the direction of superior officers (Amnesty International, 1988d). The history of the death squads goes back to the National Democratic Organization (ORDEN) founded in the 1960s by the commander of the National Guard.[2] The death squads drew most of their victims from the popular movements and especially targeted students, professors, priests, and union leaders. From 1980 to 1983, more than 37,000 civilians were killed by government security forces and death squads, at least 2,300 persons "disappeared" following abduction by the security forces, and about 20 percent of the population lived as refugees (Americas Watch, 1983).

Selective Terror, 1984 to present. The military's war against the guerrillas entered a new phase in 1984. In the rural areas, the scorched earth campaign was replaced with "search-and-destroy" operations, carried out by small mobile units (Siegel and Hackel, 1988). At the same time, an influx of U.S. military aid brought in new sophisticated equipment and highly trained officers.[3] Instead of indiscriminate bombings, helicopters were used to target FMLN bases. Meanwhile, the military launched civil programs designed to win the "hearts and minds" of the people. For instance, in 1986, the Salvadoran Armed Forces advanced a program known as the Counterinsurgency Campaign: United for Reconstruction (UFR). Under the UFR, the military set up civil defense forces and used psychological operations aimed at weakening the peasantry's support of the guerrillas (Siegel and Hackel, 1988). By all accounts, these "developmental" programs had little impact on the FMLN's level of rural support.

Following the 1984 election of Duarte, death squad activity dropped sharply, killings and "disappearances" became more selective, and the annual number of victims declined (Amnesty International, 1988d). But in 1987 and again in 1988, the number of death squad killings escalated. Some of the country's most notorious death squads, such as the Secret Anti-Communist Army (ESA), re-emerged. Notably, the rise in death squad activity increased dramatically in the first months of 1988, following the release of hundreds of political prisoners under the terms of the Central America Peace Agreement (Amnesty International, 1988d).

In 1989, as the government held negotiations with the FMLN, the army stepped up its harassment of trade unions and popular organizations. The number of political arrests increased, police round-ups of trade union leaders mounted, and reports of gross mistreatment and severe torture of detainees by government forces soared (García, 1990; Goldston, 1990). Following the October bombing of FENASTRA headquarters, the FMLN withdrew from negotiations and launched the November offensive in the capital. On November 12, President Cristiani declared a state of siege over the country and imposed a dusk-to-dawn curfew. The government's counterattack included heavy aerial bombing of the *barrios* of San Salvador and San Miguel, leaving thousands of civilians dead, injured, or displaced.

PERPETRATORS, VICTIMS, AND MOTIVES

The massacre, which claimed eight victims, including six Jesuit priests, was committed by members of an elite army battalion. The primary target of the massacre was Father Ellacuría, whom the military considered especially subversive. The massacre was carried out to eliminate the threat to the social order posed by the ideological rhetoric of the Jesuit priests.

Perpetrators

The elite U.S.-trained Atlacatl Battalion was responsible for carrying out the massacre. Atlacatl soldiers have been responsible for some of the worst atrocities committed in the course of the war.[4] The criminal investigation of the massacre indicated that the killings were part of a premeditated, well-conceived plan involving high-level officers. The evidence shows that, just prior to the massacre, 20 top Salvadoran commanders met at the high command to discuss strategy. Reportedly, Colonel Benavides, commander of the Atlacatl Battalion, emerged from the meeting determined that the Jesuits would die (Marquis, 1989). In pretrial dispositions made public, several of the soldiers described the priests as "terrorists" and told of receiving orders from Benavides to kill them (Miller, 1990). Although it is not known who ultimately gave the order to kill the priests, the army high command was certainly aware of the situation. At the very least, the military hierarchy and civilian government were responsible for encouraging the massacre by declaring the priests "subversives."

Victims

Father Ellacuría was the primary target of the killings. The military labeled him a hard-core Marxist who backed "the objectives of the communist revolution" (Bole, 1990). He was considered a particular threat because he promoted a negotiated peace and adamantly opposed U.S. aid. Also, two of the other priests who were killed in the massacre had been accused by the military of being the intellectual mentors of the FMLN (Baloyra-Herp, 1991). In reality, the Jesuits were not advocates of the guerrilla movement, but rather, their primary concern was the widespread poverty in the country and the economic injustices resulting from the concentration of power and wealth (Baloyra-Herp, 1991).

The identity of the victims of the massacre reflects the government's campaign of terror against leftist organizations. In particular, the government and military considered the Catholic Church to be a leftist and subversive institution. The Church's endorsement of liberation theology, which advocates the rights of the poor, directly challenged the inequitable social order. Thus, members of the Catholic Church were selectively targeted, and in the decade of the 1980s, about 600 members of the Catholic "base communities" were killed or "disappeared" (Barry, 1991).

Motives

The massacre was essentially carried out as punishment. The military believed the Jesuit priests were dedicated to the guerrilla cause and therefore needed to be punished for their subversive activity. But in a broader sense, the massacre was part of an overall terrorist strategy designed to maintain the social order. The priests represented an ideology that challenged the social order. Thus, the government and military were motivated to engage in a massacre in an attempt to eliminate the threatening ideological rhetoric promoted by the priests.

While an ideological motive underlies this particular massacre, the government primarily uses terror to serve economic interests. The social order is based on a high level of socioeconomic inequality and the concentration of wealth in the hands of a small ruling class. Terrorism is used to quiet demands for political and structural reform. In this context, the massacre of the Jesuits was economically motivated, designed to eliminate threats to the domination of economic elites.

AFTERMATH

The massacre of the Jesuits challenged the new civilian government's commitment to human rights. In the past, no military or police officer had been tried and convicted of human rights abuses against civilians (Americas Watch, 1988b). But in this case, the continuation of U.S. military and economic aid was tied to the conviction of those responsible for the killings. The ensuing investigation resulted in the conviction of two officers. Meanwhile, the ARENA government persistently ignored other human rights abuses committed by the armed forces. In 1992, the government and FMLN signed an agreement to end the country's 12 years of civil war. A year later, the Salvadoran Congress approved a general amnesty for army and rebel chiefs accused of human rights atrocities during the civil war.

Investigation and Accountability

The military's immediate response to the public announcement of the massacre was one of denials and accusations. Supported by Attorney General Mauricio Eduardo Colorado, the army claimed that the guerrillas had plotted to kill leaders of the Catholic Church to destabilize the country (Gruson, 1989). The attorney general went so far as to send a letter to the Pope asking him to withdraw from El Salvador all bishops who were "fomenting violence" (Barry, 1991). But the claim convinced few people, and after pressure from internal human rights and church groups and the U.S. Congress, the government opened an investigation into the massacre of the six Jesuit priests, their housekeeper, and her daughter. The investigation was carried out by the Special Investigations Unit (SIU), whose agents were all security force members. Judge Ricardo Zamora was assigned to the case.[5]

The investigation into the massacre was carried out alongside military attempts to cover up the crime. The destruction and disappearance of evidence was pervasive. A lieutenant colonel was charged with destroying evidence after it was discovered that he had burned military logbooks in which the name of anyone entering or leaving the UCA campus should have been recorded (*San Francisco Chronicle*, 1990). The destruction of logbooks was followed with the disappearance of Colonel Benavide's notebook, in which he kept notes of his activities and of the meetings he attended (Gruson, 1990). While hard evidence was destroyed or disappeared, military personnel allegedly involved in the massacre suddenly became unavailable for questioning. The military sent some of the accused soldiers and officers out of the country or gave them government posts. For instance, Colonel Joaquin Cerna Flores, who ordered the search at UCA, was removed from his military post and given a government job soon after the killings. Colonel Carlos Guzman Aguilar, head of the National Intelligence Directorate on the night its officers joined the search of the campus, was retired and sent out of the country as a military attache (Bronstein, 1990). Also, four cadets who were on guard duty at the school on the night of the slayings were sent out of the country, three to Fort Benning, Georgia, and the fourth to Panama (*The Washington Post*, 1990). Certainly, the investigation was limited by the lack of crucial evidence and eyewitness testimony.

The military dictated the direction of the investigation. For instance, the government's case rested on extrajudicial confessions by seven of the indicted soldiers, but a Military Honor Board provided little information on how those confessions were obtained. In addition, the army sent four cadets from the Military Academy, who had nothing to do with the case, to testify before Judge Zamora. When the army produced the cadets who were on duty the night of the murders, they claimed to know nothing about the killings (Arnson and Holiday, 1991).

The investigation also failed to explore the roles played by military intelligence or by officers who stood in the chain of command between Colonel Benavides and the lieutenants charged in the case. The SIU investigators did not question any top military officers, such as Guzman Aguilar or Cerna Flores, ignoring the possibility that the orders could have come directly from the high command (Gibb, 1990). From all appearances, the military hierarchy, not investigating authorities, controlled who was questioned, who was detained, and who was charged (Arnson and Holiday, 1991: 42).

The extensive coverup was paired with accusations concerning the attorney general's office and the U.S. Embassy. In January 1991, two principal prosecutors in the case resigned. The prosecutors accused the attorney general's office of not "pursuing a clean investigation" and charged that the military was "obstructing the case of the Jesuit priests" (Arnson and Holiday, 1991: 42-43).[6] Similar accusations and controversy surrounded the actions of the U.S. Embassy. A witness to the killings, Lucia Cerna, a housekeeper at the university, was taken to Miami under U.S. protection. The witness was interrogated by Colonel Benjamin Rivas, the head of the SIU, who was flown to Miami for the occasion. According to some Salvadoran Jesuits, the witness was subjected to days of interrogation and psychological pressure by Rivas until she finally retracted her story, which had identified members of the military as perpetrators of the crime (Gibb, 1990). Meanwhile, a U.S. military adviser, Eric Buckland, gave sworn testimony to the FBI that he had received warning of the killings. Buckland also retracted his story, and the U.S. Embassy refused to allow its officers to provide testimony in the case (Gibb, 1990).

In mid-January 1990, two months after the killings, Judge Zamora charged nine members of the army, including Colonel Benavides, with premeditated murder and ordered the men to be held for trial. Benavides was placed under "house arrest," which involved his removal from San Salvador to a coastal resort hotel (Feuerhard, 1990). Three months after the soldiers were charged, the U.S. congressional task force declared that the investigation into the massacre was "at a standstill," with no effort being taken to determine whether higher military officers were involved in the crime (Broder, 1990). In August 1990, U.S. Representative Joe Moakley accused the Salvadoran High Command of engaging in "a conspiracy to obstruct justice in the Jesuits' case" (Americas Watch, 1990b: 14).

Over a year later, in September 1991, a five-member jury found Colonel Benavides guilty of eight counts of murder for ordering the massacre, and Lieutenant Yusshy Rene Mendoza guilty of murder in the death of the daughter of the priests' housekeeper. It was the first time an army officer had been convicted of a crime involving human rights abuses. At the same time, the jury acquitted two lieutenants and five other soldiers. In January 1992, Judge Zamora sentenced Benavides and Menodoza to maximum 30-year prison terms.

Government Policies and Practices

Following the November offensive and the massacre of the Jesuits, the government and military continued the state of siege, which suspended constitutional freedoms of speech, association, press, and communication, as well as procedural due process rights. The general staff of the army promulgated new guidelines restricting access by human rights, humanitarian, and press organizations to the interior of the country as well as to "zones of conflict." As death squad killings increased, leaders of popular organizations and opposition politicians once again fled the country in fear for their lives (Goldston, 1990).

By the beginning of August 1990, the number of death squad killings reported to local human rights groups had exceeded the total reported for all of 1989 (Amnesty International, 1990a). But Cristiani's government failed to investigate any atrocities apart from the Jesuits' case. In 1990, several important human rights cases were dismissed wholly or in part. The dismissed cases included the 1988 massacre of ten captured peasants in San Sebastian, and the kidnapping-for-profit by rightists and members of the armed forces between 1982 and 1985 (Human Rights Watch, 1991).

In March 1991, municipal and legislative elections took place amid allegations of fraud and instances of electoral violence. The left-wing coalition, Democratic Convergence, won eight seats and entered the Assembly for the first time, while ARENA lost its absolute majority in the Legislative Assembly. In April, the government and the FMLN agreed to set up a Commission on the Truth of El Salvador to investigate acts of violence committed by government and FMLN forces. The three members of the commission were appointed by the UN secretary general in December. Despite negotiations, the war continued to claim scores of casualties. Several execution-style killings by FMLN members were reported, while electoral candidates perceived to be sympathetic to the FMLN were killed in circumstances suggesting military involvement.

On January 2, 1992, the government and FMLN signed an agreement to end the war. Since the February cease-fire, the number of human rights violations in El Salvador greatly diminished, in part due to the presence of the United Nations Observer Mission (ONUSAL). In March 1993, the Commission on the Truth of El Salvador publicly reported its findings and recommendations. The report, which covered abuses since 1980, blamed about 85 percent of the human rights abuses on the military and security organizations, 10 percent on rightist death squads and 5 percent on the FMLN (*San Francisco Examiner*, 1993). The commission called for the immediate dismissal of 40 senior officers who were associated with grave violations of human rights. Furthermore, the commission claimed that General Ponce had given the orders to kill the Jesuit priests. The Salvadoran Congress, outraged by the commission's report, approved a general amnesty for army and rebel chiefs accused of human rights atrocities during the civil war. Colonel Benavides and Lieutenant Mendoza were among those who were to be released under the amnesty. In May, President Cristiani, under international pressure, began removing 15 top Salvadoran military officers in a purge of human rights abusers from the army. On December 15, the civil war was formally brought to an end when the planned demobilization of guerrilla forces and active army units (including the Atlacatl Battalion) was formalized.

On April 1, 1993, Colonel Benavides and Lieutenant Mendoza were released, having served only 15 months of their sentences. They thus became the first beneficiaries of a controversial amnesty law passed by the right-wing-dominated Legislative Assembly in March, and widely seen as a device to protect members of the military accused of gross violations of human rights. Throughout the year, former rebel leaders fell victim to death squad killings, and in November, five former rebels, including two senior officials, were killed (Lang, 1993).

DISCUSSION

What led to the massacre in San Salvador? The massacre was carried out in the context of a rebel offensive and demonstrated the military's frustration with the war. The targets of the massacre were Jesuit priests, whom the government associated with the guerrilla movement. The military considered the Catholic Church in general to be a subversive institution, and it viewed liberation theology as a major threat to the current social order. This suggests that the government was motivated to use terrorist strategies in an attempt to destroy teachings that run counter to the dominant ideology.

What factors affect the character of terror? The political and economic structures in El Salvador are dominated by a small group of elites. In response to internal demands for the redistribution of land and income, the government has resorted to enforcement terror, including arbitrary arrests, torture, extrajudicial executions, and "disappearances," against members of leftist organizations. Death squads have been responsible for carrying out much of the terror. In sum, state terror is an outcome of the government's determination to maintain the domination of economic elites.

How has state terrorism affected the insurgency? The rebel forces have been able to adapt to the government's campaign of terror. Although the guerrillas abandoned their revolutionary rhetoric, they continued to pose a significant threat to the government. Both sides eventually pursued negotiations, and a peaceful settlement was reached. In the current political structure, the former rebel army has achieved legitimate status as a political party.

NOTES

1. In fact, the oligarchy numbers close to 200 families (Norton, 1991).

2. The U.S. Central Intelligence Agency organized ORDEN, which was responsible for the White Hand, one of the first Salvadoran death squads. ORDEN was run by military intelligence, whose commander at the time of the 1979 coup was Roberto D'Aubuisson (Barry, 1991; Needler, 1991).

3. From 1980 to 1987, the United States provided nearly one billion dollars to El Salvador's armed forces (J. McClintock, 1989).

4. Atlacatl soldiers were responsible for the massacre of 700 civilians in El Mozote in 1980; the killing of dozens of civilians in Tenancingo and Copapayo in 1983; and the 1984 killings of over 100 persons in Los Llanitos and the Gualsinga River (Goldston, 1990).

5. Judge Zamora handled the investigation of the 1980 assassination of Archbishop Oscar Romero, which remains unsolved.

6. Originally cited in *Foreign Broadcast Information Services,* 1991.

Part III

Comparisons and Conclusions

13

A Typology of Massacres

Are massacres unique events, or are there similarities between massacres? This descriptive chapter explores the conditions associated with each massacre. A comparison of the ten cases results in the development of a typology of massacres, based on the identity of the victims and the motives of the state. The chapter concludes with a description and summary of four types of government massacres.

VICTIM IDENTIFICATION

Victims of massacres often share some quality that makes them vulnerable to attacks by the government. In general, victims are selected on the basis of (1) their real or perceived political beliefs; or (2) their ascribed status as an ethnic, national, racial, or religious minority. The selection criteria are not mutually exclusive, as members of a minority group may also be associated with political organizations that are considered hostile to the state. However, two basic types of massacres can be delineated. Politicidal massacres refer to those cases where the victims are targeted for murder primarily because of their real or perceived opposition to the regime and dominant group, whereas in genocidal massacres, persons are killed because of their communal characteristics, such as their racial, ethnic, national, or religious status.

STATE MOTIVES

The state controls the only legitimate means of political violence. What motivates a state to engage in the indiscriminate killing of its people? Two types of motives are integral to the study of massacres. First, massacres, and state terror strategies in general, are social control mechanisms used to maintain the current political or structural order. Second, the state is motivated to engage in massacres by its desire to manipulate the balance of power, as it applies to the political and/or economic stratification system. Thus, politicidal and genocidal massacres can be further defined according to the political environment in which they occur. On the one hand, massacres that are carried out to maintain order are often executed (1) in conjunction with structural control techniques that aim to physically control a particular population; or (2) as part of an overall strategy to create an atmosphere of terror intended to deter political participation by "radical" groups, thereby maintaining oligarchic control of the political and economic systems. On the other hand, massacres carried out to manipulate the balance of power occur in the context of (1) a society polarized into hostile communities based on ethnicity and/or religion; or (2) a government in which a divided leadership is engaged in a struggle over political authority. In short, the state hopes the massacre will achieve at least one of the following:

- Consolidate the power of the central authorities (**crisis of authority massacres**).
- Maintain oligarchic control of the political and economic systems (**"dirty war" massacres**).
- Maintain or enhance the role of the dominant ethno-religious group in the stratification system (**communal massacres**).
- Establish government control over a separatist nationality or indigenous population (**pacification massacres**).

Figure 13.1 classifies the massacres based on victim identification and state motives.

POLITICIDAL MASSACRES

Massacres that target political opponents of the government can be labeled as (1) crisis of authority massacres; or (2)"dirty war" massacres. In crisis of authority massacres, a divided leadership struggles over the balance of power while the ideology that legitimizes the government erodes. "Dirty war" massacres occur in the context of class-based civil wars in which the oligarchy-dominated government and armed forces resolve to maintain order by attacking and threatening individuals and organizations calling for economic reforms or social justice.

Crisis of Authority Massacres

The killings in China and the Soviet Union were crisis of authority massacres. In the late 1980s, both governments found themselves in a deep crisis of authority that threatened the very survival of communist rule. This crisis was brought on by

Figure 13.1.
A Typology of Massacres

	Manipulate the Balance of Power	Maintain Order through Social Control
P **o** **l** **i** **t** **i** **c** **i** **d** **a** **l**	**CRISIS OF AUTHORITY MASSACRES** • *China* • *Soviet Union* <u>Context</u>: nonviolent demonstrations; demands for political reform; institutional imbalance; divided leadership	**"DIRTY WAR" MASSACRES** • *Colombia* • *El Salvador* <u>Context</u>: general class-based civil war; government and military act on behalf of oligarchy
G **e** **n** **o** **c** **i** **d** **a** **l**	**COMMUNAL MASSACRES** • *Sudan* • *India* <u>Context:</u> highly stratified and plural society dominated by one ethno-religious group; regional ethnic-based insurgency; communalized society and government	**PACIFICATION MASSACRES** • *Ethiopia* • *Iraq* • *Guatemala* • *Peru* <u>Context:</u> regional ethnic-based war; government views members of nationalist or indigenous groups as guerrillas, or potential guerrillas

an institutional imbalance, in which the economic structure was subjected to dramatic reforms, but the political system remained authoritarian. This institutional imbalance, combined with the failure of economic reforms in the Soviet Union and a sudden economic downfall in China, resulted in a divided political leadership and the emergence of popular movements.

In China, Deng Xiaoping advanced dramatic economic reforms, creating a "socialist commodity economy." The reforms, which led to a healthy rate of economic growth, also produced side effects such as rampant government corruption. Retail price reform, unleashed in 1988, resulted in an unprecedented bout of inflation, and the leadership began to split into two camps: those who desired to continue economic reforms, and those who wished to revert to central government control. Meanwhile, the influence of Western capitalism and the advance of a more open, modern society further eroded the legitimacy of communist ideology. The divided leadership soon encountered mass demonstrations calling for an end to corruption and the initiation of political reform. The authority of the Communist Party and the top leadership, now divided ideologically and generationally, was severely questioned by the populace, and a battle over political authority ensued.

In the Soviet Union, Gorbachev's economic reforms were combined with *demokratization* in an attempt to push the state into the capitalist world. But the economic reforms did not translate into economic prosperity; in fact, economic conditions worsened. On the political front, electoral changes and the legitimation of opposition organizations led to a shift of power from the central Communist Party to regional governments. But Gorbachev's policies were incongruent. For example, he encouraged popular participation in the Soviet republics while adopting decrees to curb dissent. The greater openness of the political system resulted in demands for autonomy and independence from the nationalist republics. As the Communist Party relinquished its monopoly of power, and nationalist demands could no longer be ignored, the Gorbachev administration found itself polarized into two competing groups. One faction believed that reforms had gone too far in undermining communist authority and promoted a return to centralized control. This hard-line faction was opposed by a more liberal group of elites that desired faster reforms and advanced democratic values. The battle over power indicated a crisis of authority in the political leadership of the Soviet Union.

In sum, both China and the Soviet Union used massacres in an attempt to push the balance of power to the conservatives' advantage. For the hard-liners who ordered the use of government force, the resort to violence aimed to achieve two things. First, the massacre would indicate the government's willingness to uphold its authority at all costs, and by doing so, deter further opposition. Second, the hard-liners hoped the show of force would lead to the consolidation of their power and push the leadership into a more conservative approach. The resort to violence was intended to shift the balance of power to the hard-line faction.

"Dirty War" Massacres

Another type of politicidal massacre occurs in the context of a "dirty war," in which death squads, paramilitary organizations, and the armed forces consider any critic of the government a potential target for elimination. The Colombia and El Salvador "dirty war" massacres share several themes. First, the government operates on behalf of the oligarchy, with the military supporting and promoting the interests of economic elites. Second, the state is engaged in a class war in which the government and oligarchy feel threatened by the legitimation of leftist movements. Massacres in these states were carried out with the goal of terrorizing leftist parties and rebels into submission, thereby retaining the present order of society, which benefits the oligarchy.

The elitist Colombia government reigns over an extremely violent society in which political violence—the majority of which is carried out by the armed forces and paramilitary death squads—targets guerrilla organizations and individuals associated with social movements. In the late 1980s, the guerrillas had become legitimate political threats. In particular, members of a major guerrilla group, FARC, had disarmed and formed a legal political party, the Marxist-oriented Unión Patriótica (UP), which had some success in regional elections. The success of UP was a major threat to the economic elites, who relied on the exploitation of labor to sustain their wealth. The legitimation of UP also was a source of resentment among the military, who still battled rebels who refused to participate in the UP. The Segovia massacre was an attempt to physically eliminate UP members and by doing so, to create an atmosphere of terror among all persons associated with the UP party. By physically eliminating the opposition, the military and oligarchy sought to maintain the present economic order, which favors their interests.

The Salvadoran political and economic system is dominated by the oligarchy, with the avid support of the military. In 1989, the class-based civil war was nearing an end, and the FMLN's legitimate role in the future political arrangement of the state seemed inevitable. The FMLN, influenced by the Catholic Church's liberation theology, promoted rights for the poor, land reform, and social justice. The legitimation of such an organization was a clear threat to those who benefited from the current social order. By massacring the Jesuits, the armed forces felt it could eliminate the "threatening" ideology of liberation theology and terrorize the opposition into submission, thus maintaining the current social order.

In sum, "dirty war" massacres were carried out to punish those who led an ideological battle against an elitist government. The massacres also were intended to create an atmosphere of terror, which presumably would deter the political participation of leftist groups. By authorizing the massacre, the government hoped to maintain the inequitable social order.

GENOCIDAL MASSACRES

Genocidal massacres can be classified as communal or pacification. For the most part, communal massacres occur in the context of a long history of communal violence, in which the government has encouraged the polarization of society along ethnic, racial, religious, or tribal lines. Pacification massacres are carried out as part of an overall government strategy to physically control a segment of the population through techniques such as "villagization," mass relocation, and civil patrols.

Communal Massacres

Communal massacres are an outcome of government policies that promote and exacerbate ethnic tensions. Despite the religious and ethnic nature of communalism, the conflict is essentially a battle between communities over political and economic resources. Communal massacres in Sudan and India share several themes: (1) armed opposition groups, drawn on communal lines, battle the central government in a highly polarized society; (2) political parties rely on communalism to win blocs of votes or effectively divide the opposition; (3) religion is used to exploit differences between communities; and (4) the armed forces and police perpetuate communal violence by protecting one community at the expense of another.

While the Sudanese government is vastly different from the Indian government, the two states effectively used religion to divide society in an attempt to retain the position of the ruling classes. The corrupt, patriarchal parties of the Sudanese government conspired with Islamic extremists, thus ensuring the continuation of war with the southern rebel army. The Wau massacre was a direct outcome of the military's policy of arming tribes that are traditionally hostile to the Dinka and Luo peoples, the main supporters of the rebel army (SPLA). The "divide and rule" strategy was a way for the northern Arab and Islamic elites to maintain their superior position in a social stratification system that views the tribal south as "uncivilized."

In India, the Meerut/Maliana massacre in Uttar Pradesh reflected the communal divisions of the regional administration and police. Although the battle reflected religious differences, the source of conflict between the Hindus and Muslims remains the inequitable distribution of resources and the balance of power. The minority Muslims, who hold legitimate claims of discrimination, resort to violence and extremist politics to gain social status in the political and economic system. The Hindus, feeling that the state has given minorities improper advantages, have resorted to forming political organizations along ethnic lines. The Indian state, dominated by the Congress Party since independence, has polarized these communities by bowing to pressures from both Hindu and Muslim fundamentalists. The Meerut/Maliana massacre, which occurred in the context of riots, was committed by the regional security forces as a way to keep the Muslims "in their place," which assumes Hindu domination of the economic and political structure.

Thus, communal massacres aim to punish certain groups of people for their perceived dissent. In general, communal massacres serve the purpose of maintaining or enhancing the position of the dominant group. Religious ideologies play a crucial role in dividing the population into competing groups, while the composition of the security forces increases the likelihood that terror will be used against the minority population.

Pacification Massacres

Pacification massacres occur as part of an overall repressive strategy designed to physically contain a particular ethnic or nationalist group. The massacres in Ethiopia, Iraq, Guatemala, and Peru share some important characteristics. First, each government battles armed opposition groups that draw their membership from a particular minority group. Second, the massacres are carried out in an environment where the minority population, believed to be susceptible to guerrilla "indoctrination," are forcibly moved into government-controlled villages. A third common element is the mass relocation or deportation of persons living in strategic areas, typically forcing the targeted population into urban centers or across the border. In some cases, the deportations are followed by population replacements, in which groups that are considered friendly to the government are given the confiscated lands of the "enemy." A fourth common element, and one related to the "villagization" tactic, is military control of the food supplies. The population, now living under military control, is dependent on the military for basic nourishment.

The Ethiopian regime, under the control of Mengistu Haile Mariam, engaged in a "villagization" and mass relocation plan. Famine was used to legitimize the "villagization" scheme, and food became a weapon for both sides of the conflict. Although "villagization" was not implemented in Eritrea, the Ethiopian government attempted to change the ethnic composition of Eritrea by importing Ethiopians into the region. Indiscriminate arrests, torture, and extrajudicial killings of Eritrean civilians were elements of the military's conduct of the civil war. The She'eb massacre demonstrated the government's pacification plan, which was directed against civilians based on their nationality or region of residence. In addition to physical brutality, the government pursued an administrative strategy that divided Eritrea into three regions roughly corresponding to the main ethnic clusters. An "Ethiopianization" plan also attempted to replace powerful Eritreans with Ethiopians.

The government of Iraq, headed by Saddam Hussein, engaged in similar strategies against its Kurdish residents. Entire cities and regions were bombed, forcing thousands of Kurdish civilians into "strategic villages." Indiscriminate arrests, imprisonment, torture, "disappearances," and executions were common in the Kurdish areas. In some cases, Arab peasants were brought in to occupy confiscated Kurdish land. Administratively, the government redrew the boundaries of the Autonomous Region, creating Arab majorities. The Halabja massacre, in which chemical bombs were dropped on the residential area of the city, was carried out in retribution for a successful guerrilla offensive. But the massacre also reflects an overall plan that called for the destruction of villages and the removal of Kurds to government-controlled villages.

In Guatemala, the civilian government created a facade of democratic institutions while the armed forces continued to dominate public policy. The army battled the guerrillas by controlling and pacifying the indigenous population through "model villages," civil patrols, and mass relocations. Additionally, death squads, torture, and "disappearances" are part of the system of terror and are applied selectively on political opponents as well. The El Aguacate massacre was directed at the indigenous population in an area known for its resistance to the army's civil patrol program. The massacre was intended to create a climate of fear, thus maintaining military domination and control over the indigenous peoples.

The government of Peru faces an exceedingly violent revolutionary movement, Sendero Luminoso. The guerrillas control significant rural areas, which are mostly populated by indigenous peasants and have long been neglected by the government. The army considers all indigenous peasants possible terrorists and has attempted to gain military control over the population by establishing civil patrols (*rondas*), and creating government-controlled villages in an attempt to undermine the guerrilla bases. The Cayara massacre was carried out in retribution for a Sendero attack on an army contingent, and demonstrates the military's belief that all persons living in the area are "guilty by association." "Disappearances," torture, and death squads are also used in the emergency zones and more selectively in urban areas. The indigenous population is trapped between the scourges of both the guerrillas and the military.

In sum, pacification massacres are intended to punish the guerrillas and their perceived supporters. In every case, the government targets members of the indigenous or nationalist group associated with the guerrilla insurgency. In addition, pacification massacres serve the purpose of forcing survivors into government-controlled areas. The overall goal of such policies is to establish government control over the minority population.

SUMMARY

Massacres can be categorized by the identity of the victims and the motives of the state. In politicidal massacres, the victims are targeted because of their real or perceived opposition to the regime and dominant group. Genocidal massacres are those in which the victims are characterized by their racial, ethnic, national, or religious status. The state's motives in perpetrating massacres fall into two general categories. First, the massacres may be part of the state's attempt to maintain the current political or structural order. Second, the state may engage in massacres as a means to manipulate the balance of political and economic power.

There are four types of massacres: crisis of authority massacres, "dirty war" massacres, communal massacres, and pacification massacres. Crisis of authority and "dirty war" massacres are politicidal, while communal and pacification massacres are genocidal in nature. In crisis of authority massacres, the political leadership is typically engaged in a power struggle over authority, brought on by the collapse of the dominant ideology. The divided leadership is challenged by nonviolent movements demanding political reforms. The conservative faction of the leadership directs the massacre in an attempt to put an end to the demonstrations and as a means to consolidate its base of power within the government.

In "dirty war" massacres, class-based civil wars and violence threaten the current socioeconomic order, which is based on a high degree of socioeconomic inequality. The government and economic elites have close ties, and death squads are used in conjunction with official security forces to maintain the domination of the oligarchy. In "dirty war" massacres, "subversives" are murdered in an attempt to preserve the prevailing order of society.

Genocidal massacres occur in the context of societal conflict based on ethnic, national, or religious cleavages. In communal massacres, the state has a long history of communal violence in which it has promoted and exacerbated ethnic and religious tensions. Communal violence evolves into a massacre when the government's agents protect one community at the expense of another.

Pacification massacres are carried out as part of an overall government strategy to physically control and contain a minority population. Armed opposition groups, drawn mostly from a politically marginal ethnic group, challenge the government's authority. Massacres, along with strategies of "villagization," mass relocation, and civil patrols, are used to instill a sense of fear in the target group, thus enabling the government to physically dominate the minority population.

14

The Character of State Terror

What are the strategies, targets, and motives of terror? This chapter identifies several different strategies and motives of terror, and describes three social structures that help explain the character of terror. Each social structure is reviewed in the context of state terror, and several findings are put forward. The chapter concludes with a discussion of factors that influence the character of terror.

STRATEGIES

In an earlier chapter, several types of strategies of terror were noted: information control, economic coercion, law enforcement/legal, and enforcement terror. In a variation of this scheme, three types of terror strategies are outlined below. Although each strategy is listed separately, readers should note that governments are likely to use a combination of strategies.

1. **Enforcement Terror**   arbitrary arrests, political prisoners, torture, extrajudicial executions, massacres, detention without trial, "disappearances," scorched earth strategies.
2. **Banning Terror**   prohibition of political expression, censorship, propaganda, purges, denial of freedom of assembly and speech, confession rituals.
3. **Containment Terror**   mass relocation, "villagization," population replacements, destruction of villages.

Enforcement terror, an elaboration of Sloan's (1984) use of the term, is the most severe form of terror, encompassing such acts as torture, extrajudicial executions, and "disappearances." Enforcement terror was present in each case study, as illustrated by the occurrence of government massacres. Yet enforcement terror varied by the level of government involvement and its scope. Government involvement may be official or covert, while the scope of terror can be defined in terms of indiscriminate as opposed to selective terror.

Official government forces are primarily responsible for perpetrating terrorist acts. But the government also may support covert forces, which are intended to shield the government and military from accountability. In particular, the persistence of paramilitary groups, typically referred to as death squads, and the promotion of civilian-based forces such as civil patrols and tribal militias are indicative of covert terror. Death squads carry out their activities in a highly secretive manner, while civilian-based forces operate openly. In all cases, the government and military have a direct but mostly invisible link to covert forces.

Enforcement terror may be carried out on an indiscriminate or selective basis. Indiscriminate terror targets entire sectors of the population, with little regard for the victims' age, sex, or political activity. Selective terror occurs on a smaller scale and is directed toward particular individuals. The scope of terror may vary by target. For instance, selective terror may be used against urban activists, while indiscriminate terror targets the peasant population. Also, the scope of terror is likely to vary over time.

Banning terror, which incorporates information control, as conceived by Lopez (1984), is used to limit, and ideally to prevent dissent. Several elements are worth noting. First and foremost, censorship and propaganda form the cornerstone of banning terror. At the extreme level, independent newspapers, television, and communication networks are nonexistent, and education serves as propaganda. Second, purges are used to eliminate internal threats to the authority of government leaders. Third, the prohibition of non-party members from employment in education, the media, and all vital institutions is a tool used to ensure loyalty to the party. Fourth, the restriction of freedom of assembly is designed to deter political organizing. Finally, a related technique is the confession ritual, in which persons are required to make confessions and vocally support government policies.

Containment terror includes a variety of techniques designed to control and contain a particular population. Containment terror encompasses three primary strategies: mass destruction, "villagization," and the transfer of populations. Mass destruction, which includes pacification massacres, is carried out to depopulate zones of conflict. These activities are coupled with "villagization" schemes to relocate the target population into government-controlled villages. Finally, the transfer of populations may be carried out with the intent of creating a pro-government populace.

TARGETS AND MOTIVES

By definition, state terrorism is intended to punish those already in opposition and to forestall future opposition. Accordingly, the targets of state terror are those persons or groups whom the government considers opponents of the state, and the motives appear to be simple: to punish and to deter. But how does the government define the opposition? Does the government use terrorism as a primary means to punish the opposition, or are there other motives? Following McCamant's (1991) review of struggles that lead to state terrorism, three motives and examples of expected targets are highlighted below.

- **Ideological**   attempt of an ideological party or dictator to assert supreme authority.
                          Targets: "counterrevolutionaries," critics (dissenters)
- **Cultural**   attempt of ethnic group to maintain domination over society and impose its cultural mores on other ethnic groups.
                          Targets: indigenous, ethnoclasses, nationalists (minorities)
- **Economic**   attempt of economic elites to maintain established patterns of domination.
                          Targets: union activists, movement leaders (leftists)

In this study, ideological motives refer to attempts by a party or dictator to assert supreme authority over society. The targets of terror are likely to be those who criticize or oppose the government's policies, or who promote alternative ideologies. The cultural motive is present in cases where an ethnic group seeks to maintain its domination over other ethnic groups. The targets of terror are most likely to be members of the minority population. Economic motives are defined as attempts of economic elites to maintain their domination of society. Here the government perceives challenges from leftist organizations to be dangerous threats to the social order.

The government may have several motives for engaging in terrorist strategies. For instance, an ideological party that is identified with a particular ethnic group may be motivated to use terror both to assert party authority and to maintain or enhance the power of the dominant ethnic group. The targets of terror will expand if the motives overlap.

SOCIAL STRUCTURES AND TERROR

The character of terror can best be explained by considering the type of social structure. For purposes of this review, a social structure incorporates such elements as the nature of the political system, economic relations, ethnic hegemony, and dominant ideology. The designation of types of social structure is helpful, since it is nearly impossible to discuss each element as an isolated or independent factor. In particular, it is extremely difficult to dissociate ideology from objective conditions, since ideologies are used to legitimize certain economic and social systems. For this reason, it is useful to understand how various factors interact to produce a social structure. There are three types of social structures that help explain the nature of conflict within society and provide the context in which state terrorism occurs. A brief description of these social structures, along with their corresponding cases, is presented below. Cases that are in italics indicate the presence of ethnic-based insurgencies.

- **Authoritarian**   the government is authoritarian; one party monopolizes power and controls all institutions; the government promotes revolutionary ideology (Marxism-Leninism, Maoism, Ba`thism).
  Cases: China, Soviet Union, *Ethiopia, Iraq*
- **Communal**   the government and underdeveloped economy are dominated by one particular ethno-religious group; the society is highly heterogeneous; the government fosters religious ideologies (Islam, Hinduism).
  Cases: *Sudan, India*
- **Elitist**   the political system is elitist; society has a high degree of socioeconomic inequality; the military has a close relationship with economic elites; dominant ideology is expressed in the principles of the National Security Doctrine.
  Cases: El Salvador, Colombia, *Guatemala, Peru*

The three types of social structures tend to be a consequence of historical conditions. For instance, elitist social structures have a heritage of Spanish colonialism, while revolutionary movements account for authoritarian structures. The following section uses an historical approach to review each type of social structure in terms of the character of terror.

Authoritarian States

China, the Soviet Union, Ethiopia, and Iraq are authoritarian states that share a history of revolution. In the Soviet Union, the Bolshevik revolution brought the Communist Party to power, while China's revolutionary history was marked by the 1949 founding of the People's Republic of China. Revolutions in Ethiopia and Iraq are more recent, and follow periods of European occupation. In Ethiopia, the 1974 revolution brought military and eventually dictatorial rule to the state. Iraq's history is marked by the 1958 revolutionary coup, and the 1968 coup that brought the Ba`th Party to power.

The revolutions, and subsequent development of authoritarian rule, resulted in two structural conditions. First, all institutions became centralized under the authority of the party. Second, social conflicts became defined in terms of revolutionary communist and nationalist ideologies (Marxism-Leninism, Maoism, Ba`thism). In this context, the party used terror to assert supreme authority over society. Banning terror became institutionalized. Education was used as propaganda, and the party's control of the media effectively eliminated alternative ideologies. Purges were used to crush opponents of the party and to consolidate authority within the leadership. Additionally, each government promoted its revolutionary ideology through terror campaigns that transformed the entire society. In the Soviet Union, Stalin's terrorist regime effectively consolidated the authority of the Communist Party, while in China, the Cultural Revolution established Mao as the supreme leader. In Iraq, Ba'th rule was institutionalized through a campaign of terror marked by public executions. In Ethiopia, the Red Terror eliminated opponents of the regime, effectively consolidating the base of Mengistu's power.

The institutionalization of banning terror, and the use of indiscriminate enforcement terror, greatly limited dissent in authoritarian states. In consequence, enforcement terror became more selective, targeting specific political opponents, such as "counterrevolutionaries." But when popular dissent re-emerged, or the leadership became divided in a battle over political authority, indiscriminate terror again became the norm, as witnessed by the Tbilisi and Tiananmen massacres.

Another component of the character of terror in authoritarian states is due to the prominence of nationalist groups. In general, authoritarian regimes have attempted to suppress nationalist cultures by discouraging, and in some cases, banning the native languages, religious practices, and social customs associated with nationalist groups. In Ethiopia and Iraq, nationalist groups pose a particular challenge to the regime, since separatist nationalities have resorted to violence in an attempt to gain greater autonomy or independence. In both cases, the origins of conflict lie with the founding of the modern state. Fascist Italy occupied Ethiopia for a brief period, and its independence came at the expense of Eritrea, which lost its statehood and became a province of the new state. In Iraq, an Anglo-Indian force occupied most of the country during the World War I, and Iraq's ensuing statehood crushed Kurdish hopes for an independent homeland.

The armed insurgencies in Ethiopia and Iraq have been met with a systematic program of containment terror and indiscriminate enforcement terror. Pacification massacres have become a common occurrence, and the entire Eritrean and Kurdish populations have been subjected to arbitrary acts of terror. Military troops practice collective punishment, retaliating against the nationalist population for guerrilla attacks. Survivors and refugees of the government's terror are forced across the border or transferred to government-controlled villages. From all appearances, the regime is motivated to use containment strategies by its desire to impose the culture of the dominant group on the nationalist population.

In sum, the character of state terror in authoritarian states can be described in ideological and cultural terms. The regime's primary motive is the desire to assert party authority and ideology over the entire society. Two types of strategies are important here. First, banning terror is institutionalized and used to eliminate alternative ideologies and to promote the superiority of the party. Second, indiscriminate enforcement terror is used to centralize authority, and is particularly likely to be applied in response to the emergence of popular dissent and in the context of intra-elite struggles. A secondary motive is cultural. In these cases, the strategies of terror take on an added dimension. First, nationalist groups are subjected to an elaborate version of banning terror, which seeks to undermine nationalist culture. Second, where the regime is challenged by nationalist insurgencies, containment terror and indiscriminate enforcement terror are the dominant strategies used against the nationalist population.

Communal States

India and Sudan are communal states. They are highly heterogeneous societies in which the government and economy are dominated by one particular ethno-religious group. In each case, the nature of conflict can be traced to European colonialism. India's relationship with Britain dates to the founding of the East India Company in 1612, while Sudan was an Anglo-Egyptian condominium for 54 years until self-government was granted in 1953.

The colonization of India and Sudan, and the subsequent independence of the states, had two effects. First, the political boundaries of the new states were drawn on religious and ethnic lines. Second, the political and economic systems became dominated by one particular ethno-religious group. In India, the integration of hundreds of native states into the new union led to internal divisions and the emergence of communal violence. In Sudan, the state was divided regionally, with the southern areas exploited for their natural resources. India's government is dominated by upper-class Hindus, while the Sudanese political structure is controlled by a small group of northern Arabs. Both governments are challenged by ethnic-based insurgencies that rely on terrorist tactics.

The primary motive for state terror in communal states is cultural, with the dominant ethno-religious group attempting to maintain its control of the political and economic structures. As such, the minority population is the most common target of terror. In India, the government recognizes and protects a wide variety of religious practices and customs, yet communalism divides society and benefits the dominant population. In Sudan, the cultural motive is more obvious, and is demonstrated by the imposition of Islamic law over the entire state.

The major strategy of terror is enforcement terror, although banning terror is used on a temporary basis during crises. The scope of terror tends to vary; however, indiscriminate terror seems to be the norm in Sudan. In general, enforcement terror is used indiscriminately and in a retributive manner following guerrilla attacks or intercommunal riots. The Wau massacre is a vivid example of the use of indiscriminate terror following a guerrilla attack. The government's target was the Dinka population, whether or not they were supporters of the guerrillas. Similarly, the indiscriminate killings of Sikhs following the assassination of Indira Gandhi is another case of collective retribution. Regime changes are also significant to the character of terror. For instance, Indira Gandhi's declaration of a state of emergency resulted in the large-scale arrest of opposition leaders, and the 1989 military coup in Sudan produced a new wave of indiscriminate terror.

The nature of conflict in communal states is more complex than it first appears. The battle is not simply between the government and guerrillas; rather, the entire civilian population seems embroiled in the conflict. The numerous ethnic, linguistic, and religious divisions within these societies are compounded by another feature—poverty. Thus, there is an economic motive underlying the character of terror, with each communal group vying for a better share of resources. This influences the strategies of terror, as covert forces have appeared on the landscape. In Sudan, tribal militias are responsible for a large share of the atrocities committed in the southern regions of the country. The militias enrich themselves by seizing the property of the target population. Covert forces are less pervasive in India, although the Meerut/Maliana massacre demonstrates the active involvement of civilians, and the use of security forces that are loyal to the dominant group. The promotion of communal forces increases the likelihood that acts of indiscriminate terror will be directed against the minority population.

In sum, communal states are prone to use enforcement terror against the minority population to enhance the domination of one particular ethno-religious group. The governments, opposed by ethnic-based terrorist insurgencies, resort to indiscriminate enforcement terror in response to guerrilla attacks. Under these circumstances, government forces engage in terror for the sake of retribution. Regime changes, such as leadership crises that result in states of emergency and coups d'état, directly result in the expansion of indiscriminate enforcement terror. Furthermore, covert forces and the active participation of civilians reflect an underlying economic motive, as each communal group struggles for a better share of limited resources.

Elitist States

Spanish colonialism left much of Latin America with elitist social structures. The Spaniards instituted a style of governing that was overcentralized, paternalistic, and corrupt (Sloan, 1984). The economic and political systems, which encouraged exploitation of the poor, rested on the assumption that most of the population, including Indians, peasants, and wage laborers, did not have the capacity to care for themselves or to influence public policy (Sloan, 1984). In consequence, most Latin American governments have been dominated by oligarchy-military alliances that view any policy or group that might increase the independent well-being of Indians, peasants, and/or workers as a threat to their status. The ideals of the National Security Doctrine are used to justify the existing social order. Typically, land and income inequality are the primary sources of conflict throughout much of the region.

A primary motive for state terrorism in elitist states is economic. The governments are challenged by leftist organizations and guerrillas who seek to change the distribution of wealth and power. Enforcement terror is the norm, although the scope of terror varies considerably. The use of indiscriminate enforcement terror occurs in response to an increase in guerrilla activity. In general, as the level of guerrilla violence increases, the scope of enforcement terror broadens to include a greater proportion of the population. However, there is another factor to consider here. The institutionalization of indiscriminate terror is an outcome of regime change, in particular, the designation of a state of emergency or state of siege. Typically, states of emergency are accompanied by the suspension of constitutional rights and the passage of repressive laws. More often than not, the laws allow people to be detained without warrant and held incommunicado for extended periods of time, and place civilian authorities under military rule. The result is the institutionalization of indiscriminate enforcement terror. Peru provides a case in point, as "disappearances," torture, extrajudicial executions, and massacres emerged as sections of the country were placed under military rule. Other regime changes also affected the scope of terror. For instance, intra-elite struggles resulted in the period of *La Violencia* in Colombia, and military coups in Guatemala led to the expansion of the scope of terror.

The close relationship between the military and economic elites has added another dimension to the character of terror in elitist states. Covert terror, in the form of death squad activity, is present in each state. Covert forces operate in a relatively selective manner, targeting high-profile leaders and supporters of leftist organizations and guerrillas. The Segovia massacre is an example of death squad activity directed against a leftist party. The magnitude of death squad activity seems tied to the government's ability to satisfy the interests of the military and economic elites. For instance, in El Salvador, death squad activity increased following the government's approval of provisions of the Central America Peace Plan, a move that angered conservative elites.

In addition to their economic motive, elitist states also may be compelled to use terror to assert the domination of Hispanic, or *ladino* culture. In Guatemala and Peru, the impoverished indigenous population is socially and physically isolated from the urban centers of commerce and power. The governments have neglected the needs of the indigenous population, and as a result, indigenous-based insurgencies have waged war against the government in a struggle to gain better economic opportunities and a more just society. In Peru, the insurgency has been particularly brutal, using revolutionary rhetoric and terrorist tactics.

To combat the indigenous insurgencies, the governments use containment terror and indiscriminate enforcement terror against the indigenous population. Pacification massacres, which are carried out in retribution for guerrilla attacks or anti-government activity, are not rare. In conflict areas, indigenous peasants are forced into government-controlled villages and required to participate in the civil patrol program. The government's use of containment terror effectively undermines traditional authority and generates intercommunal conflict.

In sum, elitist states use enforcement terror as a means to maintain the domination of a small group of economic elites. The governments are challenged by armed insurgencies that seek to change the distribution of wealth and power. Enforcement terror is used indiscriminately in response to the intensification of guerrilla activity. However, an intervening factor is the state of emergency, which effectively legitimizes the use of indiscriminate enforcement terror. Additionally, the close relationship between the military and economic elites adds a covert element to the character of terror, as death squads operate to eliminate leftists. In elitist states challenged by indigenous-based insurgencies, governments use containment terror and indiscriminate enforcement terror against the indigenous population. In these cases, a cultural motive underlies the conflict, as the government considers Hispanic culture superior to native customs.

FINDINGS

The relationship between social structure and the character of terror is outlined in Table 14.1. In general, the primary motive for terror in authoritarian states is ideological, with enforcement and banning terror used to uphold the dictatorship of the party. In communal states, the primary motive is cultural, with the dominant ethnic group attempting to assert its control of the political and economic systems. Elitist states are motivated to use enforcement terror for economic reasons, targeting leftists who seek the redistribution of resources. Additionally, a demographic condition, the presence of a regionally isolated minority group, affects the character of terror, regardless of social structure. In cases where the government is challenged by a nationalist or indigenous-based insurgency and members of that particular minority group are socially and geographically isolated from mainstream society, the government will use a policy of containment terror and indiscriminate enforcement terror against this segment of the population. Thus, authoritarian regimes opposed by nationalist insurgencies will target political dissenters and the nationalist population. Similarly, elitist governments challenged by indigenous insurgencies will target leftists and members of the indigenous population. The complexity of the character of terror is highlighted in the findings below.

Table 14.1.
Social Structures and the Character of State Terror

	Authoritarian	Communal	Elitist	Regionally Isolated Minority Group
Targets	Dissenters	Minorities	Leftists	Nationalist, indigenous groups
Primary Motive	Ideological	Cultural	Economic	Cultural
Strategies	Enforcement and Banning	Enforcement (Covert)	Enforcement (Covert)	Enforcement (Indisc.) and Containment

Finding 1. Authoritarian rule is associated with the institutionalization of banning terror.

Non-authoritarian states use banning terror as a temporary strategy under tenuous circumstances to restore stability. But in authoritarian states, banning terror is an essential component of party rule. The legitimacy of the party rests on the public's unquestioning support of revolutionary ideology. Alternative ideologies pose a real threat to the regime, and for this reason, speech, movement, and thought are controlled on a society-wide basis. In sum, banning terror is likely to be institutionalized in authoritarian regimes, since the government uses terror to further the party's ideological domination of society.

Finding 2. Covert terror is linked to non-authoritarian governments where there is a close relationship between the military and economic elites, or where ethnicity can be exploited to further the causes of war.

Paramilitary and civilian-based forces are primarily absent in authoritarian states. A major reason for their absence is the party's fanatic desire to control all aspects of society. Weapons in the hands of civilians, or the creation of decentralized, relatively autonomous paramilitary units, could be used to subvert the authority of the party. But in non-authoritarian states, especially democracies, covert terror has an advantage over official terror. Namely, covert forces shield the government and military from accountability. Consequently, governments can deny their involvement in terrorist acts, placing the blame on "private responses," or "communal fighting."

A close relationship between the military and economic elites is conducive to the formation of death squads. Under this condition, terror is economically motivated, as elites resort to extreme measures to maintain their domination of society. Large landowners and businessmen directly benefit from death squad activity, which tends to target labor activists and peasant leaders, while individual officers benefit financially from their relationship with the elites. Covert forces, in the form of civilian-based forces, such as tribal militias and civil patrols, operate in communal and elitist states where ethnic-based insurgencies challenge the government. Here, economic motives are tied with cultural motives, as the government promotes hostility between ethnic groups to ensure the economic and political domination of the ruling ethnic group.

Finding 3. Containment terror is associated with the geographic and social isolation of a nationalist or indigenous group.

In states that practice containment terror, there is one common feature: the geographic and social isolation of a minority group. In particular, separatist nationalities and indigenous groups tend to be isolated from mainstream society and vulnerable to this type of terror. The geographic isolation of the minority population is particularly critical, as it enables the government to direct its containment terror to certain regions of the country, where its policies can be carried out on an indiscriminate basis. The use of containment terror is culturally motivated and displays government insensitivity toward the culture of the target population.

DISCUSSION

In the literature, state terrorism is considered to be a response to internal threat and/or regime changes. This study finds that internal threats and regime changes do not account for variations in the strategies of terror, but rather, help explain the resort to the indiscriminate use of enforcement terror. Gurr (1986) claimed that the state will use terrorist strategies to counter challengers who rely on terrorist and guerrilla tactics. While this claim cannot be disputed, it is the level of guerrilla violence that influences the scope of enforcement terror. Gurr (1986) also argued that governments were more likely to use terror against politically marginal groups. But this study shows that terror has been used against politically prominent groups, such as students and intellectuals in China, and Jesuit priests in El Salvador. Instead, indiscriminate enforcement terror is likely to be used against ethnically marginal groups. Furthermore, an additional strategy, containment terror, will be used against socially and physically isolated minority groups, such as separatist nationalities and indigenous populations. Thus, the resort to indiscriminate enforcement terror is considered a reaction to (1) an increase in the level of guerrilla violence; and (2) the ethnic marginality of the challenger.

Lopez (1984) and Donnelly (1989) stressed regime changes as a factor that leads to the initiation of state terror. Again, regime changes help explain the use of indiscriminate enforcement terror but do not account for overall variations in the strategies of terror. While intra-elite struggles and military coups were associated with the expansion of the scope of terror, the regime change most significant to this study was the resort to emergency rule. In essence, state of emergency rule abdicates civilian authority in favor of military rule and sacrifices legal protections and constitutional rights. States of emergency thereby result in the institutionalization and legitimation of indiscriminate enforcement terror. Thus, regime changes, such as intra-elite struggles, military coups, and emergency rule, account for the indiscriminate use of enforcement terror.

While the scope of enforcement terror tends to be an outcome of situational factors, the overall character of terror is influenced by the type of social structure. McCamant (1991) noted three motives that proved relevant to this study. In general, ideological, cultural, and economic motives were found to be highly related to three types of social structures: authoritarian, communal, and elitist. Authoritarian states are associated with ideological motives, communal states primarily use terror to serve cultural motives, and elitist states are economically motivated to use terror. However, the motives tend to overlap in states whose government is opposed by an ethnic-based challenger. In particular, cultural motives interact with economic motives in cases where ethnic identity is related to economic opportunity. Economic and ideological motives may also become secondary to cultural motives in the context of nationalist and indigenous-based insurgencies.

Furthermore, the targets and motives of terror are highly associated with the strategies of terror. To be more precise, ideological motives lead to the institutionalization of banning terror, cultural motives are associated with both indiscriminate enforcement terror and containment terror, and economic motives are linked to the use of enforcement terror by covert forces. In conclusion, situational factors, such as the nature of the challengers and regime changes, affect the intensity and scope of enforcement terror, but the overall character of terror is a byproduct of social structure.

SUMMARY AND CONCLUSIONS

Three major types of terror strategies were noted: enforcement terror, banning terror, and containment terror. Enforcement terror varies by the level and scope of government involvement. Three motives and target groups were identified. Ideological motives refer to attempts by a party or dictator to assert supreme authority over society. Cultural motives refer to the attempts of an ethnic group to maintain domination over society and impose its cultural mores on other ethnic groups. Economic motives are found in the attempts by economic elites to maintain their domination of society. Corresponding to these types of motives, the targets of terror are likely to be dissidents, minorities, and leftists, respectively.

Social, political, and economic conditions tend to interact with ideology to produce a definite social structure. Three social structures were developed and discussed in regard to the character of state terror: authoritarian, communal, and elitist. In authoritarian states, one party monopolizes all power and ideology plays a dominant role in the character of terror. Communal states, which are highly heterogeneous societies dominated by one particular ethno-religious group, are culturally motivated to use terrorist strategies. Economic motives are associated with elitist states, which are characterized by a high degree of socioeconomic inequality and the close relationship between the military and economic elites.

Three findings were highlighted. First, authoritarian rule is associated with the institutionalization of banning terror. Second, covert terror is linked to non-authoritarian governments where there is a close relationship between the military and economic elites, or where ethnicity can be exploited to further the causes of war. Third, containment terror is associated with the geographic and social isolation of a nationalist or indigenous group.

In conclusion, this study finds that the character of terror is highly associated with the type of social structure in that state. Furthermore, the motives of terror tend to influence the strategies so that ideological motives lead to institutionalized banning terror, cultural motives are linked to indiscriminate enforcement terror and containment terror, and economic motives are associated with covert terror. However, an important exception to this generalization must be noted. Geographically and socially isolated minority groups are especially vulnerable to extreme forms of terror, regardless of social structure. This study finds that situational factors (that is, the nature of challengers and regime changes) affect the intensity and scope of terror, but the overall character of terror is largely determined by the nature of the social structure.

15

The Outcomes of State Terrorism

What are the outcomes of terror? In human terms, state terrorism has resulted in countless numbers of murdered citizens and tortured survivors. The state has justified its policy of terror by claiming it to be a necessary tool to conquer the opposition. Thus, a basic question must be: Does state terrorism deter opposition violence, or does it stimulate further opposition? This chapter evaluates the relationship between state terrorism and opposition violence. The discussion is organized by the type of social structure and the nature of challengers. The chapter concludes that the strategies of terror influence the outcome of state terrorism.

AUTHORITARIAN STATES

Authoritarian states depend on terrorism to maintain the tyranny of the party or dictator. The four authoritarian states in this study used similar terrorist strategies, with very different outcomes. In the Soviet Union and Ethiopia, the states were overcome by nationalist interests and civil war, respectively. In China and Iraq, the party has been able to maintain authority by increasing its level of terrorism. How have varying strategies and levels of state terror affected the opposition? To address this question, it is useful to organize the discussion around the types of challengers each government faced. In China and the Soviet Union, the major challenger came in the form of popular non-violent movements, whereas the governments of Iraq and Ethiopia were challenged by ethnic-based insurgencies.

Popular Movements

In general, China and the Soviet Union have relied on a combination of banning terror and selective enforcement terror to maintain communist rule. When the government has relaxed its censorship and propaganda campaigns, popular movements have emerged to challenge the party's authority. In typical fashion, the party has responded to the movements by arresting movement leaders, purging dissidents from the party, strengthening ideological indoctrination, and widening the scope of enforcement terror. In the past, these techniques have proved successful, and dissent has been limited and controlled.

The Tiananmen and Tbilisi massacres can be considered pivotal acts of terror, since the events changed the direction of conflict. The Chinese leaders took a number of steps to discourage dissent following the Tiananmen massacre. The government arrested thousands of people and reimposed state controls over all aspects of free expression. The movement was criminalized, and those who supported the demonstrators were purged from the party. On the ideological front, students and workers were required to attend political meetings, and a new wave of censorship was launched. In the Soviet Union, the central government declared a state of emergency in Georgia following the Tbilisi massacre, and arrested movement leaders. But unlike the Chinese government, the Soviet leaders did not establish a definite policy of terror, or liberalization, and the nationalities problem grew worse. The regime moved in contradictory directions, creating an executive presidency and ruling by emergency decree in the republics, while ending the Communist Party's monopoly of power. In Georgia, the reformist movement radicalized its agenda and declared independence two years from the date of the Tbilisi massacre.

How were the Chinese leaders able to maintain their authority, while the Soviet Union fell apart? A major reason was the consistent and systematic use of terror in China, compared with the sporadic and half-hearted Soviet efforts. In hindsight, the Soviet regime may have been militarily incapable of resorting to the kind of systematic indiscriminate terror used in China. In both states, a primary factor in the survival of authoritarian rule was the consolidation of a strong leadership. In China, Deng launched a campaign of purges that led to the consolidation of power among the hard-liners. Purges over the next few years eventually led to the emergence of a leadership that promoted economic reforms and protected communist rule. In the Soviet Union, Gorbachev did not have a strong political base and was unable to build an alliance among either faction of the political leadership. Gorbachev advanced a liberal agenda but came to the aid of key conservative members. He did not follow the Tbilisi massacre with a consistent pattern of purges. The result was a weak Soviet leadership and the intensification of the crisis of authority. The 1991 coup attempt, led by members of the president's inner circle, signaled the end of the Soviet state.

Another factor that may play a secondary role in the demise of authoritarian rule is the economy. In China, the government's economic reforms were relatively successful, and dissent was limited to the urban student movement. But in the Soviet Union, the failure of economic reforms resulted in a disillusioned public. The inability of the central government to spur the economy encouraged widespread dissent and was a factor in the republics' demands for greater autonomy. The continuation of authoritarian rule would have been difficult to justify, given the government's poor economic record.

In sum, the consistent and systematic use of banning and enforcement terror can deter opposition activity. However, several conditions must be met. First, a strong consolidated leadership with clear policies is an absolute necessity. Second, the leadership must be willing to implement and capable of carrying out a comprehensive and systematic policy of terror. Finally, the authoritarian leadership should have some legitimate claims on the right to rule, such as the ability to stimulate the economy. The Soviets' sporadic and wavering use of terror, and the government's eventual collapse, attest to the significance of these conditions.

Ethnic-Based Insurgencies

While the systematic use of terror can deter opposition activity in general, how successful is state terrorism when an authoritarian government is challenged by an ethnic-based insurgency? Ethiopia and Iraq have relied on a policy of terror to maintain the authority of dictatorial rulers. Banning terror has been institutionalized to deter public criticism of the party. An elaborate terror network, responsible for carrying out acts of enforcement terror and the use of containment terror on separatist nationalities, are features of both states. Despite similarities, the Iraqi government continues to be ruled by Saddam Hussein and the Ba`th Party, while in Ethiopia, Chairman Mengistu was forced to flee the country and Eritrea was declared an independent state. What accounts for this dramatic variance?

The Iraqi and Ethiopian governments' use of terrorist strategies, and the effect they had on the insurgencies, can be explained best by reviewing external factors, in particular, opposition unity and foreign assistance. In the case of Iraq, foreign support of the Kurdish insurgency complicates the assessment of the outcome of terrorist strategies. In the early 1980s, when Western military aid poured into Iraq, the government launched a new wave of terror against the Kurds. Meanwhile, the Kurdish rebel groups were divided and lacked the capability of launching a concerted effort. Consequently, the guerrilla movement was ineffective until the two major rebel groups united under a single front. However, the Kurds depended on military support from Iran, and when the war ended, the Kurds found themselves isolated and ill-equipped to battle Hussein's forces. Following the conclusion of war, Hussein turned his weapons against Iraqi Kurdistan, engaging in a genocidal policy designed to decimate the Kurdish population. The leadership of the Kurdish movement was forced into exile, and by all accounts, the Kurds were at the mercy of the Iraqi government. But the Kurdish movement was able to survive, and when international forces routed Iraqi troops from Kuwait, the Kurds were given a degree of protection, enabling them to regroup and reassert demands for autonomy. Thus, state terror was most effective when the Kurdish rebels were divided and when they lost foreign military assistance. The influx of foreign aid to the Iraqi regime led to an intensified campaign of indiscriminate enforcement terror, effectively crushing the opposition, at least temporarily.

In Ethiopia, Eritrean forces defeated government troops in the 1970s, but when the various rebel groups could not reach consensus on territorial claims, the Ethiopians reclaimed Eritrea, thanks in part to an influx of Soviet and Cuban military support. Years later, a strong and united Eritrean front emerged to wage a new battle against government forces. In the mid-1980s, the Ethiopian government lost major Soviet aid and faced the prospects of widespread regional war as well as famine. At the close of the decade, an attempted military coup brought Mengistu's authority into doubt, and eventually he was forced to flee the country. Clearly, the effectiveness of state terror depended on the unity of rebel forces, as well as the government's procurement of foreign military and economic assistance.

Why did the Ethiopian government fall while authoritarian rule in Iraq continued, despite similar terror strategies? Three reasons help explain the downfall of the Mengistu regime. First, Ethiopia, unlike Iraq, was challenged by widespread popular dissent as well as several regional insurgencies. The high level of dissent can be attributed to the government's poor handling of the famine. Second, the Ethiopian government was dependent on the outside world for economic and military survival, and when foreign aid was cut off, the Ethiopian government could no longer acquire the firepower needed to destroy the insurgents. Third, the Ethiopian regime allowed its internal terror network to erode, a result of an earlier decision to strip authority from the *kebeles*.

In contrast, Iraq's supreme leader, Saddam Hussein, maintained absolute authority. Unlike Mengistu, Hussein has been able to secure military loyalty, largely due to control of the armed forces and secret police by members of his clan. He has continually enhanced the terror network through purges and is not dependent on foreign military assistance. Hussein has also been able to concentrate his military efforts on the Kurdish population, since popular rebellions from other communities have been limited. Thus, Hussein has used state terrorism to his advantage.

COMMUNAL STATES

India and Sudan are communal states with numerous ethnic, religious, tribal, and caste divisions. This characteristic has made democratic rule exceedingly difficult, and in consequence, each state shares the experience of weak coalition governments. Both governments are challenged by terrorist organizations, and communal violence is rampant. In general, the governments have relied on repressive legislation and the indiscriminate use of enforcement terror against members of the minority community. Has state terrorism been an effective strategy? In India, opposition terrorism and communal violence have intensified, while in Sudan, a military coup brought a new wave of state terror to the country, and the insurgency was forced on the defensive.

India has resorted to repressive legislation to fight terrorist organizations, especially in the Punjab. Legislation has been accompanied by a systematic policy of torture, "encounter" killings, and more recently, "disappearances." The insurgents have responded with an increase in terrorist activity. In particular, armed insurgency was provoked by the 1984 army assault on the Golden Temple, which resulted in over 1,000 deaths. Insurgent terrorism, demonstrated by the assassinations of Indira Gandhi, and later, Rajiv Gandhi, continues unabated. How did state terrorism affect communal relations? The indiscriminate use of enforcement terror, and in particular, the prevalence of government massacres in the context of riots, led to the intensification of communal violence. In the political arena, Hindu fundamentalists gained seats in the federal government and successfully controlled several state governments, including Uttar Pradesh. In 1992, communal violence peaked following the destruction of the Babri mosque. For all practical purposes, the use of enforcement terror failed to deter terrorist insurgencies, and in fact, stimulated communal violence.

In Sudan, the implementation of *sharia* was directly responsible for the emergence of insurgent terrorism. The government's war against the insurgency has been fought with tribal militias, which have engaged in acts of indiscriminate enforcement terror against the Dinka population. In the mid-1980s, the guerrillas controlled major areas of the south, and communal violence was out of control. But in 1989, a military coup ended democracy, and a new regime responsive to Islamic ideals engaged in a particularly brutal policy of banning terror, indiscriminate enforcement terror, and military offensives. In 1991, internal divisions led the rebel organization to split into several factions, and its effectiveness was greatly reduced. The movement's weakness, at a time of strengthened government leadership, led to the intensification of war in the south. The guerrillas also were affected by the change of government in Ethiopia, which meant they could no longer operate from bases there. The government was able to take advantage of these conditions and regained most of the rebel-held territory. In 1993, a cease-fire was declared, and negotiations were held. Meanwhile, the military began to pave the way for democracy.

Thus, state terror in communal states is likely to lead to the intensification of insurgent terrorist activity and communal violence. It may also lead to an increase in the dominant group's support of extremist parties. However, the case of Sudan provides important insights. First, state terror may be effective in eliminating the opposition when the government has a strong military leadership that is willing to engage in a high level of banning terror and enforcement terror. Second, divisions within the rebel organization and the loss of foreign military support are likely to make state terror a more effective tool.

ELITIST STATES

Colombia, El Salvador, Guatemala, and Peru can be categorized as elitist states. Colombia and El Salvador are challenged by class-based insurgencies, while Guatemala and Peru struggle with ethnic-based insurgencies. These states systematically engage in arbitrary arrests, extrajudicial executions, torture, and "disappearances," and tend to rely on death squads for selective acts of terror. Additionally, Guatemala and Peru use containment terror against the indigenous population.

Class-Based Insurgencies

Colombia and El Salvador are characterized by a high level of land and income inequality. The governments are dominated by economic elites and the military, and there is little tolerance for leftist parties. Both governments are opposed by class-based insurgencies. In Colombia, there are several regional guerrilla groups that rely on various strategies in an attempt to change the economic and social conditions of the country. In El Salvador, the government has been challenged by a well-organized rebel army that has fought a long-standing civil war in an attempt to gain social and political reform.

From 1978 to 1982, Colombia placed whole sections of the country under military rule, resulting in the emergence of paramilitary death squads, and the systematic use of "disappearances" and massacres. These acts of enforcement terror did not significantly deter guerrilla activity. From 1982 to 1986, the government changed the direction of its policies and reached truce agreements with three major guerrilla groups, including FARC. But one event in particular, the army's 1985 assault on the Palace of Justice, led to an increase in guerrilla activity. From 1986 to 1990, the government restored a state of siege, massacres became widespread, and the military resorted to scorched earth strategies. At the same time, the leadership pursued negotiations with various guerrilla organizations, and in 1990, three rebel groups agreed to peace. Yet, the remaining guerrilla groups managed to launch a major offensive in 1991, and the following year, guerrilla and military operations increased throughout the country. From all appearances, the state's use of enforcement terror failed to deter opposition violence, and in fact stimulated guerrilla activity.

In El Salvador, a major impetus for the emergence of armed insurgency was the military's systematic use of enforcement terror against popular organizations. From 1980 to 1983, El Salvador's armed forces engaged in a policy of indiscriminate terror, relying on scorched earth tactics, air attacks, and death squad killings. The result was the destruction of the popular movement and the weakening of FMLN activities in the "zones of control." However, enforcement terror did not deter guerrilla activity. Instead, the rebels revised their war strategy, expanding their movement geographically and relying on smaller-scale actions. In the mid-1980s, the government carried out enforcement terror on a more selective basis and pursued negotiations. In 1989, selective acts of enforcement terror, in the context of negotiations, led to the resumption of hostilities, culminating in the massacre of the Jesuits. The massacre and the continued use of enforcement terror weakened the government's position, and peace was declared in 1992. By all accounts, the use of enforcement terror did not result in the elimination of opposition violence. In fact, specific acts of enforcement terror stimulated insurgent activity.

In both states, terrorist strategies failed to deter the legitimation and participation of leftist parties. The government's use of terror may have limited popular organizing but failed to halt guerrilla activities. In response to indiscriminate enforcement terror, the insurgents were able to revise their strategies and proved adaptable to the changing environment. Furthermore, enforcement terror, in the context of negotiations and cease-fires, directly resulted in the intensification of guerrilla violence. In each case, the government made concessions that led to the legitimation of leftist groups.

Ethnic-Based Insurgencies

Guatemala and Peru are elitist states, although Peru's political system has been more open than those of other Latin American states. However, Peru is nonetheless a state based on a relatively high degree of socioeconomic inequality and the predominance of the military. Guatemala has one of the most atrocious human rights records, although Peru may have surpassed this mark in the latter part of the 1980s. Both states rely on selective acts of enforcement terror against the general population. Additionally, the governments engage in a systematic policy of containment terror, in conjunction with indiscriminate enforcement terror, against the indigenous population.

In the early 1980s, the Guatemala military engaged in a scorched earth campaign that heavily damaged the highlands. The military also adopted a strategy of containment terror, using "model villages" and civil patrols to control the indigenous population. The high level of indiscriminate terror led to a significant decline in opposition violence, and by the mid-1980s, the government no longer considered the guerrillas to be a major threat. In 1987, the military conducted an "end of the year offensive," designed to eliminate the last vestiges of the guerrilla movement. But the military assault failed, and in 1988, the guerrillas launched their first joint offensives, with the number of operations doubling the following year. In 1991, President Serrano held negotiations with the rebel organization. Serrano's efforts at a peaceful settlement were accompanied by a renewed campaign of death threats against union leaders and members of the left. In 1993, Serrano carried out a "self-coup" and governed briefly by decree. The ensuing designation of a new president increased the prospects of a peaceful conclusion to the war.

In Peru, the government has been opposed by the revolutionary Sendero Luminoso since 1980. The government's war has been carried out with a systematic policy of torture, "disappearances," and extrajudicial executions. The military has incorporated a strategy of containment into its war plan, subjecting the indigenous population to "strategic hamlets," civil patrols (*rondas*), and mass relocations. But indiscriminate terror failed to deter Sendero, which expanded its operations into the cities. In fact, the government's handling of prison riots, which resulted in a massacre of inmates, created a backlash of sympathy for the revolutionary movement. In 1988, the Cayara massacre proved to be a turning point in which the government essentially legitimized the military's conduct of the war. In 1992, President Fujimori carried out a "self-coup" and dissolved Congress. The government dealt a major blow to Sendero when it captured its Maoist leader and his top followers. Still, Sendero continues to operate, although its effectiveness and support have declined.

If state terrorism were an effective strategy in deterring opposition violence, Guatemala and Peru would be the test cases. Both governments have relied on the most extensive and brutal forms of terror available. Extremely high levels of indiscriminate enforcement terror and the systematic use of containment terror did result in a decline in opposition violence. However, the rebel organizations were never fully destroyed and were able to rebound when the political environment was more favorable. In Guatemala, the insurgents were able to gain a negotiating position, while in Peru, revolutionary struggle continues. It is surprising that both government leaders resorted to "self-coups" in an effort to eliminate the guerrillas or control domestic problems. The Peruvian case suggests that acts other than state terror, in particular, the capture of revolutionary leaders, may be more fruitful to the cause of peace.

FINDINGS

In this section, four general findings are presented. Each finding is reviewed in terms of the specific strategies of terror, and exceptions are noted. The first generalization addresses the emergence of opposition violence, while the remaining findings are concerned with the effect of state terror on opposition violence in the context of armed conflict.

Finding 1. In general, state terrorism encourages the emergence of armed insurgencies.

In theory, the widespread use of terrorist strategies should act as a deterrent. But in reality, governments are incapable of spreading terror throughout entire societies indefinitely. Eight of the ten governments in this study were challenged by armed insurgencies. The emergence of these organizations can be traced to a pattern of state terror. For instance, the rebel movements in Colombia and El Salvador are a direct outcome of the governments' use of state terror against popular organizations and the exclusion of leftist parties from participation in the political systems. Similarly, in Ethiopia and Iraq, the governments' attempts to eradicate the unique cultures of the Eritreans and Kurds led to the emergence of nationalist insurgencies. In general, then, state terror has encouraged the emergence of opposition violence. However, there are two important exceptions to the catalytic effect of state terrorism. First, the institutionalization of banning terror may have a deterrent effect. Second, selective enforcement terror may deter opposition activity, at least temporarily.

A characteristic of authoritarian states is the institutionalized use of banning terror and a corresponding lack of popular dissent. For instance, historically, China and the Soviet Union have been relatively free of dissent and opposition violence. But the situation is tenuous. When authoritarian regimes relax their control over society, popular movements emerge to challenge the authority of the party. In fact, a closer examination shows that banning terror has failed to preclude dissent from nationalist groups. Each authoritarian state has been continually challenged by nationalist movements that have a long history, such as the Tibetan movement in China and the Kurdish insurrection in Iraq. Thus, the institutionalization of banning terror appears to deter dissent from the general populace but has a limited impact on nationalist groups.

Selective enforcement terror also may deter opposition activity, but the effect is likely to be temporary. The covert and official use of selective enforcement terror aimed at movement activists has resulted in a decline in popular organizing. But in actuality, enforcement terror does not altogether eliminate dissent; rather, it pushes popular movements underground. For instance, in El Salvador, military attacks against leaders of the popular movement led to the formation of clandestine organizations that evolved into rebel forces. Thus, selective enforcement terror may have a short-term deterrent effect on opposition activity. However, the opposition is likely to resurface, and quite possibly, resort to violent tactics.

If state terrorism acts as a catalyst to the emergence of opposition violence, how does it affect opposition violence once armed conflict has erupted? Is state terrorism an effective strategy in defeating armed insurgencies? Or does state terrorism result in the intensification of guerrilla activity? To address these questions, it is important to recognize the complexity of armed conflict. Throughout war, the intensity of conflict varies. Territory is won and lost, cease-fires and negotiations are interspersed with military offensives, and strategies are modified. Here I will focus on those conditions that influence the intensity of guerrilla violence.

Finding 2. Mass indiscriminate enforcement terror, bordering on genocide or politicide, weakens guerrilla activity.

When indiscriminate enforcement terror has been used on a massive scale, guerrilla activity has declined. The most obvious example of this generalization is the Iraqi use of chemical weapons to depopulate Kurdistan. Another example is the destruction of the Guatemalan highlands, which resulted in a weakened guerrilla front. Similarly, the Sudanese military regime's use of brutal indiscriminate enforcement terror greatly limited the effectiveness of the rebels. But an exception to this finding is Peru, where Sendero was able to increase its activity despite the military's reliance on a high level of indiscriminate terror. This anomaly suggests that even the most brutal forms of state terrorism may not weaken revolutionary movements.

While the systematic use of indiscriminate enforcement terror tends to weaken armed insurgencies, there is some inconsistency in this tendency. Particularly ruthless acts of indiscriminate terror have been known to strengthen guerrilla resolve and increase public support for the guerrillas. These acts may be called pivotal acts of terror, since they are responsible for changing the intensity of the conflict. Government massacres are likely to fall into this category. In this study, there are several examples of pivotal terror: the assassination of Archbishop Romero in El Salvador, Colombia's attack on the Palace of Justice, India's assault on the Golden Temple, prison massacres in Peru, and Guatemala's burning of the Spanish Embassy. These symbolic acts of terror were directly responsible for an increase in guerrilla activity.

Thus, a high level of indiscriminate enforcement terror effectively weakens guerrilla activity for the most basic reason: It disrupts the organizational capacity of the guerrilla movement. However, revolutionary ethnic-based insurgencies are least susceptible to even the most extreme forms of terror. Also, singular events of indiscriminate terror, such as highly publicized massacres, may actually stimulate guerrilla activity.

Finding 3. Opposition unity and foreign assistance may determine the effectiveness of state terrorism.

While a high level of indiscriminate enforcement terror tends to weaken guerrilla activity, the outcome of state terrorism is heavily influenced by external factors. Two factors proved to be critical in determining the effectiveness of state terrorism in the context of armed conflict: opposition unity and foreign assistance. In general, state terrorism is most effective when the rebel organization is divided into competing factions and/or has lost the support of a major foreign contributor. Similarly, state terrorism is least likely to be effective when the government is divided and indecisive and/or loses a major source of foreign assistance. This finding was substantiated by the relationship between state terror and guerrilla activity in Ethiopia, Iraq, and Sudan.

Finding 4. State terrorism has failed to eliminate armed insurgencies.

Finally, if there is one definitive finding from this study, it is the remarkable resilience of armed insurgencies. The insurgencies have proved to be adaptable to almost any situation and have survived under the harshest conditions. In Ethiopia, the Eritrean rebels were successful in their struggle against the terrorist regime, while in El Salvador, a negotiated settlement led to peace. Meanwhile, armed insurgencies continue in Iraq, India, Peru, Guatemala, Colombia, and Sudan. It is significant that the governments have failed to defeat armed insurgencies, even when they have resorted to extreme forms of indiscriminate terror. From a policy standpoint, it would be wise for governments to pursue alternative strategies.

DISCUSSION

The literature suggested three arguments: (1) State terrorism acts as a deterrent to opposition violence; (2) state terrorism stimulates opposition violence; and (3) there is a curvilinear relationship between state terrorism and opposition violence. This study finds that the relationship between state terrorism and opposition violence is complex and must be discussed in terms of the effect of terror in the context of both non-violent opposition, and armed conflict.

The deterrent effect of state terrorism rests on the argument that terrorism disrupts the organizational capacity of the opposition and raises the expected costs of opposition activities (Snyder and Tilly, 1972; Hibbs, 1973; Tilly, 1978). This argument has some merit as it relates to the emergence of opposition violence. First, the institutionalization of banning terror appears to have a deterrent effect on the general population, primarily because it disrupts the capacity to organize. Second, the selective use of enforcement terror may have a short-term deterrent effect by raising the costs of opposition activity. However, in general, state terrorism stimulates the emergence of opposition violence. In particular, the government's use of terror against popular organizations and political groups, and the use of state terror against minority populations, have led to the emergence of guerrilla armies. Thus, by limiting non-violent options for participation, state terrorism compels the opposition to resort to violence (Eckstein, 1965; Gurr, 1969).

While the stimulative effect of state terrorism accounts for the opposition's use of violent rather than non-violent tactics, it is not relevant in the context of armed conflict, where violent opposition already is the norm. There is some evidence to support the claim that there is an inverted U-shaped relationship between state terror and guerrilla violence (Bwy, 1968; Gurr 1969, 1970; Feierabend and Feierabend, 1972; Muller, 1985; Mason and Krane, 1989). In particular, there appears to be a threshold at which state terror negatively affects guerrilla violence, but that threshold approaches genocide or politicide. Furthermore, the relationship is more complex than indicated by the curvilinear model. For instance, the level of enforcement terror, in terms of number of victims, may remain constant. Yet guerrilla violence may increase, perhaps due to a particularly symbolic act of state terror, or it may decrease, possibly as a result of loss of foreign aid to the rebels. In other words, the relationship between state terror and guerrilla violence is compounded by both the character and context of terror, and external factors. The inverted U-shaped relationship must take into account these deviations. Finally, this study notes that state terrorism, regardless of strategies and scope, has failed to eradicate armed insurgencies.

SUMMARY AND CONCLUSIONS

The relationship between state terrorism and opposition violence was reviewed by the type of social structure and the nature of challengers. Outcomes varied considerably, depending on a number of factors. In authoritarian states opposed by popular non-violent movements, the effectiveness of terror depended on the consolidation of the government leadership and the consistency with which terror was used. In authoritarian regimes opposed by nationalist insurgencies, the continuation of party rule was influenced by the level of popular dissent and the loyalty of the security agencies. The outcome of state terror in communal states, where the primary challengers were ethnic- and religious-based insurgencies, was influenced by the strength of the government leadership and the unity of the guerrilla army. In elitist states opposed by class-based insurgencies, state terror failed to deter the legitimation of leftist parties. In elitist states challenged by indigenous-based insurgencies, extreme levels of state terror weakened but did not eliminate guerrilla activity.

Four findings are highlighted in this study. First, state terrorism encourages the emergence of armed insurgencies. Second, mass indiscriminate enforcement terror, bordering on genocide or politicide, weakens guerrilla activity. Third, opposition unity and foreign assistance may determine the effectiveness of state terrorism. Fourth, state terrorism has failed to eliminate armed insurgencies.

This study supports the claim that, in general, state terrorism acts as a catalyst to the emergence of opposition violence. In the context of armed conflict, there appears to be an inverted U-shaped relationship between the scope of enforcement terror and the level of guerrilla violence. However, this relationship must be modified to account for several deviations. In particular, guerrilla violence seems to be reduced only after the state engages in an extremely high level of indiscriminate enforcement terror, bordering on genocide or politicide. Furthermore, selective enforcement terror, when carried out in the context of cease-fires or negotiations, and pivotal acts of enforcement terror, lead to an increase in guerrilla violence. The complexity of this relationship is further compounded by external factors, especially opposition unity and foreign assistance. In conclusion, state terrorism has failed to eradicate guerrilla violence.

16

Government Accountability and the Pursuit of Justice

Government massacres occurred under all types of government. But our expectations of how a government will respond to a massacre are influenced by the degree of democracy in a particular state, since democracy is considered the ideal political arrangement to secure civil and political rights. However, democracies tend to be evaluated by their electoral procedures, not by their commitment to human rights. This chapter reviews the legal and political systems of authoritarian and democratic states in relation to government responses to massacres; however, a note of caution is warranted here. In general, most massacres receive little notice from the government. Many of the massacres in this study were atypical in the sense that they were the focus of considerable government attention. Given this caveat, the governments' response to massacres illustrates the difficulties in the pursuit of justice.

GOVERNMENT ACCOUNTABILITY

According to common belief, democracy represents an ideal condition in which human rights are respected and government officials are directly accountable for their actions. Indeed, Gurr (1986) claims that democratic principles and institutions inhibit governments from using terror. But historically, democratic heritage did not necessarily mean respect for human rights. In fact, the earliest philosophical foundations of democracy are generally traced to Greco-Roman times, while those of human rights are traceable only to the eighteenth-century Enlightenment (Aidoo, 1993). Democracies, then, do not automatically ensure human rights. Instead, human rights can be guaranteed only when they are specifically promoted and protected in law and by popular organizations (Aidoo, 1993).

The key factor that distinguishes democracy from other types of political arrangements is an independent judiciary, which is frequently cited as an essential condition for the respect and protection of human rights (Blondel, 1969; Cappelletti, 1971; Shapiro, 1981; Pritchard, 1988). An independent and competent legal system is not only possible but expected in democratic states. For purposes of definition, in a political democracy, fair elections are held regularly and the military and police are not used to gain or maintain power (Dahl, 1992; Linz, 1992). By contrast, authoritarianism is characterized by the monopolization of power by an individual or small group of leaders with ill-defined formal limits (Linz, 1992).[1] Logically, democracy should be an indicator of government accountability. However, acts of state terror seldom are punished, under any type of government. Thus, it would seem that democracy may be a prerequisite for the creation of a just society, but of greater importance is the capacity and willingness of the legal and political systems to protect human rights.

The Legal System

Authoritarian regimes are characterized by the lack of an independent judiciary. In this study, four governments had legal systems that functioned only to serve the interests of the ruling party: China, Ethiopia, Iraq, and Sudan. Three of the four states are authoritarian, while Sudan is a weak democracy. It is worth noting that the Soviet Union, which may be considered a state in transition at the time of the Tbilisi massacre, is excluded from this group since reforms resulted in the development of a relatively autonomous legal system. Also, Sudan's imposition of Islamic law severely limited its right to be called a full democracy.

These legal systems have three characteristics that impede the courts' ability to address government crimes. First and foremost, the judiciary has no independence. Judges are appointed and dismissed at the executive's discretion and are answerable to party-dominated committees or religious panels. Second, there is no adversarial system to protect the rights of the accused. Defendants are often denied legal representation, statements made under torture are admissible as evidence, and the verdict may be decided before the trial begins. Third, the security agencies have enormous discretion. In general, the police have the power to arbitrarily arrest, detain, and often execute individuals without any judicial oversight.

These characteristics directly influence the government's response to allegations of human rights violations. In the aftermath of the Tiananmen massacre, Chinese leaders justified the event, claiming that bloodshed was necessary to keep "hooligans" from destroying the government and society. In Ethiopia, the Mengistu regime denied allegations of human rights abuses in general and never acknowledged the She'eb massacre. The Hussein regime in Iraq responded to the Halabja massacre by accusing Iran of the chemical bombardment. Sudan chose not to respond to allegations of particular human rights violations, but did claim that such acts as the Wau massacre were a result of tribal fighting and beyond government control. Without exception, the governments' official response proved to be the last word, and no criminal or political inquiries were opened.

The lack of an independent legal system ensures that government and military officials will not be held accountable for their actions. But to secure human rights, the courts also must be competent and willing to address government crimes. Criminal investigations of the alleged massacres were initiated in six states: the Soviet Union, India, Guatemala, Peru, Colombia, and El Salvador. However, investigations do not necessarily result in charges being filed or trial hearings, let alone prosecutions. In cases where the crime involves government or military personnel, the obstacles can be overwhelming. On average, the legal systems in these states are severely incapacitated. There are four major factors that impede the judiciary's attempt to address human rights crimes: (1) jurisdiction; (2) investigative autonomy; (3) obstruction; and (4) corruption and fear.

The first barrier the civilian courts must overcome is legal jurisdiction. Military courts have proven, time and again, their unwillingness to reprimand any personnel involved in human rights violations. This problem is compounded by the Supreme Court's reluctance to order civilian trials for members of the armed forces. Colombia's landmark Supreme Court decision, which gave the civilian courts the authority to try military personnel in the Segovia case, is a notable improvement to the problem of jurisdiction. However, on the whole, the civilian courts remain hesitant to pursue cases involving members of the military.

A second factor that impedes the ability of the legal system to prosecute crimes involving military personnel is the autonomy of the policing system. The police are primarily responsible for gathering evidence, interviewing witnesses, and documenting the crime scene. But in some states, the police and security forces are centralized and report to the military hierarchy. If the civilian courts have no independent investigative powers, they must ultimately depend on the police and military to implicate themselves in the crime. The arrangement in Guatemala typifies this problem and demonstrates the need for an independent policing system.

A third factor to consider is the dominance of the military in the legal process, which leads to obstruction of justice. The criminal investigations in this study were characterized by the harassment of witnesses, the withholding and destruction of evidence, the disappearance of corpses, murder and disappearance of key witnesses, death threats, and the military's refusal to cooperate. None of the investigations were free of military attempts to cover up the crime. Furthermore, the military hierarchies ensured that any investigations would be restricted to lower-level officers. The judiciary is at a distinct disadvantage.

A fourth general problem is corruption and fear in the legal system. The courts are severely underfinanced, and corruption and complicity are rampant. A climate of fear permeates the courts. Judges and prosecutors have no assurance of protection and are likely to be subjected to threats and violence if they pursue human rights cases involving the military. The competence of any legal system operating under such conditions must be seriously challenged.

The problems facing the civilian courts are reflected in the outcomes of criminal investigations into government massacres. In the Soviet Union, the criminal case on the Tbilisi massacre was closed due to lack of evidence. A High Court judge in India probed the killings at Maliana, but no charges were filed. In Guatemala, the El Aguacate case was closed without any charges being filed. In Colombia, two officers were charged for events preceding the Segovia massacre, but no one was ever charged with the killings. In Peru, the prosecutor made strong accusations against a general for his involvement in the Cayara massacre, but the case was eventually dropped. El Salvador is the only case where military personnel were convicted of crimes related to a massacre.

Can the El Salvador case be used as a benchmark to judge all other cases? The investigation, like all other investigations, was marked by military and government obstruction. Evidence was destroyed or disappeared, the military and U.S. Embassy refused to cooperate with investigators, and the probe was limited to lower-level officers. Given the government's record, the prosecution and conviction of officers were anomalies, carried out for two principal reasons. First, the U.S. Congress linked the continuation of military aid on the successful conviction of those responsible for the murders. Second, the ARENA government's political future was based on its ability to bring a peaceful end to the decade-long civil war. The failure to prosecute the case would have further damaged negotiations between the government and rebels. Also, the high social status of the murdered Jesuit priests is a factor to consider. It is extremely doubtful the United States would have pressured the El Salvador government to investigate the massacre if the victims had not been of such high stature.

In sum, the civilian courts must take several steps before they can habitually protect human rights. The courts first must demand jurisdiction over human rights cases involving military or police personnel. Next, the investigative function must be carried out by an autonomous policing system or by an independent criminal investigative team. Any investigation then must overcome military attempts to obstruct the case. And finally, the courts must prove to be willing, dedicated, and courageous in their desire to achieve justice.

The Political System

The political system has an important role in the area of government accountability. In particular, the political system has the responsibility of promulgating legislation designed to protect human rights. The political system also has the authority to oversee the activities of government and military officials.

Two factors that are important to this discussion are authoritarianism and partisanship.

In authoritarian states, there is no independent legislature, and the political bodies have no real power to take actions contrary to the wishes of the party leadership. Again, the exception is the transitional Soviet state, where the Communist Party monopolized power, but regional political bodies and a new supreme legislature had a degree of autonomy. In China, Ethiopia, and Iraq, political authority is based on patriarchalism and personal influence. Younger, inexperienced politicians advance through the system by showing their support of elder statesmen. Family and personal relationships play a key role, and the succession process secures political loyalty to the top echelon of leaders. Criticism of government policy or leaders is grounds for removal from the party. In brief, the political systems in authoritarian states do not provide any means for the redress of human rights abuses carried out under government order.

In a democratic state, the legislature has the capacity to make the protection of human rights a top priority. But several of the democracies in this study are closed, elitist, parochial, and corrupt. For instance, in Sudan, the political parties buy votes in their election campaigns and favor family members of the traditional leaders. Also, Latin American governments, with the exception of Peru, are known for their closed political system, which excludes leftist parties. Partisanship is another factor that affects legislative responsiveness to human rights concerns. The legislative inquiries into government massacres demonstrate the difficulty of procuring consensus and action.

Three of the governments in this study authorized legislative inquiries into the events surrounding alleged massacres: India, the Soviet Union, and Peru. Each of the inquiries was politically charged, and the findings were dictated by partisanship rather than factual evidence. In India, the regional commission failed to disclose the role of the police in the killings at Meerut. In the Soviet Union, key hard-liners discredited the committee's report into the Tbilisi massacre. In Peru, the majority party came to the defense of the military in the incident at Cayara, contradicting findings from the minority parties. By all accounts, party politics influenced the investigation, findings, and recommendations of the legislative inquiries. Furthermore, party partisanship determined the acceptability of any decisions resulting from the inquiry.

In sum, political systems have the capacity and responsibility to hold government and military personnel accountable for their actions. But the political system first must have an independent legislature. This legislature then must be composed of competent legislators who represent a wide spectrum of views. Finally, legislators must take a nonpartisan approach to the problem of human rights.

THE PURSUIT OF JUSTICE

How can justice be served in the context of state terrorism? First, it is essential that governments recognize the value of human rights. Some degree of universal rights must be agreed upon, even if it includes freedom from only the most severe violations. Furthermore, the universality of these basic rights must be guaranteed for all members of the state, not just a segment of first-class citizens.

Second, an independent and competent legal system must pursue human rights cases involving military and police personnel. Within this ideal, the agency responsible for investigations into such crimes must be autonomous, persons who obstruct the pursuit of justice must be reprimanded, the courts have to be properly financed, and finally, participants in the legal system must be assured of their safety. If these conditions are met, the prospects of bringing human rights abusers to justice will be improved dramatically.

Third, the political system must advocate the cause of human rights. Emergency regulations that place military authority over civilian authority must not be sanctioned. The legislature must enact laws that protect all citizens from the scourges of the state. Legislators must address specific human rights concerns from an objective, nonpartisan angle. Finally, the political system must ensure that military and police personnel who are guilty of human rights violations are removed from service. These recommendations are outlined below.

1. **The government must recognize the universality of basic human rights.**
   - The government must ensure at least a core set of human rights, such as freedom from torture, extrajudicial executions, and "disappearances."
   - Governments should demonstrate their support of human rights by ratifying international instruments, such as the United Nations Convention Against Torture.
   - The government should support the monitoring function of domestic and international human rights organizations.
   - Governments must accept the universality of human rights for all members of the state.

2. **The government must establish an independent and competent legal system that includes the following.**
   - The civilian courts must have jurisdiction over human rights crimes involving military and/or police personnel.
   - The police, or criminal investigative unit, must be autonomous.
   - The judiciary must be adequately financed, and corruption in the courts must be eliminated.
   - Judges, prosecutors, witnesses, and victims must be protected and assured of their safety.
   - The military and police must cooperate with civilian authorities and be reprimanded if they fail to do so.

3. **The political system must establish policies that protect human rights under all circumstances.**
    - Civilian authority must override military authority, regardless of circumstance.
    - The executive and legislative branches must codify laws that protect citizens from arbitrary police and military action.
    - The legislature must address human rights issues in a nonpartisan fashion.
    - Military and police personnel found guilty of human rights violations must be removed from service.

SUMMARY AND CONCLUSIONS

This chapter reviewed the characteristics of legal and political systems in the context of human rights. Governments that lacked an independent legal system typically asserted that human rights crimes, such as massacres, were either justified or not the responsibility of the regime. In states where an independent judiciary did exist, criminal investigations into the massacres most often were terminated without any charges being filed. In general, the civilian courts were impeded by (1) military claims to jurisdiction in cases involving members of the armed forces; (2) the lack of an independent criminal investigative unit; (3) military and government obstruction; and (4) corruption and fear in the courts.

The judiciary cannot protect human rights without the support of the political system. The political system as a whole has the responsibility of legislating human rights protections. But many states have no independent legislature or are characterized by closed, corrupt, and elitist political systems that have no capacity to address human rights from a critical perspective. In political systems that do address the problem of human rights, partisanship impedes the goal of government accountability.

This study concludes that democracy is no guarantee of the protection of human rights. Rather, the creation of a just society hinges on three conditions. First, the government must recognize the universality of basic human rights. Second, the government must establish an independent and competent legal system. Third, the legislature must play an active role in safeguarding human rights.

NOTE

1. Totalitarianism is an extreme form of authoritarianism. Its usage is subjective; there is little consensus on which regimes should be classified as totalitarian. Therefore, this study focuses on the broader phenomenon of authoritarianism.

Appendix

Location[1]	Dates(s)	Number Dead	Agents
AFRICA:			
BENIN			
Savé	March 1989	10	armed forces
BURUNDI			
Ntega and Marangara	August 1988	hundreds	armed forces
ETHIOPIA			
Metekal	Feb. 1988	200	armed forces
Qazien and Shebah	April 1988	70+	armed forces
She'eb	May 1988	200+	armed forces
Hagareselam	June 1988	340	armed forces
Maikinetal/Adua	June 1988	100	armed forces
Mai Harast	October 1988	11	armed forces
LIBERIA			
Butuo and Kamplay	Dec. 24, 1989	hundreds	armed forces
MADAGASCAR			
South and central regions[2]	1988	hundreds	armed forces
MAURITANIA			
Nere-Walo	Nov. 1989	3	armed forces
NIGERIA			
Benin City	May 6, 1987	24	prison officials

Location	Dates(s)	Number Dead	Agents
SOMALIA			
El Afwein	Oct., Dec. 1988	300+	armed forces
Ervigavo	March 16, 1989	200+	armed forces
Mogadishu	July 14-16, 1989	200	armed forces
Daname army camp	July 16, 1989	46	armed forces
Dobleh	Sept. 20, 1989	dozens	armed forces
Galkayo	Nov. 24, 1989	120	armed forces
SUDAN			
Ad-Daien	March 28, 1987	hundreds	militia
Wau	Aug. 11-12, 1987	hundreds	militia
Abri	April 23, 1989	not specified[3]	armed forces
Wau	July 19, 1989	34	armed forces
Lagawa	Oct. 1989	100+	armed forces
UGANDA			
Atira	Feb. 26 or 27, 1987	18	armed forces
Minakula	August 1988	11+	armed forces
Lukutu	Dec. 1988	45	armed forces
Bwobo	Feb. 1989	10	armed forces
Bobi	May 1989	35+	armed forces
Mukuru	July 1989	69	armed forces

THE AMERICAS:

Location	Dates(s)	Number Dead	Agents
BOLIVIA			
Villa Tunari	June 1988	7+	police
BRAZIL			
Sao Paulo	July 1987	30	prison officials
Marabá	Dec. 1987	20	military police
Benjamin Constant	March 1988	14	paramilitary
Vila Aurora	Feb. 1989	7	military police
CHILE			
not specified[4]	June 15-16, 1987	12	security forces
COLOMBIA			
Urabá/La Negra	March 1988	18	paramilitary
San Rafael	June 1988	17	armed forces
Segovia	Nov. 11, 1988	43	paramilitary
La Rochela	Jan. 1989	12	paramilitary
EL SALVADOR			
San Francisco	Sept. 1988	10	armed forces
San Salvador	Nov. 16, 1989	8	armed forces

Location	Dates(s)	Number Dead	Agents
HAITI			
Jean-Rabel	July 23, 1987	200	paramilitary
Fort Dimanche	Nov. 28, 1987	46	security forces
Port-au-Prince	Nov. 29, 1987	30+	army and militia
Port-au-Prince	Aug. 14, 1988	4	armed forces
MEXICO			
Xoxocotla	Jan. 1989	4	police
PERU			
Cayara	May 1988	28	armed forces
Pucallpo	Feb. 9, 1989	23	police
Calabaza	May 17, 1989	11	armed forces
Santa Ana	June 13, 1989	4	armed forces
Santa Ana/Pampamarca	June 1989	17	armed forces
SURINAME			
Brownsweg/Pokigron	Sept. 11, 1987	19	armed forces
VENEZUELA			
near Colombia border	Oct. 1988	14	security forces
Petare	March 1, 1988	5	armed forces

ASIA AND THE PACIFIC:

Location	Dates(s)	Number Dead	Agents
AFGHANISTAN			
Mushwani village	August 1987	17	armed forces
Kolalgu	Jan. 16, 1988	9	armed forces
BANGLADESH			
Chittagong	Jan. 1988	8-22	security forces
Langadu	May 1989	36	local patrols
BURMA			
Shan state	April 1988	8	armed forces
Insein prison	April, August 1988	hundreds	security forces
Kayin	Dec. 1, 1989	6	armed forces
CHINA			
Lhasa (Tibet)	Oct. 1, 1987	several	police
Lhasa (Tibet)	March 5, 1988	12+	police
Lhasa (Tibet)	March 7-9, 1989	16-60	police
Beijing	June 3-4, 1989	1,000+	armed forces
INDIA			
Meerut	May 22, 1987	dozens	police
Kirichatra	Sept. 1987	7	police
Oinam	1987[5]	14	armed forces

Location	Dates(s)	Number Dead	Agents
PHILIPPINES			
Namulangayan	Feb. 10, 1987	17	armed forces
Candulawan	Feb. 28, 1987	3	paramilitary
Bulacao	March 15, 1987	3	paramilitary
Cadiz and Sagay	April 1987	7	armed forces
Himamaylan	Aug. 9, 1987	6	paramilitary
Lanao del Norte	June 29, 1987	5	armed forces
Na-ilan	Feb. 1988	4	paramilitary
Aton-Aton	April 1988	5	armed forces
Carayman	Feb. 1989	8	armed forces
Buena Vista	March 1989	5	armed forces
Paombong	April 1989	9	armed forces
SRI LANKA			
Kokkaddicholai	Jan. 28, 1987	150+	special forces
Jaffna Peninsula	Oct. 12-13, 1987	40	armed forces
Valvettiturai	August 1989	46	armed forces

EUROPE:

Location	Dates(s)	Number Dead	Agents
ROMANIA			
Timisoara	Dec. 17, 1989	many	armed forces
SOVIET UNION			
Tbilisi	April 1989	20	armed forces
UNITED KINGDOM			
Gibraltar	March 1988	3	armed forces
YUGOSLAVIA			
Kosovo	March 23-28, 1989	22	armed forces

MIDDLE EAST AND NORTH AFRICA:

Location	Dates(s)	Number Dead	Agents
ALGERIA			
various cities	Oct. 6-12, 1988	176+	police
IRAQ			
Jiman	Nov. 11, 1987	100-150	armed forces
Halabja	March 16-17, 1988	5,000	armed forces
Tanjaro	April 2, 1988	400	armed forces
north	August 1988	hundreds	armed forces
Durhok	August 28, 1988	1,000	armed forces

NOTES

1. Sources: *Amnesty International Report* covering the years 1988, 1989, and 1990.

2. Massacres were reported in the provinces of Toliary, Fianarantsoa, Antananarivo, and Mahajanga.

3. Amnesty International does not specify the number of killings. Reports indicate that on April 23, 1989, members of the government militia and armed forces extrajudicially executed civilians as they destroyed a number of villages near Abri in the Nuba mountains.

4. Amnesty International does not specify the location of the killings. Reports state that 12 alleged Manuel Rodriguez Patriotic Front (FPMR) members were killed on June 15 and 16 in circumstances suggesting that they were the victims of extrajudicial executions by the state security police.

5. An exact date is not given for the killings of 14 people in Oinam village near the Nagaland border.

Bibliography

Abrams, Jim. 1990. "China pays the price for night of bloodshed," *The Times*, May 27.

Acevedo, Carlos. 1991. "El Salvador's new clothes: The electoral process." In Anjali Sundaram and George Gelber (eds.), *A Decade of War: El Salvador Confronts the Future*. New York: Monthly Review Press, pp. 19–37.

Ahmad, Imtiaz. 1980. "They have not done too badly," *New Delhi*, Sept. 1–14, p. 12.

Aidoo, Akwasi. 1993. "Africa: Democracy without human rights?" *Human Rights Quarterly* 15 (4): 703–15.

Akbar, M.J. 1988. *Riot after Riot: Reports on Caste and Communal Violence in India*. New York: Penguin Books.

Akol, Lam. 1987. "The present war and its solution." In Francis Mading Deng and Prosser Gifford (eds.), *The Search for Peace and Unity in the Sudan*. Washington, D.C.: Wilson Center Press, pp. 15–23.

al-Khalil, Samir. 1989. *Republic of Fear: The Politics of Modern Iraq*. Berkeley, Calif.: University of California Press.

Amaya, Atilio Ramírez, Miguel Angel Amaya, Carlos Alberto Avilez, Josefina Ramírez, and Miguel Angel Reyes. 1987. "Justice and the penal system in El Salvador," *Crime and Social Justice* 30: 1–27.

Americas Watch. 1983. *Human Rights in Central America: El Salvador, Guatemala, Honduras, Nicaragua*. New York: Americas Watch.

———.1987. *A Certain Passivity: Failing to curb Human Rights Abuses in Peru*. New York: Americas Watch.

———.1988a. *Closing the Space: Human Rights in Guatemala, May 1987–October 1988*. Washington, D.C.: Americas Watch.

———.1988b. *Nightmare Revisited: 1987–1988*. New York: Americas Watch.

———.1988c. *Tolerating Abuses: Violations of Human Rights in Peru*. Washington, D.C.: Americas Watch.

———.1989. *The Killings in Colombia*. New York: Americas Watch.

———.1990a. *The "Drug War" in Colombia: The Neglected Tragedy of Political Violence*. New York: Americas Watch.

———.1990b. "Slayings of Jesuits, Their Cook, Her Daughter," *News from Americas Watch*, September, pp. 12–15.

————.1992a. *Peru Under Fire: Human Rights Since the Return to Democracy*. New Haven, Conn.: Yale University Press.

————.1992b. *Political Murder & Reform in Colombia: The Violence Continues*. New York: Americas Watch.

Amnesty International. 1983. *Political Killings by Government*. London: Amnesty International.

————.1985. *Amnesty International Report, 1985*. New York: Amnesty International.

————.1987. *Violations of Human Rights in Iran [Iran Briefing]*. London: Amnesty International.

————.1988a. "Mass killings of civilians," *Amnesty International Newsletter* 28 (9): 7.

————.1988b. "Unarmed civilians killed," *Amnesty International Newsletter* 28 (6): 8.

————.1988c. "Unarmed civilians killed deliberately," *Amnesty International Newsletter*, 18 (1), p. 7.

————.1988d. *El Salvador: 'Death squads'–a government strategy*. London: Amnesty International.

————.1988e. *India: A Review of Human Rights Violations*. New York: Amnesty International.

————.1988f. *Peru: Violations of Human Rights in the Emergency Zones*. New York: Amnesty International.

————.1988g. *Amnesty International Report, 1988*. New York: Amnesty International.

————.1988h. *Philippines: Unlawful Killings by Military and Paramilitary Forces*. New York: Amnesty International.

————.1989a. *Amnesty International Report, 1989*. New York: Amnesty International.

————.1989b. *'Caught between Two Fires' [Peru Briefing]*. New York: Amnesty International.

————.1989c. *Colombia: Human Rights Development: "Death Squads" on the Defensive?* New York: Amnesty International.

————.1989d. *Guatemala: Human Rights Violations under the Civilian Government*. New York: Amnesty International.

————.1989e. *Guatemala: Recent Human Rights Developments*. Washington, D.C.: Amnesty International.

————.1989f. *Peru: Human Rights in a State of Emergency*. New York: Amnesty International.

————.1989g. "Soldiers using spades and gas blamed for deaths," *Amnesty International Newsletter* 19 (6): 8.

————.1989h. *Sudan: Human Rights Violations in the Context of Civil War*. New York: Amnesty International.

————.1989i. *U.S.S.R.: Human Rights in a Time of Change*. New York: Amnesty International.

————.1989j. *U.S.S.R.: Human Rights in Transition*. New York: Amnesty International.

————.1990a. *El Salvador: Killings, Torture and "Disappearances."* New York: Amnesty International.

————.1990b. *Sudan: A Permanent Human Rights Crisis, the Military Government's First Year in Power*. New York: Amnesty International.

————.1990c. *Amnesty International 1990 Report*. New York: Amnesty International.

————.1991a. *Ethiopia: End of an Era of Brutal Repression, A New Chance for Human Rights*. New York: Amnesty International.

————.1991b. *Peru: Human Rights in a Climate of Terror.* New York: Amnesty International.

————.1992a. *The 1992 Report on Human Rights Around the World.* New York: Amnesty International.

————.1992b. *People's Republic of China: Continued Patterns of Human Rights Violations in China.* New York: Amnesty International.

————.1992c. *Peru: Human Rights during the Government of President Alberto Fujimori.* New York: Amnesty International.

————.1992d. *India: Torture, Rape and Deaths in Custody.* New York: Amnesty International.

————.1992e. *Sudan, a Continuing Human Rights Crisis.* New York: Amnesty International.

Akol, Lam. 1987. "The present war and its solution." In Francis Mading Deng and Prosser Gifford (eds.), *The Search for Peace and Unity in the Sudan.* Washington, D.C.: Wilson Center Press, pp. 15–26.

Andean Commission of Jurists. 1991. *Colombia: The Right to Justice.* New York: Lawyers Committee for Human Rights.

Anderson, John Ward, and Molly Moore. 1992. "Religious riots across India–200 more die," *San Francisco Chronicle*, December 8.

Anderson, Kenneth. 1989. *Maximizing Deniability: The Justice System and Human Rights in Guatemala.* Washington, D.C.: International Human Rights Law Group.

Anderson, Ken, and Jean-Marie Simon. 1988. "Guatemala democracy is an army in disguise," *Los Angeles Times*, May 29.

Andreas, Peter R., and Kenneth E. Sharpe. 1992. "Cocaine politics in the Andes," *Current History* 91 (562): 74–79.

An-na'im, Abdullah A. 1992. "Islam and national integration in the Sudan." In John O. Hunwick (ed.), *Religion and National Integration in Africa: Islam, Christianity, and Politics in the Sudan and Nigeria.* Evanston, Ill.: Northwestern University Press, pp. 15–26.

Ansari, Iqbal A. 1990. "Discrepant perceptions of Hindus and Muslims in India on communally sensitive issues: A note," *Journal–Institute of Muslim Minority Affairs* 11 (1): 4–14.

Arendt, Hannah. 1966. *The Origins of Totalitarianism.* New York: Harcourt Brace Jovanovich.

Arnson, Cynthia, and David Holiday. 1991. *El Salvador and Human Rights: The Challenge of Reform.* New York: Americas Watch.

Arzt, Donna. 1990. "The application of international human rights law in Islamic states," *Human Rights Quarterly* 12 (2): 202–30.

Asia Watch. 1990. "Punishment season: Human rights in China after martial law." In George Hicks (ed.), *The Broken Mirror: China after Tiananmen.* Chicago, Ill.: St. James Press, pp. 369–89.

Assam, Mukhtar Al. 1989. "Bureaucracy and development in the Sudan," *Journal of Asian and African Studies* 24 (1–2): 28–48.

Atarodi, Habibollah. 1991. "The Kurds: A nation of 30 million denied its freedom," *The Journal of Social, Political and Economic Studies* 16 (3): 273–285.

Balagopal, K. 1987. "Meerut 1987: Reflections on an inquiry," *Economic and Political Weekly* 23 (16): 768–71.

Baloyra-Herp, Enrique. 1991. "The persistent conflict in El Salvador," *Current History* 90 (554): 121–24, 132–33.

Banu, Zenab. 1989. *Politics of Communalism*. Bombay: Popular Prakashan Private Ltd.

Barry, Tom. 1991. *Central America Inside Out*. New York: Grove Weidenfeld.

———.1992. *Inside Guatemala*. Albuquerque, N.M.: Inter-Hemispheric Resource.

Barry, Tom, and Deb Preusch. 1986. *The Central America Fact Book*. New York: Grove Press.

Barsh, Russel Lawrence. 1993. "Measuring human rights: Problems of methodology and purpose," *Human Rights Quarterly* 15 (1): 87–121.

Bartram, Roger. 1991. "Reflections on human rights issues in prewar Iraq," *Journal of Palestine Issues* 20 (3): 89–97.

Bechtold, Peter K. 1990. "More turbulence in Sudan: A new politics this time?" *Middle East Journal* 44 (4): 579–95.

Beissinger, Mark R. 1988. "Political reform and Soviet society," *Current History* 87 (531): 317–20, 345.

Bennett, Philip. 1990. "Burying the Jesuits," *Vanity Fair*, November.

Bernstein, Jacob. 1993. "Guatemalans perplexed in wake of coup," *San Francisco Examiner*, May 26.

Bhatnagar, Ashwini. 1987. "Trail of hate," *The Illustrated Weekly of India* 108 (26): 20–23.

Blondel, J. 1969. *An Introduction to Comparative Government*. New York: Praeger.

Bole, William. 1990. "Top military leaders had labeled slain Jesuit a Marxist," *National Catholic Reporter*, May 18.

Bollen, Kenneth A. 1986. "Political rights and political liberties in nations: An evaluation of human rights measures, 1950 to 1984," *Human Rights Quarterly* 8 (4): 579–82.

Bourque, Susan C., and Kay B. Warren. 1989. "Democracy without peace: The cultural politics of terror in Peru," *Latin American Research Review* 24 (1): 7–34.

Bradshaw, David. 1991. "After the Gulf War: The Kurds," *The World Today* 47 (5): 78–80.

Brass, Paul R. 1985. *Caste, Faction and Party in Indian Politics, Vol. II: Election Studies*. Delhi: Chanakya Publications.

Brockett, Charles D. 1991. "Sources of state terrorism in rural Central America." In P. Timothy Bushnell et al. (eds), *State Organized Terror: The Case of Violent Internal Repression*. Boulder, Col.: Westview Press, pp. 59–76.

Broder, Jonathan. 1990. "Jesuits' death inquiry stalled," *San Francisco Examiner*, April 30.

Bronstein, Phil. 1990. "Conspiracy suspected in Salvador massacre," *San Francisco Examiner & Chronicle*, April 15.

Brook, Timothy. 1992. *Quelling the People: The Military Suppression of the Beijing Democracy Movement*. New York: Oxford University Press.

Brown, Cynthia G. 1990. *In Desperate Straits: Human Rights in Peru after a Decade of Democracy and Insurgency*. New York: Americas Watch.

Bulloch, John, and Harvey Morris. 1992. *No Friends but the Mountains: The Tragic History of the Kurds*. New York: Oxford University Press.

Burg, Steven L. 1989. "The Soviet Union's nationalities question," *Current History* 88 (540): 341–44, 359–62.

Burton, John W. 1991. "Development and cultural genocide in the Sudan," *The Journal of Modern African Studies* 29 (3): 511–520.

Bushnell, P. Timothy, Vladimir Shlapentokh, Christopher K. Vanderpool, and Jeyaratnam Sundram. 1991. "State organized terror: Tragedy of the modern state," In P. Timothy Bushnell et al. (eds), *State Organized Terror: The Case of Violent Internal Repression*. Boulder, Col.: Westview Press, pp. 3–22.

Bwy, Douglas. 1968. "Political instability in Latin America: The cross-cultural test of a causal model," *Latin America Research Review* 3: 17–66.

Cáceres, Jorge. 1989. "Violence, national security and democratisation in Central America." In Catholic Institute for International Relations (ed.), *States of Terror: Death Squads or Development*. London: Catholic Institute for International Relations, pp. 95–114.

Candor, Joseph. 1988. "Communalism in India," *Impact* 23 (1): 20–23.

Cappelletti, M. 1971. *Judicial Review in the Contemporary World*. Indianapolis: Bobbs-Merrill.

Carr, Mathew. 1991. "Guatemala: State of terror," *Race and Class* 33 (1): 31–56.

Chakravartly, Nikhil. 1987. "How the terror was let loose," *The Times of India*, June 14.

Chalabi, Ahmad. 1991. "Iraq: The past as prologue?" *Foreign Policy* 83: 20–29.

Chalk, Frank, and Kurt Jonassohn. 1990. *The History and Sociology of Genocide: Analyses and Case Studies*. New Haven, Conn.: Yale University Press.

Chand, David D. 1989. "The Sudan civil war: Is a negotiated solution possible?" *Africa Today* 36 (3,4): 55–63.

Chandra, Bipar. 1987. *Communalism in Modern India*. New Delhi: Vikas Publishing House.

Chhibber, Pradeep K., and John R. Petrocik. 1990. "Social cleavages, elections and the Indian party system." In Richard Sisson and Ramashray Roy (eds.), *Diversity and Dominance in Indian Politics, Vol. 1*. Newbury Park, Calif.: Sage Publications, pp. 105–22.

Chiang, Harriet. 1990. "Peruvian prosecutor seeks U.S. asylum," *San Francisco Chronicle*, March 22.

Chomsky, Noam, and Edward S. Herman. 1979. *The Washington Connection and Third World Fascism, The Political Economy of Human Rights, Vol. I*. Boston: South End Press.

Clapham, Christopher. 1988. *Transformation and Continuity in Revolutionary Ethiopia*. New York: Cambridge University Press.

Claude, Richard P., and Thomas B. Jabine. 1986. "Editors' introduction to symposium: Statistical issues in the field of human rights," *Human Rights Quarterly* 8 (4): 551–66.

Colburn, Forrest D. 1992. "The fading of the revolutionary era in Central America," *Current History* 91 (562): 70–73.

Comite pro Justicia y Paz de Guatemala (Pro Justice and Peace Committee of Guatemala). 1986. *Human Rights in Guatemala*. Presented to the Commission on Human Rights of the United Nations, 42nd session, February-March.

———.1989. *International Bulletin* (Mexico), August 25.

Commission for the Study of Violence. 1992. "Organized violence." In Charles Bergquish, Ricardo Peñaranda, and Gonzalo Sánchez (eds.), *Violence in Colombia: The Contemporary Crisis in Historical Perspective*. Wilmington, Del.: Scholarly Resources Inc., pp. 261–72.

Conquest, Robert. 1968. *The Great Terror: Stalin's Purges of the Thirties*. New York: Macmillan.

Cook, Rebecca J. 1993. "Women's international human rights law: The way forward," *Human Rights Quarterly* 15 (2): 230–61.

Cosman, Catherine. 1991. *Glasnost in Jeopardy: Human Rights in the USSR*. New York: Helsinki Watch.

Cox, Cindy. 1989–90. "Chronology of events related to the 1989 Tiananmen Square incident," *World Affairs* 152 (3): 129–34.

Crabtree, John. 1992. *Peru under García: An Opportunity Lost*. Pittsburgh: University of Pittsburgh Press.

Crouch, Martin. 1989. *Revolution and Evolution: Gorbachev and Soviet Politics*. New Delhi: Prentice-Hall of India.

Cultural Survival Quarterly. 1988. "Sudan's secret slaughter," 12 (2): 41–47.

Dahl, Robert A. 1992. "Democracy and human rights under different conditions of development." In A. Eide and B. Hagtvet (eds.), *Human Rights in Perspective: A Global Assessment*. Oxford: Basil Blackwell Ltd., pp. 235–51.

Dallin, Alexander, and George Breslauer. 1970. *Political Terror in Communist Systems*. Stanford, Calif.: Stanford University Press.

Datta, Prabhat K. 1991. *Politics of Region and Religion in India*. New Delhi: Uppal Publishing House.

Davis, Sheldon. 1985. "Civil patrols–Armed peace in Northern Huehuetenango," *Cultural Survival Quarterly* 9 (4): 38–39.

Dawisho, Adeed. 1986. "The politics of war: Presidential centrality, party power, political opposition." In Frederick W. Axelgard (ed.), *Iraq in Transition: A Political, Economic, and Strategic Perspective*. Boulder, Col.: Westview Press, pp. 21–32.

Day, Mark R. 1988. "Peasants bear the brunt of Peru's brutal rebellion," *Los Angeles Times*, June 5.

De Waal, Alex. 1991. *Evil Days: Thirty Years of War and Famine in Ethiopia*. New York: Human Rights Watch.

d'Encausse, Hélène Carrère. 1993. *The End of the Soviet Empire: The Triumph of the Nations*. Translated by Franklin Philip. New York: Basic Books.

Denmark, Robert A., and Howard P. Lehman. 1984. "South African state terror: The costs of continuing repression." In M. Stohl and G. Lopez (eds.), *The State as Terrorist: The Dynamics of Governmental Violence and Repression*. Westport, Conn.: Greenwood Press, pp. 143–66.

Deng, Francis Mading. 1990. "War of visions for the nation," *Middle East Journal* 44 (4): 596–609.

———.1991. "War of visions for the nation." In John O. Voll (ed.), *Sudan: State and Society in Crisis*. Bloomington, Ind.: Indiana University Press, pp. 24–42.

Deng Xiaoping. 1989–90. "Deng's June 9 speech: We faced a rebellious clique and dregs of society," *World Affairs* 152 (3): 154–55.

Dietz, Henry. 1990. "Peru's Sendero Luminoso as a revolutionary movement," *Journal of Political and Military Sociology* 18 (1): 123–50.

Dines, Mary. 1988. "Ethiopian violation of human rights in Eritrea." In Lionel Cliffe and Basil Davidson (eds.), *The Long Struggle of Eritrea for Independence and Constructive Peace*. Nottingham, England: Spokesman, pp. 139–61.

Dittmer, Lowell. 1989. "The Tiananmen massacre," *Problems of Communism* 38 (5): 2–15.

————.1990. "China in 1989: The crisis of incomplete reform," *Asian Survey* 30 (1): 25–41.

Dix, Robert H. 1987a. *The Politics of Colombia*. New York: Praeger.

————.1987b. "Social change and party system stability in Colombia," *Government and Opposition* 25 (1): 98–114.

Doninelli, Factor Méndez. 1989. "The unofficial story: The El Aguacate massacre," *Report on Guatemala* 10 (1): 3–5.

Donnelly, Jack. 1984. "Cultural relativism and universal human rights," *Human Rights Quarterly* 6 (4): 400–19.

————.1989. "Repression and development: The political contingency of human rights trade-offs." In David P. Forsythe (ed.), *Human Rights and Development: International Views*. New York: St. Martin's Press, pp. 305–28.

Dreyer, June Teufel. 1989. "The People's Liberation Army and the power struggle of 1989," *Problems of Communism* 38 (5): 41–48.

Drinan, Robert F., S. J., and Teresa T. Kuo. 1992. "The 1991 battle for human rights in China," *Human Rights Quarterly* 14: 21–42.

Duff, Ernest A., and John F. McCamant. 1976. *Violence and Repression in Latin America*. New York: Free Press.

Duffield, Mark. 1990. "Absolute distress: Structural causes of hunger in Sudan," *Middle East Report*, Vol. 20 (5): 4–11.

Duvall, Raymond D., and Michael Stohl. 1988. "Governance by terror." In M. Stohl (ed.), *The Politics of Terrorism*, 3rd edition. New York: Marcel Dekker, pp. 179–219.

Eckstein, Harry. 1965. "On the etiology of internal wars," *History and Theory* 4: 133–63.

Economic and Political Weekly. 1987. "State and communalism," 22 (22): 823.

Elst, Koenraad. 1990. *Ram Janmabhoomi vs. Babri Masjid: A Case Study in Hindu–Muslim Conflict*. New Delhi: Voice of India.

Engineer, Asghar Ali. 1987a. "Meerut: The nation's shame," *Economic and Political Weekly* 22 (25): 969–71.

————.1987b. "Communalism, communal violence and human rights." In Upendra Baxi (ed.), *The Right to be Human*. New Delhi: Lancer International, pp. 161–72.

————.1988. "Meerut–Shame of the nation." In Asghar Ali Engineer (ed.), *Delhi-Meerut Riots: Analysis, Compilation and Documentation*. Delhi: Ajanta Publications, pp. 16–32.

————.1989. *Communalism and Communal Violence in India: An Analytical Approach to Hindu-Muslim Conflict*. Delhi: Ajanta Publications.

Entessar, Nader. 1992. *Kurdish Ethnonationalism*. Boulder, Col.: Lynne Rienner.

————.1989. "The Kurdish mosaic of discord," *Third World Quarterly* 11 (4): 83–100.

Falk, Richard. 1979. "Responding to severe violations." In J. Domínguez, N. Rodley, B. Wood, and R. Falk (eds.), *Enhancing Global Human Rights*. New York: McGraw-Hill, pp. 205–57.

————.1988. "The rights of peoples (in particular indigenous peoples)." In James Crawford (ed.) *The Rights of People*. Oxford: Clarendon Press, pp. 17–37.

Farouk-Sluglett, Marion, and Peter Sluglett. 1991. "The historiography of modern Iraq," *American Historical Review* 96 (5): 1408–21.

Faucher, Philippe, and Kevin Fitzgibbons. 1989. "Dissent and the state in Latin America." In C. E. S. Franks (ed.), *Dissent and the State*. Toronto: Oxford University Press, pp. 138–68.

Feierabend, Ivo, and Rosalind Feierabend. 1972. "Systematic conditions of political aggression: An application of frustration aggression theory." In I. K. Feierabend, R. L. Feierabend, and T. R. Gurr (eds.), *Anger, Violence and Politics: Theories and Research.* Englewood Cliffs, N.J.: Prentice-Hall, pp. 136–83.

Fein, Esther B. 1989 "Moscow tightens Georgia security," *The New York Times,* April 12.

Fein, Helen. 1979. *Accounting for Genocide: National Response and Jewish Victimization during the Holocaust.* New York: Free Press.

————.1984. "Scenarios of genocide: Models of genocide and critical responses." In I. W. Charny (ed.), *Toward the Understanding and Prevention of Genocide: Proceedings of the International Conference on the Holocaust and Genocide.* Boulder, Col.: Westview Press, pp. 3–31.

Fellner, Jamie. 1986. *The Central-Americanization of Colombia?* New York: Americas Watch.

Feuerhard, Joe. 1990. "Stalling alleged in murder probe," *National Catholic Reporter,* March 23.

Fish, Joe, and Cristina Sganga. 1988. *El Salvador: Testament of Terror.* New York: Olive Branch Press.

Fitzpatrick, Catherine A. 1989. *USSR: Human Rights Under Glasnost.* New York: Helsinki Watch.

Foreign Broadcast Information Services. 1991. "Prosecutors cite 'irregularities' " (San Salvador Radio Cadena Sonara), Jan. 10, p. 20.

Fluehr-Lobban, Carolyn. 1991. "Islamization in Sudan." In John O. Voll (ed.), *Sudan: State and Society in Crisis.* Bloomington, Ind.: Indiana University Press, pp. 71–89.

García, José Z. 1990. "Tragedy in El Salvador," *Current History* 89 (543): 9–12, 40–41.

Gargan, Edward A. 1992. "Militants want a Hindu state," *San Francisco Chronicle,* December 8.

Gastil, Raymond D. 1985. "The comparative study of freedom," *Freedom at Issue* 82.

Gelber, Harry G. 1990. "China's new economic and strategic uncertainties and the security prospects," *Asian Survey* 30 (7): 646–68.

Ghareeb, Edmund. 1981. *The Kurdish Question in Iraq.* Syracuse, N.Y.: Syracuse University Press.

Ghosh, S. K. 1987. *Muslim Politics in India.* New Delhi: Ashish Publishing House.

Gibb, Tom. 1990. "What probe of El Salvador Jesuit killings has revealed," *San Francisco Chronicle,* December 14.

Girdner, Eddie J., and Kalim Siddiqui. 1990. "The political economy of communalism in India," *Asian Profile* 18 (2): 147–62.

Gitelman, Zvi. 1990. "The nationalities." In Stephen White, Alex Pravda, and Zvi Gitelman (eds.), *Developments in Soviet Politics.* Durham, N.C.: Duke University Press, pp. 137–58.

Glaser, Kurt, and Stefan T. Possony. 1979. *Victims of Politics: The State of Human Rights.* New York: Columbia University Press.

Goldman, Merle. 1989. "Vengeance in China," *The New York Review,* November 9, p. 5.

Goldstein, Robert Justin. 1978. *Political Repression in Modern America: From 1870 to the Present.* Cambridge, Mass.: Schenkman Publishing.

————.1983. *Political Repression in 19th Century Europe.* Totawa, N.J.: Barnes and Noble.

————.1986. "The limitations of using quantitative data in studying human rights abuses," *Human Rights Quarterly* 8 (4): 607–27.

Goldston, James. 1990. *A Year of Reckoning: El Salvador a Decade after the Assassination of Archbishop Romero.* New York: Human Rights Watch.

Gong, Gerrit W. 1990. "Tiananmen: Causes and consequences," *The Washington Quarterly* 13 (1): 79–95.

Goodwin, Jeff. 1993. "Why insurgencies persist, or the perversity of indiscriminate state violence." Paper presented at the American Sociological Association meeting. Miami Beach, Fla.

Gowers, Andrew, and Richard Johns. 1988. "Iraq bombs its citizens with lethal chemicals," *Financial Times*, March 23.

Graham, Carol. 1992. *Peru's APRA: Parties, Politics, and the Elusive Quest for Democracy.* Boulder, Col.: Lynne Rienner.

Gramsci, Antonio. 1992. *Prison Notebooks.* Translated by Joseph A. Buttigieg and Antonio Callari. New York: Columbia University Press.

Gruson, Lindsey. 1989. "Bishop links military to killing of 6," *The New York Times*, November 20.

————.1990. "Crucial evidence vanishes in case of 6 slain Jesuits," *The New York Times*, May 7.

Guatemala Human Rights Commission/USA. 1989a. *A Report on the Massacre at El Aguacate, Guatemala: The Findings of an Independent Investigation.* Washington, D.C.: Guatemala Human Rights Commission/USA.

————.1989b. *Information Bulletin*, Vol. 7, No. 5, October/November.

Guatemalan Church in Exile. 1988. "The army's war against the Guatemalan campesinos," Nicaragua, August.

Guocang, Huan. 1989. "The events of Tiananmen Square," *Orbis* 33 (4): 487–500.

Gurr, Ted Robert. 1969. "A comparative study of civil strife." In H. D. Graham and T. R. Gurr (eds.), *Violence in America: Historical and Comparative Perspectives.* New York: Signet.

————.1970. *Why Men Rebel.* Princeton, N.J.: Princeton University Press.

————.1986. "The political origins of state violence and terror: A theoretical analysis." In M. Stohl and G. Lopez (eds.), *Government Violence and Repression: An Agenda for Research.* Westport, Conn.: Greenwood Press, pp. 45–71.

Gurr, Ted Robert, and James R. Scarritt. 1989. "Minorities rights at risk: A global survey," *Human Rights Quarterly* 11 (3): 375–405.

Hajda, Lubomyr. 1988. "The nationalities problem in the Soviet Union," *Current History* 87 (531): 325–28, 347, 352.

Hanle, Donald J. 1989. *Terrorism: The Newest Face of Warfare.* Washington, D.C.: Pergamon-Brassey's International Defense Publishers.

Harbeson, John W. 1988. *The Ethiopian Transformation: The Quest for the Post-Imperial State.* Boulder, Col.: Westview Press.

Harding, Colin. 1987. "The rise of Sendero Luminoso." In Roy Miller (ed.), *Region and Class in Modern Peruvian History.* Liverpool: University of Liverpool, Institute of Latin American Studies Monograph No. 14, pp. 179–207.

————.1991. "A chronicle of death in Segovia," *Index on Censorship* 20 (9): 27.

Harff, Barbara. 1988. *Genocide and Human Rights: International Legal and Political Issues*. Denver, Col.: Monograph Series in World Affairs, Graduate School of International Studies, University of Denver.

———.1992. "Recognizing genocides and politicides." In Helen Fein (ed.), *Genocide Watch*. New Haven, Conn.: Yale University Press, pp. 27–41.

Harff, Barbara, and Ted R. Gurr. 1988. "Toward empirical theory of genocides and politicides: Identification and measurement of cases since 1945," *International Studies Quarterly* 32: 359–71.

Hartford, Kathleen. 1990. "The political economy behind Beijing spring." In Tony Saich (ed.), *The Chinese People's Movement: Perspectives on Spring 1989*. Armonk, N.Y.: M. E. Sharpe, pp. 50–82.

Hasan, Mushirul. 1991. "Adjustment and accommodation: Indian Muslims after partition." In K. N. Panikkar (ed.), *Communalism in India: History, Politics and Culture*. New Delhi: Manohar, pp. 62–79.

Hasan, Zoya. 1991. "Changing orientation of the state and the emergence of majoritarianism in the 1980s." In K. N. Panikkar (ed.), *Communalism in India: History, Politics and Culture*. New Delhi: Manohar, pp. 142–52.

Hayes, Monte. 1992. "Top man, military take over in Peru," *San Francisco Examiner*, April 6.

Held, David. 1989. *Political Theory and the Modern State: Essays on State, Power, and Democracy*. Stanford, Calif.: Stanford University Press.

Henkin, Louis. 1990. *The Age of Rights*. New York: Columbia University Press.

Henze, Paul. 1985. *Rebels and Separatists in Ethiopia: Regional Resistance to a Marxist Regime*. Santa Monica, Calif.: RAND.

———.1989a. *Mengistu's Ethiopian Marxist State in Terminal Crisis: How Long Can it Survive? What will be its Legacy?* Santa Monica, Calif.: RAND.

———.1989b. *Ethiopia in Early 1989: Deepening Crisis*. Santa Monica, Calif.: RAND.

Herman, Edward S. 1982. *The Real Terror Network: Terrorism in Fact and Propaganda*. Boston: South End Press.

Hibbs, Douglas A., Jr. 1973. *Mass Political Violence: A Cross National Causal Analysis*. New York: Wiley Interscience.

Hirst, Paul. 1991. "The state, civil society and the collapse of Soviet communism," *Economy and Society* 20 (2): 217–42.

Holley, David. 1992. "Chinese remove key hard-liners," *San Francisco Chronicle*, October 19.

Hood, Lucy, and Derrill Bazzy. 1988. "Guatemala army tries to end rebel war," *Christian Science Monitor*, January 20.

Hore, Charlie. 1991. *The Road to Tiananmen Square*. Chicago, Ill.: Bookmarks.

Horowitz, Irving Louis. 1989. *Taking Lives: Genocide and State Power*. New Brunswick, N.J.: Transaction Publishers.

Hoskin, Gary. 1988. "Colombia's political crisis," *Current History* 87 (525): 9–12, 38–39.

Hough, Jerry F. 1991. "Assessing the coup," *Current History* 90 (558): 305–10.

House, William J. 1989. "Population, poverty, and underdevelopment in the southern Sudan," *The Journal of Modern African Studies* 27 (2): 201–31.

Howard, Rhoda E. 1986. *Human Rights in Commonwealth Africa*. Totowa, N.J.: Rowman and Littlefield.

————.1988. "Repression and Terror in Africa: The Case of Kenya." Paper presented at a conference on "State Organized Terror: The Case of Violent Internal Repression." Michigan State University, Nov. 2–5.

————.1991. *International Human Rights as a Social Problem*. Montreal: Montreal Institute for Genocidal Studies.

————.1993. "Cultural absolutism and the nostalgia for community," *Human Rights Quarterly* 15 (2) : 315–38.

Hubbell, Stephen. 1990. "Color Sudan 'Islamic' green," *The Nation* 251 (2): 46–50.

Human Rights Watch. 1990. "Special issue: The crackdown in China," *Human Rights Watch* 3: 1–7.

————.1991. *Human Rights Watch World Report 1990*. New York: Human Rights Watch.

————.1992. *Human Rights Watch World Report 1993*. New York: Human Rights Watch.

Humana, Charles. 1986. *World Human Rights Guide*. New York: Facts on File.

Hundley, Tom. 1992. "Riots in India may foretell a worse future," *San Francisco Examiner*, December 20.

Hunter, Shireen T. 1990. "Soviet politics: Breakdown or renewal?" *Current History* 89 (549): 309–12, 339–40.

Huntington, Samuel P. 1968. *Political Order in Changing Societies*. New Haven, Conn.: Yale University Press.

————.1991. *The Third Wave: Democratization in the Late Twentieth Century*. Norman, Okla.: University of Oklahoma Press.

Hunwick, John O. 1992. "Introduction." In John O. Hunwick (ed.), *Religion and National Integration in Africa: Islam, Christianity, and Politics in the Sudan and Nigeria*. Evanston, Ill.: Northwestern University Press, pp. 1–9.

Hussain, Monirul, 1989. "The Muslim question in India," *Journal of Contemporary Asia* 19 (3): 279–96.

ICCHRLA Newsletter (Inter-Church Committee on Human Rights in Latin America). 1989. "Peru," Nos. 1 and 2.

International League for Human Rights. 1989. *Massacre in Beijing: The Events of 3–4 June 1989 and their Aftermath*. New York: International League for Human Rights and the Ad Hoc Study Group on Human Rights in China.

Jackson, Steven, Bruce Russett, Duncan Snidal, and David Sylvan. 1978. "Conflict and coercion in dependent states," *Journal of Conflict Resolution* 22: 627–57.

Jayawickrama, Nihal. 1990. "Human rights exception no longer." In George Hicks (ed.), *The Broken Mirror: China after Tiananmen*. Chicago, Ill.: St. James Press, pp. 345–68.

Jencks, Harlan W. 1991. "Civil-military relations in China: Tiananmen and after," *Problems of Communism* 40 (3): 14–29.

Johnson, Chalmers. 1966. *Revolutionary Change*. Boston: Little, Brown.

Johnson, Douglas H. 1988. *The Southern Sudan*. London: The Minority Rights Group, Report No. 78.

Jonas, Susanne. 1991. *The Battle for Guatemala: Rebels, Death Squads, and U.S. Power*. Boulder, Col.: Westview Press.

Kaplan, Robert D. 1991. "New world orphan," *The New Republic* 204 (25): 16–18.

Kazer, William. 1990. "China frees 97 more Tiananmen activists," *San Francisco Examiner*, June 7.

Kebbede, Girma. 1987. "State capitalism and development: The case of Ethiopia," *The Journal of Developing Areas* 22 (1): 1–24.

——.1992. *The State and Development in Ethiopia.* Atlantic Highlands, N.J.: Humanities Press International.

Keller, Bill. 1989a. "Soviets report use of toxic gas in putting down strife in Georgia," *The New York Times*, April 20.

——.1989b. "Soviets identify a 2d gas used in Georgian strife," *The New York Times*, May 6.

Keller, Edmond J. 1988. *Revolutionary Ethiopia: From Empire to People's Republic.* Bloomington, Ind.: Indiana University Press.

——.1990. "Constitutionalism and the national question in Africa: The case of Eritrea." In Marina Ottaway (ed.), *The Political Economy of Ethiopia.* New York: Praeger, pp. 95–113.

Kelsey, Tom. 1989. "Resettled Kurds mourn lost mountains," *The Independent* (London), August 19.

Kendall, Sarita. 1989. "The commonplace of massacre in Colombia," *Financial Times*, January 3.

Khalid, Mansour. 1985. *Nimeiri and the Revolution of Dis-May.* London: KPI.

Khan, Rasheeduddin. 1989. "Communalism and secularism in Indian polity: Dimensions of challenges." In R. C. Dutt (ed.), *Challenges to the Polity: Communalism, Casteism and Economic Challenges.* Lancer, India: Lancer, pp. 3–23.

Kidron, Michael, and Ronald Segal. 1987. *The New State of the World Atlas.* New York: Simon & Schuster.

Knorr, Klaus. 1976. *Historical Dimensions of National Security Problems.* Kansas City: University Press of Kansas.

Kriesberg, Louis. 1982. *Social Conflicts.* Englewood Cliffs, N.J.: Prentice-Hall.

Kristof, Nicholas D. 1990. "China's untold story: Who died in the crackdown," *The New York Times*, June 3.

Krueger, Chris, and Kjell Enge. 1985. *Security and Development Conditions in the Guatemalan Highlands.* Washington, D.C.: Washington Office on Latin America (WOLA).

Kumar, B. Gopalakrishna. 1989. "Tiananmen and the uncertain legacy of reform," *Economic and Political Weekly* 24 (27): 1511–12.

Kuper, Leo. 1981. *Genocide: Its Political Use in the Twentieth Century.* New York: Penguin Books.

——.1985. *The Prevention of Genocide.* New Haven, Conn.: Yale University Press.

Lambelin, Charles. 1988. "42 dead in Bogota raid," *San Francisco Examiner & Chronicle*, November 13.

Lane, David. 1992. *Soviet Society under Perestroika.* New York: Routledge.

Lang, Thomas. 1993. "Salvador charges U.S. with death-squad lies," *San Francisco Examiner*, November 1993.

Larmer, Brook. 1988. "Guatemala's moderate chief went too far for far right," *Christian Science Monitor*, May 17.

——.1989a. "New doubts surface in Guatemala," *Christian Science Monitor*, February 14.

——.1989b. "Guatemala democracy bows to military-business alliance," *Christian Science Monitor*, March 14.

Latin American Regional Reports, Andean Group. 1989. "Troops use 'terror against terror' in Peru," December 14.

Latin American Weekly Report. 1988. "Colombia: Death squads take up total war call," November 24.

Latinamerica Press. 1988a. "Peru's general are trying to cover up dirty war, human rights groups charge," August 4.

————.1988b. "Peru under Alan García," September 15.

Lawyers Committee for Human Rights. 1990. *Abandoning the Victims: The UN Advisory Services Program in Guatemala.* New York: Lawyers Committee for Human Rights.

Lee, Ta-ling, and John F. Cooper. 1991. *Failure of Democracy Movement: Human Rights in the People's Republic of China, 1988/89.* Baltimore, Md.: School of Law, University of Maryland.

Leonard, Richard. 1988. "Popular participation in liberation and revolution." In Lionel Cliffe and Basil Davidson (eds.), *The Long Struggle of Eritrea for Independence and Constructive Peace.* Nottingham, England: Spokesman, pp. 105–35.

Lesch, Ann Mosely. 1986. "Party politics in the Sudan," *USFI Reports* 9.

Lichbach, Mark I., and Ted R. Gurr. 1981. "The conflict process: A self-generating model," *Journal of Conflict Resolution* 21: 3–29.

Lih, Lars T. 1989. "The transition era in Soviet politics," *Current History* 88 (540): 333–36, 353–54.

Linz, Juan J. 1992. "Types of political regimes and respect for human rights: Historical and cross-national perspectives." In A. Eide and B. Hagtvet (eds.), *Human Rights in Perspective: A Global Assessment.* Oxford: Basil Blackwell Ltd., pp. 177–222.

Lopez, George A. 1984. "A scheme for the analysis of government as terrorist." In M. Stohl and G. Lopez (eds.), *The State as Terrorist: The Dynamics of Governmental Violence and Repression.* Westport, Conn.: Greenwood Press, pp. 59–81.

Lopez, George A., and Michael Stohl. 1984. "Studying the state as terrorist: A conclusion and research agenda." In M. Stohl and G. Lopez (eds.), *The State as Terrorist: The Dynamics of Governmental Violence and Repression.* Westport, Conn.: Greenwood Press, pp. 183–90.

————.1985–86. "State terrorism: From Robespierre to Nineteen Eighty-Four," *Chitty's Law Journal*, winter.

Mahmud, Ushari Ahmad, and Suleyman Ali Baldo. 1987. *Human Rights Abuses in the Sudan 1987: The Diein Massacre and Slavery in the Sudan.* Khartoum.

Malik, Yogendra K., and Dhirendra K. Vajpeyi. 1989. "The rise of Hindu militancy: India's secular democracy at risk," *Asian Survey* 29 (3): 308–25.

Malwal, Bona. 1991. "The challenge of the south to Sudanese national politics." In Georges Nzongola-Ntalaja (ed.), *Conflict in the Horn of Africa.* Atlanta: African Studies Association Press, pp. 117–28.

Mannheim, Karl. 1949. *Ideology and Utopia.* Translated by Louis Wirth and Edward Shils. New York: Harcourt, Brace.

Manuel, Anne, and Eric Stover. 1991. *Guatemala: Getting Away with Murder.* New York: Americas Watch and Physicians for Human Rights.

Markakis, John. 1989. "Nationalities and the state in Ethiopia," *Third World Quarterly* 11 (4): 118–30.

Marquis, Christopher. 1989. "Salvador gunmen kill 6 priests," *Miami Herald*, November 17.

Marr, Phebe. 1985. *The Modern History of Iraq*. Boulder, Col.: Westview Press.

———.1991. "Iraq's uncertain future," *Current History* 90 (552): 1–4.

Martz, John D. 1989. "Colombia's search for peace," *Current History* 88 (536): 125–28, 145–47.

———.1991. "Colombia at the crossroads," *Current History* 90 (553): 69–72, 80–81.

———.1992. "Party elites and leadership in Colombia and Venezuela," *Journal of Latin American Studies* 24: 87–121.

Mason, T. David. 1989. "Nonelite response to state-sanctioned terror," *Western Political Quarterly* 42 (4): 467–92.

Mason, T. David, and Dale A. Krane. 1989. "The political economy of death squads: Toward a theory of the impact of state-sanctioned terror," *International Studies Quarterly* 33 (2): 175–98.

Masterson, Daniel M. 1991. *Militarism and Politics in Latin America: Peru from Sánchez Cerro to Sendero Luminoso*. New York: Greenwood Press.

Mathur, Kuldeep. 1992. "The state and the use of coercive power in India," *Asian Survey* 32 (4): 337–49.

Mauceri, Philip. 1991. "Military politics and counter-insurgency in Peru," *Journal of Interamerican Studies and World Affairs* 33 (4): 83–109.

Mawson, Andrew N. M. 1991. "Murahaleen raids on the Dinka, 1985–89," *Disasters* 15 (2): 137–49.

McCamant, John F. 1984. "Governance without blood: Social science's antiseptic view of rule; or, the neglect of political repression." In M. Stohl and G. Lopez (eds.), *The State as Terrorist: The Dynamics of Governmental Violence and Repression*. Westport, Conn.: Greenwood Press, pp. 11–42.

———.1991. "Domination, state power, and political repression." In P. Timothy Bushnell et al. (eds), *State Organized Terror: The Case of Violent Internal Repression*. Boulder, Col.: Westview Press, pp. 41–58.

McClintock, Cynthia. 1983. "Sendero Luminoso: Peru's Maoist guerillas," *Problems of Communism* 32 (5): 19–34.

———.1984. "Why peasants rebel: The case of Peru's Sendero Luminoso," *World Politics* 37: 48–84.

———.1989. "The prospects for democratic consolidation in a "least likely" case: Peru," *Comparative Politics* 21 (2): 127–48.

McClintock, John M. 1989. "Fingerprints found at site of Salvadoran killings," *Baltimore Sun*, November 20.

McDowall, David. 1991. "The Kurds: An historical perspective," *Asian Affairs* 22 (3): 293–302.

———.1992. "The Kurdish question: A historical review." In Philip G. Kreyenbroek and Stefan Sperl (eds.), *The Kurds: A Contemporary Overview*. New York: Routledge, pp. 10–32.

Miami Herald. 1988. "Peruvians set inquiry into killings," May 20.

Middle East Watch. 1990. *Human Rights in Iraq*. New Haven, Conn.: Yale University Press.

Mill, John Stuart. 1950. *Philosophy of Scientific Method* (edited by E. Nagel). New York: Hafner (originally the 1881 edition of *A System of Logic*).

Miller, Judith, and Laurie Mylroie. 1990. *Saddam Hussein and the Crisis in the Gulf.* New York: Random House.

Miller, Marjorie. 1990. "Colonel, 8 others formally charged with the murder of 6 Jesuit priests," *Los Angeles Times,* January 20.

Millett, Richard L. 1991. "Guatemala: Hopes for peace, struggles for survival," *Survival* 33 (5): 425–41.

Mitchell, Christopher, Michael Stohl, David Carleton, and George A. Lopez. 1986. "State terrorism: Issues of concept and measurement." In M. Stohl and G. Lopez (eds.), *Government Violence and Repression: An Agenda for Research.* Westport, Conn.: Greenwood Press, pp. 1–26.

Moore, Barrington, Jr. 1966. *Social Origins of Dictatorship and Democracy.* Boston: Beacon Press.

Muhsin, Jabr, George Harding, and Fran Hazelton. 1989. "Iraq in the Gulf War." In Philip G. Kreyenbroek and Stefan Sperl (eds.), *The Kurds: A Contemporary Overview.* New York: Routledge, pp. 229–41.

Mukhoty, Gobinda. 1990. "Human rights in India." In *Human Rights Year-Book 1990.* New Delhi: International Institute of Human Rights Society, pp. 28–35.

Muller, E. N. 1985. "Income inequality, regime repressiveness, and political violence," *American Sociological Review* 50: 47–61.

Munro, Robin. 1990. "Who died in Beijing and why," *The Nation,* June 11.

Nairn, Allan, and Jean-Marie Simon. 1986. "The bureaucracy of death," *New Republic,* June 30.

National Catholic Reporter. 1989. "Fear, accusations and multiple arrest follow Jesuit murders in El Salvador," November 24.

Nduru, Moyiga. 1991. "Sudan: Laying down the law for Allah," *Index on Censorship* 20 (2): 17–20.

Needler, Martin C. 1991. "El Salvador: The military and politics," *Armed Forces and Society* 17 (4): 569–88.

Network in Solidarity with the People of Guatemala (NISGUA). 1989a. News release, February.

———.1989b. *Report on Guatemala,* Vol. 10, No. 1 (January–March).

The New York Times. 1989a. "Thousands march at Soviet victim's funeral," April 16.

———.1989b. "Gas killed Georgian protesters, republic's party chief confirms," April 25.

Noorani, A. G. 1987. "Amnesty report on Meerut killings," *Economic and Political Weekly* 22 (50): 2139–40.

———.1989 "Telling the world about human rights in India," *Economic and Political Weekly* 24 (32): 1811.

Norton, Chris. 1991. "The hard right: ARENA comes to power." In Anjali Sundaram and George Gelber (eds.), *A Decade of War: El Salvador Confronts the Future.* New York: Monthly Review Press, pp. 196–215.

O'Donnell, Guillermo. 1973. *Modernization and Bureaucratic-Authoritarianism.* Berkeley, Calif.: University of California Press.

Olcott, Martha Brill. 1991. "The slide into disunion," *Current History* 90 (558): 338–44.

Osterling, Jorge P. 1989. *Democracy in Colombia: Clientelist Politics and Guerilla Warfare.* New Brunswick, N.J.: Transaction Publishers.

Ottaway, David B. 1989. "Expert says Soviets used toxic gas," *The Washington Post,* May 26.

Ottaway, Marina. 1987. "State power consolidation in Ethiopia." In Edmond J. Keller and Donald Rothchild (eds.), *Afro-Marxist Regimes: Ideology and Public Policy.* Boulder, Col.: Lynne Rienner, pp. 25–42.

Oxfam America. 1985. "Violence, repression afflict resilient peasants in Guatemala," *Oxfam America Special Report* No. 3, Fall.

Painter, James. 1987. *Guatemala: False Hope, False Freedom.* London: Latin America Bureau.

Palmer, David Scott. 1986. "Rebellion in rural Peru: The origins and evolution of Sendero Luminoso," *Comparative Politics* 18 (2): 127–46.

Pateman, Roy. 1990a. "The Eritrea war," *Armed Forces and Society* 17 (1): 81–98.

———.1990b. *Eritrea: Even the Stones are Burning.* Trenton, N.J.: Red Sea Press.

———.1991. "Eritrea and Ethiopia: Strategies for reconciliation in the Horn of Africa," *Africa Today* 38 (2): 43–55.

Pearce, Jenny. 1990. *Colombia: Inside the Labyrinth.* London: Latin America Bureau.

People for a Just Peace. 1988. *The Proliferation of Chemical Warfare: The Holocaust at Halabja.* Washington, D.C.: People for a Just Peace.

Pendzich, Christine. 1990. *Peru in Crisis: Challenges to a New Government.* Washington, D.C.: Washington Office on Latin America.

Perdue, William D. 1989. *Terrorism and the State: A Critique of Domination Through Fear.* New York: Praeger.

Perlmutter, Amos. 1981. *Modern Authoritarianism: A Comparative Institutional Analysis.* Yale University Press.

Petras, James. 1987. "The anatomy of state terror: Chile, El Salvador and Brazil," *Science and Society* 51 (3): 314–38.

———.1988. "Colombia: Neglected dimensions of violence," *Contemporary Crises* 12 (3): 191–93.

Pion-Berlin, David. 1984. "The political economy of state repression in Argentina." In M. Stohl and G. Lopez (eds.), *The State as Terrorist: The Dynamics of Governmental Violence and Repression.* Westport, Conn.: Greenwood Press, pp. 99–122.

———.1989. *The Ideology of State Terror: Economic Doctrine and Political Repression in Argentina and Peru.* Boulder, Col.: Lynne Rienner.

———.1991. "The ideological governance of perception in the use of state terror in Latin America: The case of Argentina." In P. Timothy Bushnell et al. (eds), *State Organized Terror: The Case of Violent Internal Repression.* Boulder, Col.: Westview Press, pp. 135–52.

Pomeranz, Ken. 1990. "China since the Square: Political repression, economic austerity," *Dissent* 37 (2): 243–46.

Popkin, Margaret. 1991. "Human rights in the Duarte years." In Anjali Sundaram and George Gelber (eds.), *A Decade of War: El Salvador Confronts the Future.* New York: Monthly Review Press, pp. 58–82.

Prah, K. K. 1989. "Ethnicity, politics and human rights in the southern Sudan." In David P. Forsythe (ed.), *Human Rights and Development: International Views.* New York: St. Martin's Press, pp. 263–78.

Premo, Daniel L. 1988. "Coping with insurgency: The politics of pacification in Colombia and Venezuela." In Donald L. Herman (ed.), *Democracy in Latin America: Colombia and Venezuela.* New York: Praeger, pp. 219–44.

Pritchard, Kathleen. 1988. "Comparative human rights: Promise and practice." In D. L. Cingranelli (ed.), *Human Rights: Theory and Measurement*. London: Macmillan Press, pp. 139–53.

Puri, Balraj. 1987. "Communalism and regionalism," *Economic and Political Weekly* 22 (28): 1132–36.

Rajgopal, P. R. 1987. *Communal Violence in India*. New Delhi: Uppal Publishing House

Reed, Jon. 1989. "Reign of terror escalates in wake of coup attempt," *Guardian*, July 5.

Remnick, David. 1989a. "Area military leader blamed for use of poison gas to quell protests," *The Washington Post*, October 12.

———.1989b. "Soviet aides blamed in Georgian deaths," *The Washington Post*, December 22.

Renteln, Alison Dundes. 1990. *International Human Rights: Universalism Versus Relativism*. Newbury Park, Calif.: Sage Publications.

Report on Guatemala. 1989. "The unofficial story: The El Aguacate massacre," 10 (1): 3.

Restrepo, Luís Alberto. 1992. "The crisis of the current political regime and its possible outcomes." In Charles Bergquish, Ricardo Peñaranda, Gonzalo Sánchez (eds.), *Violence in Colombia: The Contemporary Crisis in Historical Perspective*. Wilmington, Del.: Scholarly Resources, pp. 273–92.

Robison, Gordon. 1992. "Sudan: A cause for concern," *The World Today* 48 (4): 61–64.

Roxburgh, Angus. 1991. *The Second Russian Revolution: The Struggle for Power in the Kremlin*. London: BBC Books.

Rubin, Barnett R., and Paula R. Newberg. 1980. "Appendix: Statistical analysis for implementing human rights policy." In Paula R. Newberg (ed.), *The Politics of Human Rights*. New York: New York University Press, pp. 268–84.

Rummel, R. J. 1984. "Libertarianism, violence within states, and the polarity principle," *Comparative Politics* 16 (4): 443–62.

Russell, John. 1991. "The Georgians," *A Minority Rights Group Soviet Update* (London).

Saeedpour, Vera Beaudin. 1988. "The world must speak out for our Kurds," *Our Times*, September 12.

———.1992. "Establishing state motives for genocide: Iraq and the Kurds." In Helen Fein (ed.), *Genocide Watch*. New Haven, Conn.: Yale University Press, pp. 59–69.

Safran, William. 1981. "Civil liberties in democracies: Constitutional norms, practices, and problems of comparison." In V. Nanda, J. Scarritt, and G. Shepherd, Jr. (eds.), *Global Human Rights: Public Policies, Comparative Measures and NGO Strategies*. Boulder, Col.: Westview Press, pp. 206–9.

Saiyed, A. R. 1988. "Changing urban ethos: Some reflections on Hindu-Muslim riots." In K. S. Shukla (ed.), *Collective Violence: Genesis and Response*. New Delhi: Indian Institute of Public Administration, pp. 97–119.

Salih, Kamal Osman. 1990. "The Sudan, 1985–9: The fading democracy," *The Journal of Modern African Studies* 28 (2): 199–224.

Samatar, A. I. 1991. "Horn of Africa: The exigencies of self-determination." In G. Nzongola-Ntalaja (ed.), *Conflict in the Horn of Africa*. Atlanta: African Studies Association Press, pp. 67–88.

San Francisco Chronicle. 1990. "Evidence reported that Salvador army covered up slayings," May 30.

San Francisco Examiner. 1992. "India targets warring zealots," December 14.

———.1993. "El Salvador approves amnesty for rights abuse," March 21.

Saxena, N.C. 1988. "Development, change and collective violence." In K. S. Shukla (ed.), *Collective Violence: Genesis and Response*. New Delhi: Indian Institute of Public Administration, pp. 181–212.

Schapiro, Leonard. 1972. *Totalitarianism*. London: Pall Mall Press.

Schirmer, Jennifer. 1989. "Waging war to prevent war," *The Nation* 248 (14): 478–79.

Schmidt-Lynch, Corrine. 1992. "Shining Path leader given life sentence," *San Francisco Examiner*, October 8.

————.1993. "Human rights scandal rocks Peru," *San Francisco Examiner*, May 26.

Schoultz, Lars. 1982. *Human Rights and United States Foreign Policy Toward Latin America*. Princeton: Princeton University Press.

Schwab, Peter. 1985. *Ethiopia: Politics, Economics and Society*. London: Frances Pinter.

Scobell, Andres. 1992. "Why the People's Army fired on the people: The Chinese military and Tiananmen," *Armed Forces and Society* 18 (2): 193–213.

Scoble, Harry M., and Laurie S. Wiseberg. 1981. "Problems of comparative research on human rights." In V. Nanda, J. Scarritt, and G. Shepherd, Jr. (eds.), *Global Human Rights: Public Policies, Comparative Measures and NGO Strategies*. Boulder, Col.: Westview Press, p. 167.

Shakir, Moin. 1986. *State and Politics in Contemporary India*. Delhi: Ajanta Publications.

Shambaugh, David. 1991. "China in 1990: The year of damage control," *Asian Survey* 31 (1): 36–49.

————.1992. "China in 1991: Living cautiously," *Asian Survey* 32 (1): 19–31.

Shapiro, M. 1981. *Courts: A Comparative and Political Analysis*. Chicago: Chicago University Press.

Shawky, Ahmed. 1988. *Difficulties Facing Democracy in Sudan*. Cairo: Cairo University.

Sherzad, A. 1992. "The Kurdish movement in Iraq: 1975–88." In Philip G. Kreyenbroek and Stefan Sperl (eds.), *The Kurds: A Contemporary Overview*. New York: Routledge, pp. 134–42.

Shi, Hong. 1990. "China's political development after Tiananmen: Tranquility by default," *Asian Survey* 30 (12): 1206–17.

Siegel, Daniel, and Joy Hackel. 1988. "El Salvador: Counterinsurgency revisited." In Michael T. Klare and Peter Kornbluh (eds.), *Low-Intensity Warfare: Counterinsurgency, Proinsurgency, and Antiterrorism in the Eighties*. New York: Pantheon, pp. 112–35.

Simon, Jean-Marie. 1987. *Guatemala: Eternal Spring–Eternal Tyranny*. New York: W. W. Norton and Co.

Singer, Max. 1990. "Militarism and democracy in El Salvador," *Society* 27 (6): 49–56.

Singh, Mahendra Prasad. 1992. "The dilemma of the new Indian party system: To govern or not to govern?" *Asian Survey* 32 (4): 303–17.

Sisson, Richard. 1990. "India in 1989: A year of elections in a culture of change," *Asian Survey* 30 (2): 111–25.

Skocpol, Theda. 1973. "A critical review of Barrington Moore's *Social Origins of Dictatorship and Democracy*," *Politics and Society* 4 (3): 1–34.

————.1984. "Emerging agendas and recurrent strategies in historical sociology." In T. Skocpol (ed.), *Vision and Method in Historical Sociology*. New York: Cambridge University Press, pp. 356–91.

Sloan, John W. 1984. "State repression and enforcement terrorism in Latin America." In M. Stohl and G. Lopez (eds.), *The State as Terrorist: The Dynamics of Governmental Violence and Repression*. Westport, Conn.: Greenwood Press, pp. 83–98.

Smelser, Neil J. 1963. *Theory of Collective Behavior*. New York: The Free Press of Glencoe.

Smith, Carol A. 1990. "The militarization of civil society in Guatemala: Economic reorganization as a continuation of war," *Latin American Perspectives* 17 (4): 8–41.

Smith, Gordon B. 1992. *Soviet Politics: Struggling with Change*. New York: St. Martin's Press.

Snyder, David, and Charles Tilly. 1972. "Hardship and collective violence in France, 1830 to 1960," *American Sociological Review* 37: 520–32.

Southerland, Daniel. 1989a. "10,000 Chinese detained in crackdown on dissent," *The Washington Post*, July 8.

———.1989b. "Chinese cast new dragnet," *The Washington Post*, December 3.

Spalding, Hobart A. 1992. "Peru on the brink," *Monthly Review* 43 (8): 29–43.

Staub, Ervin. 1989. *The Roots of Evil: The Origins of Genocide and Other Group Violence*. Cambridge, England: Cambridge University Press.

Stavenhagen, Rudolfo. 1992. "Universal human rights and the cultures of indigenous peoples and other ethnic groups: The critical frontier of the 1990s." In A. Eide and B. Hagtvet (eds.), *Human Rights in Perspective: A Global Assessment*. Oxford: Basil Blackwell Ltd., pp. 135–51.

Stavis, Benedict. 1988. *China's Political Reforms*. New York: Praeger.

Stinchcombe, Arthur. 1978. *Theoretical Models in Social History*. New York: Academic Press.

Stix, Bob. 1989. "The El Aguacate massacre: Evidence implicates the army," *Report on Guatemala* 10 (1): 2–3.

Stone, Brewer S. 1988. "Institutional decay and the institutionalization of politics: The Uttar Pradesh Congress Party," *Asian Survey* 28 (10): 1018–30.

Sudhir, Sonalkar. 1980. "Communalism in Indian life," *Deccan Herald*, Sept. 24, p. 6.

Sun, Yan. 1991. "The Chinese protests of 1989: The issue of corruption," *Asian Survey* 31 (8): 762–82.

Ter-Grigoryan, Alexander. 1983. "Overcoming divisions," *New Times* (Moscow), June: 24–25.

Tessitore, John, and Susan Woolfson (eds.). 1988. *Issues before the 43rd General Assembly of the United Nations*. Lexington, Mass.: Lexington Books.

Thomas, Dorothy Q., and Michele E. Beasley. 1993. "Domestic violence as a human rights issue," *Human Rights Quarterly* 15 (1): 36–62.

Tilly, Charles. 1978. *From Mobilization to Revolution*. Reading, Mass.: Addison-Wesley.

Tishkov, Valerii. 1989. "*Glasnost* and the nationalities within the Soviet Union," *Third World Quarterly* 11 (4): 191–207.

Trimble, Jeff. 1989. "The Soviet agony over states' rights," *U.S. News & World Report* 106 (16): 34–35.

Tseggai, Araya. 1988. "The history of the Eritrean struggle." In Lionel Cliffe and Basil Davidson (eds.), *The Long Struggle of Eritrea for Independence and Constructive Peace*. Nottingham, England: Spokesman, pp. 67–84.

Tullock, Gordon. 1971. "The Paradox of Revolution," *Public Choice* 11: 89–99.

van den Berghe, Pierre L. 1990. "The Ixil Triangle: Vietnam in Guatemala." In Pierre L. van den Berghe (ed.), *State Violence and Ethnicity*. Niwot, Col.: University Press of Colorado, pp. 253–88.

Voll, John O. 1990. "Political crisis in Sudan," *Current History* 89 (546): 153–56, 178–80.

Vyas, Neena, and Nilanjan Mukhopadhyay. 1988. "Learning to live with official lies." In Asghar Ali Engineer (ed.), *Delhi-Meerut Riots: Analysis, Compilation and Documentation*. Delhi: Ajanta Publications; originally appeared in *Statesman*, June 27, 1987, pp. 128–31.

Wakoson, Elias Nyamlell. 1987. "The dilemmas of South–North conflict." In Francis Mading Deng and Prosser Gifford (eds.), *The Search for Peace and Unity in the Sudan*. Washington, D.C.: Wilson Center Press, pp. 90–106.

Walder, Andrew G. 1989. "The political sociology of the Beijing upheaval of 1989," *Problems of Communism* 38 (5): 30–40.

Walter, Eugene Victor. 1969. *Terror and Resistance*. New York: Oxford University Press.

Warburg, Gabriel R. 1991. "The *Sharia* in Sudan: Implementation and repercussions." In John O. Voll (ed.), *Sudan: State & Society in Crisis*. Bloomington, Ind.: Indiana University Press, pp. 90–107.

Washington Office on Latin America (WOLA). 1988. *Who Pays the Price? The Cost of War in the Guatemalan Highlands*. Washington, D.C.: Washington Office on Latin America.

————.1989. *Colombia Besieged: Political Violence and State Responsibility*. Washington, D.C.: Washington Office on Latin America.

————.1990. *The Administration of Injustice: Military Accountability in Guatemala*. Washington, D.C.: Washington Office on Latin America.

The Washington Post. 1989. "The Kremlin's ethnic strains," April 19.

————.1990. "Christiani assails U.S. critics of Jesuits' murder probe," April 15.

Watson, Cynthia A. 1990. "Political violence in Colombia: Another Argentina?" *Third World Quarterly* 12 (3): 25–39.

Webster, Katharine. 1990. "Deception in Guatemala: How the U.S. media bought a cover-up," *The Progressive* 54 (2): 26–32.

Weisskopf, Michael. 1989. "8 sentenced to death by court in Beijing," *The Washington Post*, June 18.

Werlich, David P. 1991. "Fujimori and the "disaster" in Peru," *Current History* 90 (553): 61–64, 81–83.

Whittleton, Celine, Jabr Muhsin, and Fran Hazelton. 1989. "Whither Iraq?" In Philip G. Kreyenbroek and Stefan Sperl (eds.), *The Kurds: A Contemporary Overview*. New York: Routledge, pp. 242–52.

Willerton, John P., Jr. 1990. "The political leadership." In Stephen White, Alex Pravda, and Zvi Gitelman (eds.), *Developments in Soviet Politics*. Durham, N.C.: Duke University Press, pp. 48–66.

Wirpsa, Leslie. 1989. "Military implicated in massacres," *Miami Herald*, January 23.

Woldemikael, Tekle Mariam. 1991. "Political mobilization and nationalist movements: The case of the Eritrean People's Liberation Front," *Africa Today* 38 (2): 31–42.

Wolpin, Miles. 1986. "State terrorism and repression in the Third World: Parameters and prospects." In M. Stohl and G. Lopez (eds.), *Government Violence and Repression: An Agenda for Research*. Westport, Conn.: Greenwood Press, pp. 97–164.

Wong, Jan. 1990. "How many did the Chinese army actually kill?" *San Francisco Examiner*, June 5.

Woodward, Peter. 1990. *Sudan, 1898–1989*. Boulder, Col.: Lynne Rienner Publishers.

Woy-Hazleton, Sandra, and William A. Hazleton. 1990. "Sendero Luminoso and the future of Peruvian democracy," *Third World Quarterly* 12 (2): 21–35.

————.1992. "Shining Path and the Marxist Left." In David Scott Palmer (ed.), *The Shining Path of Peru*. New York: St. Martin's Press, pp. 207–24.

Yarbro, Stan. 1990. "U.S. accused over human rights in Colombia," *Los Angeles Times*, October 23.

Yim, Kwan Ha (ed.). 1991. *China Under Deng*. New York: Facts on File.

Youngers, Coletta. 1989. "Will Colombia stand up to paramilitary?" *Los Angeles Times*, August 31.

Yusuf, Syed. 1987. "Meerut, Maliana ... Pac role x-rayed," *Radiance Viewsweekly*, June 21–27, pp. 1, 13.

Zaher, U. 1989. "Political developments in Iraq 1963–1980." In Committee Against Repression and for Democratic Rights in Iraq (CARDRI) (eds.), *Saddam's Iraq: Revolution or Reaction*. London: Zed Books, pp. 30–53.

Zuckerman, Mortimer B. 1990. "China myth, China reality," *U.S. News & World Report* 108 (10): 55–56.

Zwick, Jim. 1984. "Militarism and repression in the Philippines." In M. Stohl and G. Lopez (eds.), *The State as Terrorist: The Dynamics of Governmental Violence and Repression*. Westport, Conn.: Greenwood Press, pp. 123–42.

Index

About the Author

BRENDA K. UEKERT holds a Ph.D. in Sociology from Syracuse University. She has spent several years as a Senior Research Analyst at the University of California and is currently an adjunct instructor at the University of Wisconsin at Green Bay.